TWO ESSAYS ON THE
PHILOSOPHY OF MENTAL HEALTH

Two Essays on the Philosophy of Mental Health

Reflections on the Hermeneutics of Psychopathology and Psychotherapy

Claude A. Della Zazzera & David J. Crowe

Miamine Press
Ottawa, Ontario

Della Zazzera, Claude A.
&
Crowe, David J.

Two Essays on the Philosophy of Mental Health:
Reflections on the Hermeneutics of Psychopathology and Psychotherapy

A Miamine Press Book

Library and Archives Canada
Legal Deposit, 2015
ISBN: 978-0-9940910-0-0

Front cover image,
Painted Ship (acrylic on wood),
by Anna Della Zazzera

Dedicated to
Bruce Schowalter, friend and colleague,
who expressed with charm and intuition
much of what we attempt to put into words here.

Neque enim quaero intelligere ut credam,
sed credo ut intelligam. Nam et hoc credo,
quia, nisi credidero, non intelligam.

Nor do I seek to understand that I may believe,
but I believe that I may understand.
For this, too, I believe, that unless I first believe,
I shall not understand.

Anselm of Canterbury

CONTENTS

INTRODUCTION

The writings in this book are based on an on-going dialogue the two of us have had over many years, a dialogue focused on our clinical practice as psychologists. In our discussions, we have considered, not only clinical material and psychological theory, but also philosophical questions. Indeed, we have come to see the consideration of philosophical issues as essential to navigating the mental health field. Consequently, we have sought to investigate philosophical principles that are relevant to an evaluation of those basic mental health notions on which we focus our attention in the regular practice of psychological assessment and treatment: notions such as normality, abnormality, and psychotherapeutic healing.

This book is essentially comprised of two essays on the philosophy of mental health, both of which emphasise the importance of applying a *hermeneutics of belief* to the subjects of psychopathology and psychotherapy.[1] We basically propose that, in order to interpret (i.e. apply hermeneutics to) mental health issues in an effective and meaningful manner, one requires *belief in trusted connection*.

In relating belief to interpretation we are alluding to Paul Ricoeur's distinction between the hermeneutics of belief and the hermeneutics of suspicion. He famously refers to the three *Masters of Suspicion*, Marx, Nietzsche and Freud, and sees their unmasking of false consciousness as a principal task for hermeneutics. Ricoeur does not accept the three masters in an uncritical manner, however. In his own hermeneutics he seeks a balance between belief and suspicion, although he does tend to follow the Masters *part-way* by giving priority to suspicion.[2]

We look more broadly at the meaning of belief and suspicion and extend the scope of interpretation or hermeneutics beyond questions of whether consciousness is false, ideology mystifies, institutional practices alienate or conventional beliefs prove inauthentic. The subjects to which these questions refer are examples where one commonly applies a *hermeneutics of suspicion*. Our desire for a broader, more inclusive focus,[3] on the other hand, leads us to give priority to a *hermeneutics of belief,* by which we mean an interpretive process that arises from a recognition of the basic ontological accord or complementarity between the distinction and relation of persons – and analogous complements such as freedom and commitment, right and obligation, uniqueness and solidarity. We view this complementarity as the basic framework of human experience.

By *basic ontological accord of the distinction and relation of persons* we are proposing that human experience depends on an intimate connection (accord) between being a person and being in relationship with another. It follows, therefore, that to be oneself (to be unique and exercise freedom) and to be in relationship with another (to care for and love the other, and to be cared for and loved by the other) are complementary, mutually supportive aspects of being. We will be elaborating on these themes in the course of the two essays in this book. It is this accord or complementarity at the heart of being that provides the context for the *belief in trusted connection*, noted above. Thus, belief in trusted connection is the interpretative key (or hermeneutics) we propose.

We go on to elaborate how this ontological accord forms the basis of a philosophical understanding of normality and healing, an understanding that serves to anchor psychological or psychotherapeutic theory and practice. Since the accord or complementarity of distinction and relation (of persons) provides a basis for normality, we define abnormality or psychopathology in terms of, or by reference to the disaccord of these complements or factors. In addition, although we emphasise belief as a central feature of the interpretive process, we also see an apt, if secondary, role for the hermeneutics of suspicion, and, therefore, for doubt and critique – approaches that, in a general way, resonate with suspicion.[4] Accordingly, we argue for the priority of belief in the interpretive process, but not for its exclusivity. While we go on to challenge approaches in the mental health field that give priority to suspicion, we nevertheless specify a role for suspicion in exposing instances where the disaccord of complements occurs.[5]

The first essay, "Applying a Hermeneutics of Belief to the Understanding of Psychopathology," begins with an exploration of the psychoanalytic concepts of object and defence. We argue that the predominant tendency in psychoanalysis is to approach these concepts in the context of a hermeneutics of suspicion: that is, the tendency in psychoanalytic thought is to grant the internal or mental object (i.e. the representation within oneself of others, as *objects* of the mind, a representation that forms a part of the structure of one's interior life) a primarily separating and ego-defensive function. We, on the other hand, in giving priority to a hermeneutics of belief, wish to emphasise the connecting role of the internal object vis-à-vis real relationship. Furthermore, in keeping with this emphasis, we propose expanding the notion of defence to extend beyond the sole defence of ego.

We do not exclude the possibility that the ego may react defensively, nor that the properties of the internal object may be influenced by ego-defence; however, in view of the fundamental role of relationship or *complementarity* in human existence, we see the notion of defence as having greater scope than sole ego-defence, and we see the internal object as dependent on relation *before* there is threat to self, and *before* there is opposition or division (between self and other). We therefore speak of defence of *relationship* as being more fundamental than *ego*-defence and as providing the latter its context. We argue for a basic accord between the *independence* (distinction, freedom) and *relation* (connection, commitment) of persons with respect to one another, and see the internal object as arising in the context of this accord, and not, primarily, as the product of alienation in, or from relationship. In order to provide a philosophical basis for our proposals, we explore and discuss the work of three contemporary thinkers who address whether and in what manner entities can be both independent and related: Graham Harman, Kenneth Gergen and Kenneth Schmitz.

We consider how Harman, in his object oriented philosophy, affirms the independent, distinct, unique, ontological reality of each entity, thing or object, while seeing relation as something that only touches the surface of entities.[6]   Gergen, from a constructionist perspective, proposes a somewhat opposite emphasis: a dissolution of all entities into what he calls "relational being."   Although he speaks of *being* he eschews all ontology, and he rejects the notion of distinct, independent entities.[7]   Schmitz, on the other hand, in emphasising the metaphysics of existential act and personalism, offers a perspective that we interpret as affirming both the distinction of entities or objects *and* their in-depth relation to one another – in what he calls a *community of beings*. Moreover, his proposals allow one to consider two fundamental aspects of relating: an epistemological aspect and an ontological aspect. We elaborate on how the epistemological speaks to the relation of one as a *subject of consciousness* to the other as an *object of consciousness*, and the ontological to the relation of one as a *subject of being* to the other, as a *subject of being*. Schmitz also emphasises the intrinsic openness of being to thought. Consequently, in his philosophy, there is, in our view, more *bridge* than *chasm* between thought and reality (between the epistemological and ontological moments of human experience, and therefore, in analogous psychological terms, between the internal object and the actual relationship with another).[8]

These reflections on the philosophical implications of how one accounts for what it means *to be* and *to relate* allow us to consider, in a corollary or analogous way, how one might challenge the psychoanalytic tendency to view the internal object as being primarily the product of ego-defence. We argue that the internal object is rooted in the primacy of relationship – or, more to the point, in the *accord* or *complementarity* that has distinction and relation of persons *co*-exist in human experience. It is on the basis of this primacy of accord or complementarity that we propose the expansion of the psychoanalytic notion of defence, noted above: the notion of defence, in this expanded view, is not limited to defence of ego but becomes defence of the accord of distinction and relation of self and other. In other words, defensive process applies not only to the ego but also, and more intrinsically, to the relationship of persons.

We go on to see psychopathology in terms of the failure of the accord of distinction and relation, and analogous or associated complements such as independence and solidarity, freedom and commitment.... On this basis we consider how healing calls for an extraction of the normal (expressive of accord) from the experience of the abnormal (expressive of disaccord), a theme which we also address, and upon which we elaborate, in our second essay, which focuses on the hermeneutics of psychotherapeutic healing.

In addition, for the reader who would like to more quickly consider the main themes and arguments presented in this first essay, "Appendix A" provides a synopsis or digest.

The second essay, "The Hermeneutics of Psychotherapy: Healing through Belief," is, in some ways, a development and application of the conclusions reached in the first essay. The second essay presents a theoretical framework within which we seek to identify principles of healing that underlie psychotherapeutic process. We view psychological wounds as expressions of a tension between the normal and the abnormal, and elaborate on how a *horizontal* complementarity and a *vertical* hierarchy provide the basic framework within which the healing tendency associated with the wound finds expression. By *horizontal* we are referring to the notion of complementarity developed in the first essay: that is, we mean a dimension of encounter among persons characterised by an equality (of value or meaning) between person and relationship, between *one and many*, between uniqueness and solidarity.... By *hierarchy* we are referring to the human experience of the distribution of power, and, in our understanding of this dimension, we focus especially on questions regarding how competitive and co-operative expressions of power are to be hierarchically ordered with respect to one another. We go on to propose that *horizontal*, relational equality provides the norm for the *vertical*, hierarchical ordering of human experience, and discuss how this normalising influence might affect the healing process of psychotherapeutic change. Moreover, the priority of belief over suspicion has implications for how one is to order power, freedom, rights, obligations and knowledge in human relationship, and we consider how this *hierarchical ordering* challenges one to interpret troubled feelings in terms of an inherent response to, and quest for the meaning that characterises human life. In view of this emphasis on *meaning*, we also discuss the relevance and impact of Viktor Frankl's logotherapy[9] on our proposals.

We consider that the breakdown of complementarity and hierarchy threatens normality, yet calls for healing. We discuss how this breakdown represents neither a circumscribed nor fatalistic process (even if, during times of discouragement, one may feel that there is *no light at the end of the tunnel*). Rather, we consider how one may uncover healing properties that both dwell within and transcend temporal features of the psychological experience of feeling troubled and being wounded: these healing properties influence the nature of the exchange between the accord and disaccord of the complementary, and between the integration and disintegration of the hierarchical: that is, between the normal and the abnormal. We conclude that the salutary potential of this exchange in the human experience of the *mix of reality*[10] makes of the psychotherapeutic process a hopeful enterprise.

As with the first essay, for the reader who wants a quicker overview of the issues and themes presented in this second essay, we have added a synopsis: "Appendix B."

Appendix C, entitled, "Some Reflections on the Compatibility of Thought and Being, Idea and Reality, Internal Representation and Actual Relationship" completes the book. This appendix revisits the discussion in the first essay regarding the association between epistemological and ontological questions. We consider the implications this association has for understanding how, in our view, the internal or mental object of psychoanalysis ought to be seen as arising from, depending on, and referring to actual relationship. We also revisit the discussion, from the second essay, regarding the *compatibility* between the human experience of *complementarity* (e.g. trusted connection between self and other) and the human experience of the *hierarchy* of power and meaning. We explore, in a more explicit fashion than was done in the original essays, how the notions of *complementarity*, *hierarchy* and *compatibility* may contribute to seeing epistemological and psychological aspects of human experience as essentially and intrinsically compatible with the ontological-relational foundations of that experience. We conclude with a consideration of the hierarchical ordering of the realm of thought: we view thought oriented to *thankfulness* and *wonder* as having intrinsic priority over thought characterised by *possession* and *control*. When it comes to the human connection to truth, deferral informs mastery.

We should clarify that, although we speak in this book of the hermeneutics of belief and give priority to belief over suspicion, ours is not a work about religious belief, nor about the psychological effect of religious belief. We do adopt, however, an approach that does not see only an extrinsic relation between the scientific study of psychology and psychopathology, on the one hand, and philosophical and theological questions that might arise in relation to the human experience of abnormality, on the other.[11] Each science has its metaphysical *moment* on the basis of which it establishes an essential grasp of the reality or subject matter it explores. In this work we invoke a consideration of the rupture or breach between the complements of person and relationship as defining a crucial (metaphysical) *moment* for the understanding and treatment of psychopathology. In the second essay we propose that this rupture or breach presents not simply as division, but essentially as *wound*. The *wound* is a sign of division but also contains within itself a healing tendency. We further consider how it is this normalising, healing tendency – as an inherent or intrinsic feature of the wound – that allows us, in approaching the subject matter of psychopathology, to speak of the priority of a hermeneutics of belief over one of suspicion.

In this context, we concern ourselves with metaphysical or philosophical issues because we understand these to be central to a consideration of our subject matter: psychopathology and its healing or treatment. As indicated above, we see the relation between the philosophical and psychological to be *intrinsic* as opposed to *extrinsic*. Here we may refer to work of Michael Hanby who speaks of *intrinsic* relations among science, metaphysics and theology.[12] We, likewise, explore our subject matter in a manner that does not view philosophical – or even religious – considerations as something to be excluded from, or extrinsic to the understanding of psychological experience. In contradistinction to an *extrinsicist* approach, we see an *intrinsic* association that allows, among other things, for the integration of the empirical and the ontological aspects of the human enterprise.[13] Our position is, broadly speaking, in keeping with what has been described as *post-secular*. From this perspective one recognises an *intrinsic* connection between the metaphysical and the natural, between the religious and the secular, while also recognising that each of these various visions and dimensions of reality enjoys its own autonomy.[14]

Claude A. Della Zazzera &
David J. Crowe
April 2, 2015

Acknowledgements

There are many who have been helpful and influential in our work. First of all we recognise our patients who, by placing their trust in us and allowing us to share in their problems and struggles, have taught us about the importance of understanding the meaningfulness of mental health symptoms. We are also deeply appreciative for the privilege of working for over three decades with colleagues from various mental health professions, who have been models for us of quality patient care. We are grateful to those who took the time to read and discuss parts of our manuscript. In particular, we wish to thank Sylvie Richard for her willingness to carefully explore an earlier version of our first essay and offer helpful comments and suggestions. Finally we wish to consider family and friends who have been supportive and encouraging, not only through what they have done, but also by their faithful presence. For all these sources of trust, support and inspiration we are thankful.

---

[1] The term *hermeneutics* refers to the theory or philosophy of interpretation that one applies in approaching the subject matter of one's enquiry. As we

will discuss in the course of the writings in this book, we give priority to a *hermeneutics of belief* over a *hermeneutics of suspicion* (see below for a discussion of Paul Ricoeur's use of these terms). The priority of belief in our approach to interpretation implies a certain kind of openness to the *understanding* of psychopathology (cf. first essay) and to the *healing* of psychopathology (cf. second essay). By such an *open hermeneutical approach* we intend an approach that allows one to consider that both breach and healing are ever present in the experience of a wounded state (i.e. a state involving psychopathological symptoms). We will elaborate on how disorder or distress, on the one hand, and a longing for *trusted connection*, on the other, both call for interpretation. We will also show, however, that, with the *hermeneutical* priority of belief over suspicion, *trusted connection* has priority over breach; and this is the case both with respect to making symptoms intelligible/meaningful, and with respect to advancing this (*hermeneutically-* or *belief-informed*) way of healing.

[2] Ricoeur, Paul, "Hermeneutics and Critique of Ideology," in J. B. Thompson (Ed. and Trans.), *Paul Ricoeur: Hermeneutics and the Human Sciences*, Cambridge, Cambridge University Press, 1981 (original published, 1973), p. 100; Ricoeur, Paul, *Freud and Philosophy*, (translated by D. Savage), New Haven and London, Yale University Press,1970, p.28, p. 32-36; Scott-Baumann, Alison, *Ricoeur and the Hermeneutics of Suspicion*, London, Continuum International Publishing Group, 2009, p. 115-116, p. 118; Itao, Alexis Deodato S., "Paul Ricoeur's Hermeneutics of Symbols: A Critical Dialectic of Suspicion and Faith," *Kritike*, vol. four, number two, 2010, p. 11-13; Kaplan, David M., *Ricoeur's Critical Theory*, Albany, New York, State University of New York Press, 2003, p. 41-45.

[3] We mean here an *ontological* inclusiveness.

[4] Scott-Bauman (*Ricoeur and the Hermeneutics of Suspicion*, p. 40) draws important distinctions between suspicion and critique. We do not wish to suggest equivalence among suspicion, critique and doubt, only indicate a broad semblance.

[5] We should clarify that our purpose in this book is not to focus on the topic of *hermeneutics as such*. We do consider, however, the consequences of two hermeneutical positions – suspicion and belief – and proffer the argument that belief has priority over suspicion.

[6] Harman, Graham, "On Vicarious Causation," in Robin MacKay (Ed.), *Collapse Vol. II: Speculative Realism*, Falmouth, Urbanomic, 2007, p. 189.

[7] Gergen, *Relational Being: Beyond Self and Community*, Oxford, Oxford University Press, 2009, p. xx-xxi.

[8] Schmitz, Kenneth L., "The First Principle of Personal Becoming," *Review of Metaphysics, 47-4*, 1994, p. 761-762; Schmitz, Kenneth, L., "Transcendentalism or Transcendentals? A Critical Reflection on the

Transcendental Turn," *The Review of Metaphysics, 58*, 2005, p. 560;
Schmitz, Kenneth L., "Enriching the Copula," *The Review of Metaphysics:
A Commemorative Issue. Thomas Aquinas, 1224-1247, 27*, 1974, p. 511-
512.

[9] Frankl, Viktor, *Man's Search for Meaning*, translated by Ilse Lasch,
Boston, Beacon Press, 2006 (first published in English, 1959; originally
published in German in 1946).

[10] Kenneth Schmitz speaks of the "mixture of reality" by which he refers to
"those clouds and shadows that are part of the reality of the make-up of
each of us," that involve negations and privations through which the
"texture of being [nevertheless] shines with its positive values" (Schmitz,
Kenneth L, *Person and Psyche*, Arlington, Virginia, The Institute for the
Psychological Sciences Press, 2009, p. 31).

[11] For an elucidation of the distinction between *extrinsic* vs. *intrinsic* forms
of relation among natural science, metaphysics and theology, see: Hanby,
Michael, *No God, No Science? – Theology, Cosmology, Biology*,
Chichester, West Sussex, Blackwell Publishing Ltd., 2013, p. 10-45.

[12] Ibid. As Hanby elaborates, an *extrinsicist* position would see
metaphysics/theology *dictate* to natural science or natural science *dictate* to
metaphysics/theology, or view each field as radically separate from the
other.

[13] Consider this comment by Michael Hanby on empirical experience or
appearance in Aristotle: "Since truth is not exhausted in appearance it
needs to be unpacked, not because truth lurks obscurely 'behind'
appearances (where it can never logically be reached), but because it
overwhelms appearances, as the light of the sun overwhelms the eye of the
owl (Aristotle, Metaph II, 933b10)." See: Hanby, *No God, No Science?*, p.
16.

[14] A post-secular approach may refer to both an emerging historical phase
(occurring in the context of the post-modern, while also transcending it) in
which the secular world-view is no longer given an absolute status (but
understood to have its own metaphysical/theological underpinnings or
implications), and to any historically antecedent viewpoint which allows
one to distinguish domains of human knowledge (e.g. natural science,
philosophy, theology) and yet remain open to a consideration of the
intrinsic relations among them (Hanby, *No God, No Science?*).

Consider Margaret Somerville's question regarding whether "an
aggressively 'secular' society is proving inhospitable to the human spirit."
She also asks whether we could imagine a "post-secular" society in which
one might find a "shared ethics." She proposes notions such as the *human
spirit* and the *secular sacred* as providing a non-exclusive common ground
(neither excluding religious nor non-religious beliefs) for exploring and

deciding ethical issues ("Building Ethical Bridges in a Secular Age" *Comment, Public Theology for the Common Good*, September 1, 2014, published by Cardus, http://www.cardus.ca/comment/article/4373/building-ethical-bridges-in-a-secular-age/).

Consider, as well, the work by John R. Betz, in which he explores J. G. Hamann's (1730-1788) philosophy in terms of how it allows one to "get beyond postmodernity" and holds possibilities for a *post-secular vision* (*After Enlightenment: The Post-Secular Vision of J. G. Hamann*, Chichester, West Sussex, Wiley-Blackwell, 2009, p. 319).

In *The Self: Beyond the Postmodern Crisis*, Paul C. Vitz speaks of what he terms a *transmodern* conception of self as an answer to the problems associated with modern and postmodern conceptions of self. This has some analogy with the post-secular visions we note above (Vitz, Paul C. & Felch, Susan M., Eds., *The Self: Beyond the Postmodern Crisis*, Wilmington, Delaware, ISI Books, 2006; see: "Introduction: From Modern and Postmodern Selves to the Transmodern Self," p. xi-xxii).

We are not necessarily endorsing the particular post-secular positions noted above, but only suggesting that a post-secular view permits a degree of freedom towards our subject matter (i.e. psychopathology and its treatment) that we would not have if we had to exclude a-priori, non-secular considerations – or if we had to accept the metaphysical and religious underpinnings of an exclusive secularism and thus adopt an *extrinsicist* (cf. Hanby, *No God, No Science?*) understanding of the association between our subject matter and metaphysical/theological considerations.

I

APPLYING A HERMENEUTICS OF BELIEF TO THE UNDERSTANDING OF PSYCHOPATHOLOGY

A *The Ambiguity in the Psychoanalytic Understanding of the Internal Object*

In this essay[1] we propose a philosophical/psychological theory[2] in which we define normality in terms of the basic accord one experiences between *being* (a person) and *relating* (to other persons), and abnormality in terms of the disaccord or rupture that one may experience between these complements. This leads us to consider the question of normality in terms of basic ontological-relational issues. In other words, we do not see the matter of what is psychologically normal or abnormal as referring solely to phenomena that one may define as statistical/empirical, subjectively generated or socio-historically relative.[3] We propose, rather, a more fundamental formulation on the basis of which one might evaluate such other definitions.

In exploring these issues we focus particular attention on the psychoanalytic notions of object and defence.[4] We see these notions as having a rich impact on matters that pertain to the theory of psychopathology and healing. We also see, however, an ambiguity in psychoanalytic formulations of the origin and meaning of *object relations*. In psychoanalytic theory the concept of object relations, broadly speaking, refers to interpersonal or social relationships, both as actually occurring and as internally structured, pondered and represented in the psyche.[5] There is, therefore, an initial ambiguity with the use of the term, *object*, in that psychoanalysts employ it to refer to the actual other, with whom one relates, as well as to the internal form or representation of that other in the psyche.[6]   The problem of ambiguity we wish to highlight, however, lies not so much with the matter of distinguishing the internal from the external object as with the way in which the two are said to be related. The textual context will normally indicate whether one or the other meaning is intended, but a greater or more significant ambiguity lies in the basic psychoanalytic view that the internal object is said to develop, in significant ways, as a consequence of ego defensive withdrawal from the actual object (i.e. from real relationship).[7]

In our view the internal object thereby takes on an ambiguous status. On the one hand, psychoanalysts appear to understand it as a sign of the impact of actual human relationship on the internal development of the psyche, thus as the structural expression of a *link* with the other.[8]   On the other hand, they view it as a product of defence of self or ego *from* relationship: that is, they tend to understand the development of the internal object as occurring in reaction to frustrations, conflicts or failures in relationship, which prompt some form of movement *away* from actual relationship (i.e. *back* to self or ego).

Thus, the internal object supports both linkage and separation, although the tendency, in basic psychoanalytic theory, is to resolve this ambiguity by ultimately viewing the genesis or formation of the internal object as being more the consequence of separation than connection.[9]   Indeed, in some ways the ambiguity associated with the internal object will appear to vary depending on the part of the theory (or practice) of psychoanalysis to which one attends. In what follows we will explore this *variable ambiguity* and its implications for how one may understand the dynamic tension in the mix of normal and abnormal aspects of human experience. We will begin below by investigating two factors that in psychoanalytic theory are closely associated with object relations: motivational structure and developmental process.

According to Freud object cathexis or object love (i.e. the investment of libido or energy by the ego in something or someone outside the ego) is preceded by autoerotic and narcissistic stages of development in which the individual invests libido primarily within him or herself.[10]   For example, Freud writes that the ego-ideal "is the heir to the original narcissism in which the childish ego found its self-sufficiency."[11]   Thus, the ego-ideal expresses some aspect of the ambiguity of which we speak: it is based on identification with a real person or external object, but its function as an internal object (or internal expression of that relationship) depends more on a presumed original cathexis by the ego of itself, and less, it would seem, on the *attraction* of the other.[12] All forms of internal object development associated with object love appear to retain or express basic features of the primary narcissism and pleasure-oriented autoerotism that precede and underlie them. This is the case even though the internal object may be based on identification with, and introjection of others, such as parents and significant social influences, as is the case with the ego-ideal and the superego. For Freud primal forms of motivation (drive reduction, autoerotism) are clearly linked to a primal mode of object relation (narcissism). Thus, Freud may speak of "the force behind all human activities" as the "striving towards the two [auto-oriented] convergent aims of profit and pleasure."[13]

This strong emphasis on an underlying a-relational or auto-orientated form of motivation[14] would appear to dispel the ambiguity of the internal object to which we are alluding: that is, there would be no ambiguity if the meaning of relationship (both with an external real person and in the way this relationship might be pondered, represented or structured internally) is essentially explained on the basis of an a-relational primary narcissism, the underpinning of which is an even more a-relational state of autoerotism.   A strict interpretation of psychoanalytic theory tends towards the view that all interest in others is self-interest: the interest in or cathexis of real objects (i.e. others), which characterizes human development, is primarily viewed as a detour from an originally self-oriented form of human desire or motivation. For example, to allow for such relations as familial, non-erotic affection, the actual instinctual aim is said (by Freud) to be inhibited.[15]

The idea that we are to explain human behaviour on the basis of some form of self-interest that discounts other forms of motivation is found not only with Freud, however; it is so widespread in the understanding of human affairs that to suggest otherwise (i.e. to suggest that relational meaning cannot be simply or universally reduced to self-interest) seems to violate some basic axiom of the modern or contemporary mindset or zeitgeist.[16]

The very nature and course of development, which is summed up succinctly in Freud's dictum "Where id was there ego shall be,"[17] seems to reinforce the notion that human psychological development originates in and remains fundamentally tied – not only with respect to origin, but also in principle – to an a-relational source.[18] The ego forms from the id (and the superego from the ego); development is rooted in a primitive and non-relational state (which is how Freud describes the id).[19]   Although the implication is that human development involves a movement from the non-relational to the relational (e.g. the transformation of narcissistic libido into object libido),[20] this seems more like an assertion or declaration than explanation of how the human being *comes to be* relational, and if, as we noted above, all human activity is actually motivated by "profit and pleasure," then the actuality or authenticity of human relation has already come into question or, as we will later elaborate, under *suspicion*.[21]

Many psychoanalysts incorporate some version of the idea of an a-relational beginning into their theories of development.[22]   This incorporation is reflected in the names that they give to early stages of infant development. Consider the following examples: Winnicott speaks of the "unintegrated phase";[23]   Hartmann of the "undifferentiated phase";[24] Spitz of the "objectless stage";[25] Kernberg, Mahler and Jacobson of an "initially undifferentiated stage" (of self-object fusion or autism);[26] Lacan of the "body in bits and pieces" (not yet unified; he proposes that unity occurs with the advent of the "mirror stage" at six months).[27]

Although these designations all emphasize a non- or a-relational beginning to psychological development, one may detect some shift from Freud's formulations: his understanding of the origins of psychological development put the emphasis on the enduring role of early, instinctually-based forms of motivation (e.g. the id as ruled by pleasure, the ego as starting out in primary narcissism), whereas other analysts seem to focus more on the psyche's early lack of boundaries and definition as a stage on the path towards later differentiation and connection.[28]   One may speculate here about whether the developments in object relations and ego psychology that followed

Freud were, in some sense, part of an attempt to loosen the hold of the idea that an a- or non- or even anti-relational motivational force or process underlies and rules all human behaviour. These later theoretical considerations tended to put greater emphasis on the developing of connections with others and reality as features of psychological motivation and functioning. Indeed, Freud's own theory evolved towards a greater emphasis on object-relations, expanding his earlier emphasis on instinctual drive.[29]

The importance of relation is also noted in the central role Freud gives to Eros – the life force and uniting power of desire – as that which orients human beings to connection with one another (we will elaborate on this below). One may also consider how psychoanalysis itself is practised in a relational (interpersonal) context between analyst and analysand; it is after all, a *talking cure*. Furthermore, one may consider the requirement of a training analysis for any would-be analyst, established early in the history of psychoanalysis, as yet another indication of acknowledgement, from within the psychoanalytic movement, of the importance of interpersonal relations, in this case with respect to the professional development of the psychoanalyst.[30] Yet here too one may detect an emphasis on an *a-relational* origin.

There is an interesting parallel or analogy, which one may draw between the psychoanalytic emphasis on an a-relational origin to psychological development, and the apparent claim to an a-relational origin to psychoanalysis itself as an historical movement. Borch-Jacobsen and Shamdasani[31] propose that Freud and other supporters of psychoanalysis, when describing the development of the psychoanalytic movement, minimize the impact of historical influences from outside their movement, and exaggerate claims of originality. Borch-Jacobsen and Shamdasani devote particular attention to how the requirement for training analysis of each would-be psychoanalyst developed within psychoanalysis.

Initially, Freud seemed to indicate that self-analysis was sufficient for someone preparing to become a psychoanalyst. After all, this was Freud's own preparation: he had analyzed himself. But later, with divisions regarding theory (e.g. with Adler) becoming increasingly problematic, Jung (who was still a supporter of Freud at the time) proposed that each would-be analyst ought to undergo an analysis with an experienced analyst.[32]   Freud, accepted and supported Jung's suggestion that all analysts ought to undergo a training analysis in preparation to become analysts, but he, Freud, was to be exempt from such training.[33] He was the originator, and when Jung had offered to help Freud work through a psychological problem he had experienced during their 1909 visit to lecture at Clark University in the US, Freud is said to have limited Jung's intervention because he could not compromise his "authority."[34] Freud and others in the psychoanalytic movement came to define his self-analysis as a necessary origin to the psychoanalytic enterprise. Borch-Jacobsen and Shamdasani propose, however, that this emphasis on Freud's self-analysis – as playing a central role in the origins of psychoanalysis – is more legend or myth than historical event. They write, "Freud's self-analysis […] becomes the mythical origin of psychoanalysis," and they speak of the "mythification and dehistoricisation of psychoanalysis."[35] The initial acceptance that self-analysis might be sufficient for someone interested in becoming an analyst was rejected and gave way to the idea that only Freud's self-analysis was foundational. The value of other self-analyses then came under question or suspicion. For example, Freud remarked in a letter to Paul Schilder (an analyst who had only undertaken a self-analysis) that, "the first psychoanalysts who had not been analysed 'were never proud of it.'" Freud viewed his own case as an exception and so added that with respect to *his* self-analysis "'one might perhaps assert the right to an exceptional position.'"[36]

We believe it more crucial to consider, however, not the a-historical claims that may have occurred within the psychoanalytic movement, not the alleged construction of a myth, but the ambiguity expressed in psychoanalysis about the nature of the influence of actual relationship on the psychological development of an internal object world. This ambiguity seems to occur in analogous aspects of psychoanalysis: its conceptions of its own historical origins, *and* its understanding of the origins of human psychological development. The psychoanalytic theory of psychological development posits an a-relational beginning that somehow becomes relational or object-oriented: autoerotism and primary narcissism set the stage or form the background to object relations. In an analogous manner the self-analysis of Freud is said to start the chain of psychoanalytic training that calls for all future psychoanalysts to submit to an *interpersonal* training analysis, while Freud, as originator, is to be exempt. Where Borch-Jacobsen and Shamdasani see mythological, a-historical origins we see an ambiguity of relation vs. non-relation, and we see ontological and not only historical questions raised by this ambiguity (as we will consider below). In any case, our own focus is less on the claims of psychoanalysis with respect to its own historical origins, and more on its claims with respect to explaining psychological origins.

We have referred above to the ambiguity in the psychoanalytic conception of object relations as a *variable ambiguity*. As noted earlier, the ambiguity tends to be dispelled when the emphasis is primarily or exclusively on an a-relational origin or basis to psychological experience.[37] However, if in human experience there is an actual connection to the other, and if (as we will propose) the internal pondering of that relation (involving an internal object) constitutes a potential deepening of relating, then one must ask about what factors motivate and structure such actual *relational* development. It is this that introduces the ambiguity: for psychoanalysts there is a linking, relational motive – not just a self-oriented, a-relational motive – that somehow plays a role in psychological development.

As mentioned earlier, Freud recognizes the great source of this *linking motive* in Eros, but, as we will consider, his understanding of the actual expression of this life instinct follows a reductive paradigm (reduction to non- or a-relational motives and factors: discharge-seeking rather than object-seeking).[38] Although Eros is said to expand human interest towards the universal, Freud seems to understand such expansion as taking place through the inhibition of the actual aim of instinct or drive. Thus, for example, familial or even national ties are said to be the result of an inhibition of the erotic aim.[39] But why does Eros contribute to the inhibition of instinctual drive such that, for example, erotic object love may become non-erotic affection among family members (see second essay, section "H," endnote # "89," for discussion of Max Scheler's view on this question)? Why is there this *connecting*, universal direction to life? Freud says, "Why this has to be done we do not know; it is simply the work of Eros."[40]

Yet much of Freud's thinking (in view of his reductive paradigm) tends towards a denial of this universal direction, even as he asserts it. It is interesting to note that when he directly compares death and life instincts he does define the linking role of the life instinct (Eros) in unambiguous terms.[41] We propose, however, that his death instinct is already latent in the reductive way he understands the concrete expressions of the life instinct, and that this latent *undermining* (contained in his understanding of life instinct or Eros – see discussion of Graham Harman's use of "undermining" later in this essay) contributes to his eventual positing of a death instinct and to the ambiguity which we have been emphasizing.[42]

We come back to Freud's dictum: "Where id was there ego shall be." The ambiguity arises when we ask the question, "Why?" Now, however, we are not focusing, as we did previously, on the reductive origins of "[w]here id was," but on the relational implications of why "ego shall be" (and one might add, "why superego shall be"): in other words, "Why is there relation – with reality, with others, and why an internalisation of that relation?" We noted (above) Freud's answer to this question: "it is simply the work of Eros." This answer is more in the form of an observation or belief than explanation. Interestingly, the implications of the death instinct are that any development of connection is ultimately to regress back to non-connection, fragmentation and separation.[43] If, however, as we are suggesting, Freud's death instinct is already implicit in the reductive processes that are assumed to be under the rule of the life instinct, and if (as a consequence of this kind of reduction) the relation to the other is always in some fundamental way a detour from auto-orientation, then it would follow that death might be viewed as a basic goal. If the reductive expression of the life instinct is fundamental, then why stop at narcissism or auto-erotism: one would expect to see indications of motivation to return not only to self but also to before self (or ego, or id), thus to a non- or pre-life.

B *Hermeneutics of Belief and Suspicion: Speculative Realism, Constructionism and Personalism*

We have proposed in the above that the psychoanalytic understanding of the internal object presents with some ambiguity, an ambiguity that stems from a *weak/thin* recognition of the meaningfulness of relationship, and a contrasting *strong/thick* emphasis on auto-orientation with respect to explaining the basis of psychological experience. Hence a paradox arises in regards to psychoanalysis: ostensibly, psychoanalysis is to contribute to a Copernican decentring of the human being and to achieve this by viewing consciousness with suspicion while seeking explanations for human conduct in the unconscious.   Taking into consideration the emphasis on auto-orientation in the psychoanalytic paradigm, however, the proposed shifting of the centre from the conscious to the unconscious does not result in an actual *decentring*.[44]   In our view, this is because in psychoanalysis one directs doubt or suspicion more towards human relationship (and its substantive underpinnings) than towards consciousness *per se*. In any case, we believe that these matters take us beyond questions of psychological theory (and its historical development), and require a consideration of underlying philosophical issues. Let us expand on this point.

In order to address the ambiguity we have been highlighting we believe it necessary to consider whether and how relational and ontological aspects of human experience may co-occur, and in what way human thought and psychological structures like the internal object may be rooted in, and reflective of this co-occurrence. To elaborate an understanding of this *link* between being and relation (i.e. ontology), and the influence of this link on mind (i.e. epistemology, knowledge) and psyche (i.e. psychology, interior object), we will explore three contemporary systems of thought which offer interesting yet varied positions on questions regarding the ontological basis of relationship and on the implications such questions might have for understanding interior or mental activity: 1) the object-oriented philosophy of Graham Harman (which has developed in the context of a broader movement known as speculative realism),[45] 2) the constructionist approach to *relational being* of Kenneth Gergen,[46] and 3) the personalism/metaphysics of existential act of Kenneth Schmitz.[47]   We cannot offer extensive expositions of these three perspectives, but we believe that our reflections on comparisons and contrasts among them will allow us to propose a philosophical position which provides some resolution of the ambiguity on which we have been focusing.   In contradistinction to the psychoanalytic tendency, our attempt is to show that this resolution can be achieved non-reductively.

Harman's object-oriented philosophy presents a defence of the reality of objects and critically rejects any privilege given to the *relation* implied by human knowing. He is critical, therefore, of any anthropocentric, Kantian-like emphasis, in which the reality of objects is said to be essentially formed by the (human) mind (he sees this as a problem of *overmining*).[48] He is also critical of the reduction of objects to their component parts, arguing that objects are as real as the atoms, molecules or other components that may be part of their make-up (the reduction of objects to components he calls *undermining*). He is a defender, one might say, of the *distinction* or even *autonomy* of the object, the object as a *thing-in-itself*. To defend the *thing-in-itself*, however, he believes he has to limit the role of relation: "relations never directly encounter the autonomous reality of their components."[49]   He thus explains that "real things are so deeply hidden they can't touch." With respect to relation he says, "Things get at each other through their weaknesses and accidents, not through their essences,"[50] and "*all* relations translate or distort that to which they relate."[51]

We might infer, however, that Harman's assertion of the reality of objects- or things-in-themselves indicates a form of solidarity with objects, a recognition and assertion of their being, and that such solidarity constitutes a form of relation, perhaps more implied than explicit, in his approach. This implied solidarity or relation would be neither the *overmining* of mental or social construction (e.g. all is mind), nor the *undermining* of a reductive naturalism or materialism (e.g. all is made up of particles of matter). We will propose below that this solidarity involves a notion of relation that is deeper than the *epistemological* one – which seems to be the only kind of relation that Harman explicitly allows: as noted above, for Harman, essences do not touch, things get at each other only through their weaknesses and accidents, and all relations translate and distort that which they relate.[52]

Gergen presents a position which, in contrast to Harman's, appears to favour relation, and yet we believe it restricts the meaning of relation, in some ways more than Harman's does. Gergen's fundamental presupposition is that reality is a construction that arises from what he calls *unbounded, relational being*. The latter concept refers not to selves or persons in relationship, but to some sort of fluid, "generative process of relating" that leads to, or underlies human agreements about reality: constructionism requires that reality be what it is because *our* agreeing makes it so. Gergen critically approaches what he calls *bounded being*, which he says refers to separate units such as persons, individuals, moral agency, causality, traditions of truth, etc. He sees the Enlightenment as the source of the restrictive notion of separateness associated with bounded being.[53] Gergen makes frequent references to the optionality of any defined being (i.e. it could be defined differently) and from this he appears to deduce that there is a substratum of unbounded being that is both constructive (producing the options) and *relational* (prior to the separation of things into units);[54] however, his notion of relation, described in terms of unbounded being, seems to us to be problematic.

The notion of unbounded, relational being indicates more a kind of non-differentiated state (of things without boundary or definition: unbounded, optional) than what is usually understood by relation (i.e. association between or among distinct entities).[55] He writes that he wants to "generate an account of human action that can replace the presumption of bounded selves with a vision of relationship. I do not mean relationships between otherwise separate selves, but rather, a process of coordination that precedes the very concept of the self."[56] He rejects the "presumption" that relationship is derivative of independent beings and believes it is necessary to abolish independence in order to challenge this presumption. His attempt is to "generate a 'strong' relationality, one in which there is no condition of independence"; he wants to challenge the notion that relationship results from the contact of distinct entities and to posit the reverse: "that individual units are derivative of relational process."[57] It is not clear, however, what might be *co*-ordinated in his reference to "process of coordination" because all entities ("separate units"), according to Gergen, are mere options and, by definition, restrictive or limiting. The optionality inherent to unbounded being and to the "process of coordination," provide, according to Gergen, the possibility of freeing oneself from any restrictive, bounded being, such as the potential "prison" of the self.[58] The freeing associated with optionality, however, invariably leads to the restrictiveness of the actually chosen options, thus turning the ostensibly liberating freedom of (arbitrary) construction into a perennial source of restriction.

Gergen claims that the conventions of language "virtually insist that separate entities exist prior to relationship,"[59] but he, on the other hand, wants *relationship* to exist *prior* to such "separate entities." In our view, this amounts to some kind of abstracted, virtual notion of relation, in which relation and distinction do not co-occur. For Gergen relation and distinction have an exclusionary rather than complementary association: for one to be the other must flee; or the one has to be derived from and resolved back into the other.

We appreciate Gergen's critique of individualism, but we do not agree that the relational nature of the human person obviates distinction or, vice-versa, that distinction obviates relation. As well, we do not share Gergen's concern with the restrictions of conventional language; we are more concerned by how his particular critique of language seems to imply a form of relation that is actually a form of perpetual escape from relation based on a perpetual revision of options.

Although we see some affinity between Gergen's emphasis on the relational meaning of being and aspects of the position we are proposing, we also see differences. In addressing questions of bounded vs. unbounded being Gergen sees matters of ontology and truth as futile.[60] He seeks to settle theoretical debate, not in the court of truth, but in the court of "more promising outcomes."[61] He writes that "by embracing Truth we eliminate the voices of all those who do not see the world in the same way."[62] In Gergen's constructionism we cannot encounter one another on the basis of truth that makes a claim on us, but only on the basis of "truth" in so far as we claim it. For Gergen the power of optional construction is pre-emptive: any tradition of truth must be reduced to a mere option. In his system one can only construct the meaning of the other, never discover the meaning of the other, as there is no distinct other, in fact, to discover. In addition, truth cannot be part of the common ground on which one might base discourse or relation.

Because of his constructionism, Gergen has to explicitly dismiss any notion of truth that is more than a mere claim based on the power of agreement. Presumably, truth that exceeds such power cannot be tested in the court of "more promising outcomes," and perhaps, for that reason, one is to set such truth aside or disqualify it.[63] Indeed, the notion of truth that Gergen explicitly excludes from his system would have to be tested in the *court* where truth is not a mere property of reason (the Enlightenment view), nor the mere property of *social* agreements (which is Gergen's view: in some ways more in line with, than a criticism of the Enlightenment). Gergen is, of course, correct to reduce traditions of truth to mere options, if such traditions of truth are merely the result of arbitrary construction. From the self-imposed theoretical limits of his constructionism it does seem impossible to actually encounter another's tradition of truth (and perhaps to actually encounter an other) because the other's tradition of truth is pre-emptively reduced to the mere claim of truth. The claim that truth is a claim, however, does not make the truth a claim. From the perspective which he proposes, Gergen must repeatedly exclude the possibility that truth makes its own claim on discourse.[64]

In his response to reviewers of his book, *Relational Being: Beyond Self and Community*, Gergen proposes a way to proceed with debate and dialogue between positions endorsing bounded vs. unbounded being: "to deliberate on the *positive practices* issuing from the tradition of bounded being... [and to] inquire into the *problems in practice* raised by the conception of relational being" (emphasis added). He says that "[i]n this way, one would come to appreciate the existence of multiple realities, including both their potentials and limits."[65] Aside from the fact that Gergen loads the dice, as it were, in that those who enter a dialogue with him are to assess theory only in terms of practices that follow from it and presumably not inquire about its truth, there is a further problem. Even if we were to set aside the question of theoretical truth as Gergen would have us do, the problem of how to determine whether something supports "positive practices" or "more promising outcomes" remains. Here, we may challenge Gergen's pragmatism (along with that of William James): truth (of theory) cannot be set aside and replaced with the cash value[66] (or "promising outcomes") of an idea because truth is pre-required to determine whether one is dealing with counterfeit or real cash (counterfeit or real promising outcomes). Truth is, therefore, not merely a property of theories, reason, agreements or practices: it underlies and informs theories, reason, agreements or practices. From within the constructionist frame which Gergen espouses, one can only conclude that his theory is neither positive nor negative, and that it is neither promising nor unpromising, because it excludes or eclipses that which might allow one to discern such features. Stepping outside the constructionist frame, however, and in so far as Gergen's theory presents an arbitrary view of meaning that jeopardizes and obscures the common ground that, we would suggest, forms the basis of dialogue and relationship, one would have to see his theory as not supporting "more promising outcomes." It would seem that promise is excluded in principle.

Gergen makes some important points in critiquing individualism and in supporting the value of relationship (including an endorsement of what one might call *universal* values);[67] however, in our view, the constructionism[68] he endorses, along with his notion of relational, unbounded being, is incompatible with an inclusive understanding of the meaning of relationship (i.e. inclusive of being *and* relation), and with a perspective in which one understands the human experience of ideas and knowledge as influenced by and dependent on such meaning.

We have argued that Freud, Harman and Gergen present approaches that emphasize a separation or breach between distinct and relational aspects of being, and an incompatibility between the world of being and the world of knowing. In these three approaches we may speak of a hermeneutics of suspicion[69] applied to being and knowing. In psychoanalysis, there is the relationally ambiguous meaning of the internal object, in which the internal object is less a reflection or affirmation of actual relationship and more an indication of separation or division of self from relationship. With Harman's object-oriented philosophy there is ontological separation among objects, but only *epistemological* relation among them. Relation is restricted to knowing and knowing is restrictive because objects in their core remain things-in-themselves and in Kantian-like fashion *hide* from being known. With Gergen's constructionism there is no ontological level to reality, only the constructions that are produced by a relational process of agreement in which anything that might come to be in relation is itself optional.

We also note, however, that there is ambiguity in these three approaches. The development of psychoanalytic theory, as manifested in object relations theory and ego psychology, introduces greater emphasis on relationship as a basis and goal for psychological development, and as essential for understanding the structure of the psyche.[70] Harman's whole philosophy seems to us to be oriented to the *defence* of objects. To defend objects implies a solidarity with them, and, in our view, it is an ontological relation that gives rise to this implicit affirmation of solidarity (an ontological relation which in Harman is largely implicit, since he, at an explicit level, appears to restrict relation to *knowledge*).[71] Gergen, despite his insistence on the optional nature of what might be in relation and his eschewal of being, would assert the primacy of relationship, and of it as a source of *being* (i.e. he speaks of *relational being*). In any case, we have indicated that, in these systems of thought (cf. Freud, Harman and Gergen), the support of the ontological realm (of distinction and relation of persons), and of the ideational realm (that can affirm and remain compatible with the ontological) is not unambiguous.

Kenneth Schmitz presents an approach which, in our view, supports and defends *both* the ontological basis of relationship and the potential for compatibility between the ontological and the ideational: there are both ontological and ideational forms (or levels) of association among beings, and there is a basic compatibility between these forms. We read and interpret Schmitz as proposing a complementarity between the distinction of being and its relational meaning.[72] Furthermore, Schmitz differentiates between *object of consciousness* and *subject of being*[73] (this distinction will become central to our understanding of the internal object). He sees the relation between knower and known as more than one where a subject of consciousness apprehends an object of consciousness; the relation involves encounters between subjects of being.[74]   Accordingly, the relation between knower and known "is not a 'contract' [or construct] based upon the knower. It is the capacity of the knower to participate in and with the knowable as companionate member in the community of beings."[75]   And Schmitz, like Harman, does not privilege the human grasp or consciousness of the object. For example, Schmitz writes,

> Does experience begin with the presence of an object in the medium of consciousness? […] Or, rather, is it that we encounter beings in their own integrity and inherent dignity in the midst of other things (*res*), free to spontaneously exercise their own careers whether known or not? If we admit the latter *we release things from their bondage to human consciousness*…we free consciousness from the burden of strategic justification. Justification now becomes a tactical task of confirmation as verificative, touching specific questions of argument and inference and ceases to be a strategy [emphasis added].[76]

Schmitz further defends the reality of objects in the following:

> As I have argued the modern movement towards the absolute autonomy of the human subject has been complicit with the denial of the integrity to other things, reducing them to objects and even to phenomena, which are then fit members of a system that encroaches upon their integrity. As things re-emerge in their singularity from such a system, a new sense of order, sensitive to the historical condition and contingency of all things is required. This calls also for a new more concrete epistemology.[77]

Schmitz' notion of the community of beings, which is inclusive of human and non-human objects (all of which are subjects of being and, therefore, not *only* objects of, or to human consciousness), provides support for what we have called the *solidarity of objects*, which we have suggested is implied in Harman's approach. This solidarity (or relation) may include a role for, and find expression through what Harman refers to as "accidents and weaknesses" but it has, beyond these, an ontological basis.[78]   As well, Harman's defence of the object from the relation implied in *knowing* finds qualified justification in the distinction between subject of being and object of consciousness: a thing withdraws from the *mere* objectification of itself by another[79] – but as subjects of being things may stand together in solidarity.[80]   We may also find in the distinction between subject and object of consciousness a qualified justification for Gergen's critique of individualism.   Gergen would argue that objects (of consciousness) are mere constructions (i.e. "*nothing* is real unless people agree that it is").[81]   If reality were reduced to objects of consciousness, then Gergen's critique of "separate units" would have some validity.   Ironically, however, it is his exclusion of the ontological that leads to, or supports his idea of the construction of "separate units" and, consequently, their eventual, if not essential, alienation from relationship.   With Schmitz' approach, being need not withdraw from relation to retain identity (as with Harman), and it need not be resolved back to boundlessness (as with Gergen).[82]

With both Harman and Gergen one has the impression that relation is reduced to an ideational construction: that is, that ontological aspects of relation are reduced, as it were, to epistemological ones.   With Harman the intent is to protect the ontological, whereas with Gergen the ontological is simply reduced to or absorbed by the ideational.   In both cases one ends up with a reduced notion of relationship, although for different reasons.   For Harman the ontological foundations – which have things be in themselves – have to be protected, as it were, from the *overmining*, reductive effects of ideational relation.   For Gergen ideational relation (i.e. *overmining*) is all there is, and one surmises that such relation is continually forming independent realities from which relation must just as continually recoil.   If, as we have proposed, however, relation and being co-occur, then there is a sense in which relation is ontological *before* it finds epistemological expression.   Nevertheless, one may recognise that there is validity in the critique of Harman (i.e. not to reduce being to mere knowing), and that of Gergen (i.e. not to accept what is merely known as identical to being – although Gergen is misguided, in our view, in so far as he attempts to achieve this by reducing one's relation to *what or who is*, to a relation to what is arbitrarily constructed, thus eliminating the being of that to which one is related).   From these critiques we derive the conclusion that one ought not to reduce the ontological to the epistemological; one ought to consider that "realities are more important than ideas."[83]

Moreover, one may note that Schmitz has emphasised that there is a basic compatibility between thought and being, that is, between the world of knowing and the world of being.   Schmitz refers to "a pronounced modern motivation to make doubt the energy of the search for proven meaning."[84] In contrast to such a hermeneutics of suspicion,[85] he speaks of an attitude of faith based on the *ability* of being to *share* itself with thought.   Consider, for example, how Schmitz refers to the intelligible connection between thought and being as based in "a certain abundance and generosity written into being, its capacity for making a gift of itself to thought…The possibility of cognition is rooted in its ontological generosity, and in a vicariosity which permits one being to bear the presence and meaning of another."[86] G. K. Chesterton also speaks to this matter of generous origins in describing the nature of thought: "Thanks are the highest form of thought."[87] In this context, one could say that the relational quality of being is reflected in, and affirmed by thought and knowledge, because being has the "capacity for making a gift of itself to thought."   For example, Schmitz speaks to the importance of relation with respect to knowledge, saying that "the recovery of the whole relational character of knowledge is one of the most important philosophical achievements of the [twentieth] century."[88]   If knowledge expresses relation, and relation has an ontological and not only epistemological meaning, *then this indicates the possibility of interpreting reality with trust or belief.*

We could say that both Harman and Gergen, in contrast, approach the relation, intrinsic to, and associated with human knowledge, from a perspective that emphasizes doubt or critique, thus tending towards suspicion, even if they do so in different ways and for different reasons: for Harman the object withdraws from human knowledge as from all relation, and for Gergen relation produces objects – of knowledge – which are intrinsically optional.[89] Schmitz allows for criticism (or suspicion) but does not give it primacy. He writes:

> [K]nowledge contains within itself a basic aspect of trust developed in the medium of human faith. This makes the role of criticism indispensable, but it does not make it primary as it so often is in our present excessively critical temper. Rather, criticism is a sifting process based upon and subordinate to the credibility already encountered in knowledge.[90]

We will address this issue – of how the compatibility and integration of the ontological and epistemological favours belief over suspicion – more extensively in the second essay in this book, and in "Appendix C."[91]

C *Psychological and Ontological Aspects of the Internal Object*

We may apply Schmitz' understanding of the distinction between subject of being and object of consciousness to the psychological sphere in general, and, more particularly, to questions we have raised regarding the ambiguity of the internal object in psychoanalysis. Let us consider these psychological implications.

When self approaches other in an auto-oriented manner the other is seen as solely or primarily an object of consciousness. This limits openness of self to other as subject of being. Moreover, when the other is approached as an object of consciousness the self finds itself in the role of a subject of consciousness.[92] On the other hand, when self approaches other in a manner that recognizes the other, not only as object (of consciousness), but also and primarily as subject of being, then there is openness to the ontological dimension – both self and other may then be recognised as subjects of being. Furthermore, we propose that the internal object, as the structural representation of the other within the psyche, is the psychological analogue of the object of consciousness.[93] One may therefore apply what we have noted above about the object of consciousness to the internal object. When the internal object functions to eclipse or obstruct openness to the (ontological) relation of self and other as subjects of being, one may speak of its separating function or *opacity*. When the internal object functions to facilitate or allow openness to the relation of self and other as subjects of being, one may speak of its linking function or *transparency*. Furthermore, although the obstructive effect of the internal object may at times be in a tension with its linking function, we see the latter as its fundamental or primary role – this primacy has its basis in ontology: the priority of subject of being over object of consciousness, a priority based in the generosity that allows being to make "a gift of itself to thought,"[94] and that allows, therefore, the ontological relation to be reflected and affirmed in the object of consciousness as a feature of thought[95] – and thought, therefore, takes the form of thanks (cf. Chesterton).[96]

We also have noted the tendency in psychoanalysis to view the internal object in a manner that gives primacy to separation over linkage (with respect to relationship of self and other), and have argued that this involves a reductive interpretation of the internal object's origins and nature (and may involve, therefore, a reductive approach to the person in whose interior the internal object exists). We are proposing, however, that by giving primacy to linkage over separation, one may approach the question of the ambiguity of the internal object in a non-reductive manner.

In psychoanalytic theory the experience of threat associated with psychological disturbance calls for defence that is generally characterized as ego-defence[97] (this is in keeping with the psychoanalytic understanding of the human individual or organism as primarily or fundamentally auto-oriented). To the extent that the internal object is understood to be the result of ego-defensive process its formation involves some form of withdrawal from the external object; it is, therefore, viewed in terms of representing exclusion from the realm of subjects of being or actual relationship. By proposing a non-reductive understanding of the internal object as primary, however, we are indicating that the internal object's function of internalization of, or identification with the external object is inherently oriented to the deepening of relation with the real other. We are therefore critical of approaches that interpret the formation of the internal object as the product of a process that is basically self-referentially defensive, and, therefore, also essentially exclusionary with respect to relationship.

By analogy, the internal object is to relation as the eyes are to the visual world. The primary function of sight is to see clearly what is around us even if there are times when vision may fail. The primary function of the internal object is to orient the self to the other as subject of being even if it may function at times to distort and exclude such relation (and limit the other solely to object of consciousness). Thus the emphasis on an inherent openness and inclusion does not preclude failures to achieve integration and compatibility between the internal object world and the realm of subjects of being – nor does it preclude underlying failures in the relation of subjects of being. Indeed, we wish to define psychopathology or abnormality in terms of these kinds of failure, and the treatment of psychopathology or abnormality as the attempt to recover from and provide remedies for such failure. Accordingly, our psychotherapeutic focus is on how one may defend, recover or promote the accord (or solidarity) of subjects of being and the integration (transparency) of the internal object world in circumstances in which such accord and integration are threatened. We propose that this calls for the expansion of the understanding of defence such that it is not restricted to the (psychoanalytic notion of) defence of self or ego, but becomes a defence of the relation of subjects of being, and this allows one to interpret the internal object as potentially open to and affirmative of such relation.

Within this framework, one may further define normality as based in an accord between *distinction* (i.e. of self-from-other)[98] and *unity* (i.e. self-for-and-with-other), an accord which finds expression in psychic structures (including internal subjects/objects of consciousness), which affirm and resonate with such accord rather than negate it. In normal development the person achieves both a confident autonomy (i.e. independence, distinction – *to be*) *and* a connection and commitment to relationship (i.e. closeness, unity – *to relate*), such that autonomy serves commitment and commitment supports autonomy (i.e. closeness or intimacy gives rise to independence or freedom, and independence or freedom is oriented towards closeness and intimacy). Moreover, the concepts of self and other (and the whole internal object world) that one develops may reflect and affirm that accord between autonomy and relationship.

With abnormal development, a breach occurs in this accord such that relationship fails to support autonomy or autonomy fails to support relationship. It is in such circumstances that one may see the rise of a form of self-defence that eclipses the ontological basis of relationship. The intended self-affirmation degenerates into self-alienation and the intended commitment degenerates into some form of fearful (or fear-inducing) dependence. We may speak here, respectively, of ruptured or divisive separation instead of healthy, normal distinction, and of fusion or con-fusion instead of meaningful relation. In this circumstance the internal object world also becomes disordered (e.g. an excessively punishing superego, or an overly permissive one).

Meaningful or normal internal representation, on the other hand, is associated with values that favour the accord of distinction and relation of self and other as subjects of being – values such as honour, respect, loyalty, love, etc. Note, in the above, that the internal object and the accord of subjects of being come together on the basis of three factors: 1) the ontological level of the accord of subjects of being, 2) the epistemological level of the internal object to which that accord gives rise, and 3) the association or compatibility between these two levels.

From the perspective we are offering normality has ontological origins or roots that exert an influence on the human person's struggle with abnormality: one is always to confront the meaningless (or abnormal) on the basis of the meaningful (or normal). In the experience of psychopathology there is a co-occurrence of normal accord and abnormal disaccord, that gives rise to a tension. The basic aim of this tension, however, is to heal the rupture of accord.[99] Indeed, the ultimate purpose of subjecting psychological suffering and struggle to psychotherapeutic understanding and intervention is to reorient the person to the value in meaningful/normal relation (and distinction). This work will, at least implicitly, involve the three factors, noted above: 1) the ontological level of actual relationship, 2) the internal object world, and 3) the association between actual relationship and internal representation. Psychotherapeutic work addresses these three factors through the exploration of troubled thoughts, feelings and actions which express both belief and lack of belief in meaningful accord. In this process the tension of the internal world will reflect the tension of the actual world of relationship, and, as noted above, the essential aim of that tension is to heal. Thus, the challenge is to accept, interpret and apply this healing influence to one's life.

Let us consider, for example, a woman who experiences alienation, bitterness, despair and suicidal inclination which is associated with her childhood experience of abuse. She understands her discouragement and anger in terms of the injustice and betrayal she suffered in the formative years of her life. On the one hand, her symptoms signify that she decries the lack of faith in relation of subjects of being, a lack which she witnessed and suffered in her own experience of abuse; on the other hand, her own destructive inclinations involve or express such lack of faith. The challenge for her (and her therapist) is to reinterpret (or newly interpret) the self-defensive lack of belief expressed by inclinations directed against self, other and/or relationship, and work through to the latent belief contained in her protest. In this way she may uncover or reveal the implicit desire and need to reconcile self and other as subjects of being, a desire and need which her very suffering signifies.

In seeking to find meaning in distress one is not normalizing the abnormal, but extracting or seeking out the normal from the experience of the abnormal. From the intrinsic objection contained in the painful reaction to breach begins the orientation to healing, and from the intrinsic protest against the oppression of fusion begins the orientation to liberation. Emptiness, abandonment and division may, therefore, become opportunities to sense and interpret the call to express personal initiative to engage or live relationship in ways that show the need one has to refashion and integrate the internal object on the basis of a renewed or recovered accord of subjects of being.

We should note that the notion of relationship between one subject of being and another implies greater depth of relation than the notion of relationship between a subject of consciousness and an object of consciousness (and we could also speak here by analogy of the relation between ego and internal object).[100] There is greater depth because a subject of being is more than a subject/object of consciousness (since the subject of being is the thing-in-itself, and not just the thing as limited to someone's knowledge: as considered previously, reducing the reality of things to mere knowledge is what Harman calls *overmining*). When one circumscribes or limits the meaning of the object of consciousness and of its analogue, the internal object – by considering them to be mere constructions, and thus excluding their ontological foundations – one has the tendency to reduce all reality to construction or impression and to imply a fusion of being *and* relation. This is what we noted in Gergen's approach: a reduction of being to mere construction, and, therefore the *cancelling* of being or ontology.[101]

It is important to consider, however, that the relation between subjects of being does not exclude but includes the relation between a subject of consciousness and an other approached as an object of consciousness. Yet, to remain open to the realm of subjects of being, one is ever giving priority to being-in-real-or-true-relationship (i.e. relation between or among subjects of being) and, therefore, viewing objects (and subjects) of consciousness (including the psychic world of ego and internal objects) as secondary or *participatory* (i.e. having the role of *parts* rather than *wholes*). Internal objects retain meaning by remaining rooted in a context where to be and to relate are complementary, and internal objects eclipse meaning when they exclude such complementarity. In this approach, an understanding of oneself as a subject of consciousness oriented to an object of consciousness (or as ego oriented to an internal object), remains ontologically rooted in, and open to real relationship. For example, I may completely embrace my opportunity to be a loving witness and support to the life and person (subject of being) of my spouse, while also relating to my spouse as someone (object of consciousness) on whom I rely in the enterprise of managing home, family, friends, etc.

On the other hand, the more one separates the psychological realm from the ontological realm, the more one finds the internal subject/object of consciousness alienated from its ontological foundations. This is likely to occur as a result of the defence of self *against* other (i.e. against relationship), and in this self-defensive mode, one is more likely to envision relationship as occurring primarily in terms of mere construction or pragmatics. The internal object will then tend to eclipse rather than translate the relation between subjects of being. In this *self-defensive* mode of relating, the internal object takes on exclusive and reductive qualities. Conversely, the vision of self and other as subjects of being becomes expressed or evident in the *defence of the accord of subjects of being, an accord that supports the integration or compatibility between the ideational world of consciousness (and unconsciousness) and the real world of relationship* (see "Appendix C" in this book for a further development of this theme). The internal object then has the potential to express inclusive and comprehensive qualities.[102]

As implied above, we consider it normative for human beings to relate to one another and to other realities (e.g. things in nature) both as subjects of being *and* as objects of consciousness (and to develop internal objects as psychological analogues of objects of consciousness). The prototypical psychological example of how human relational existence involves a connection to both an object of consciousness (or internal object) and a subject of being is perhaps that of infant and mother (two subjects of being). The infant encounters the mother as an object of desire based in its interests and needs, but also as a subject of being that informs it from beyond its wishes. In feeding, for example, the infant is relating to the mother via the breast. The breast is akin to an object of consciousness for the infant, and may become an internal object: the breast is sometimes called a *part-object* in psychoanalytic terms. In the context of love between mother and child the breast is a unifying object (both as external and internal), permitting child to connect to mother and mother to child. As we have indicated, however, an internal object may also function as an obstacle to authentic relationship if it loses transparency, as it were; in that case it may divide rather than authentically unite self and other (consider, for example, the *bad breast* in Melanie Klein's object relations theory).[103] As we will discuss below, it is this obstructive, eclipsing status of the internal object and not its *essential* or *original* meaning that gives rise to its *ambiguity*.

To further delineate the ontological features associated with defensive responses, and the role the interpretations of these responses have in the treatment of psychopathology, we will provide an example in which we will highlight psychopathological vs. normal object relations. Let us consider the example of a man who is chronically anxious, and who associates his anxiety with childhood experiences of having been mistreated and bullied. He believes that it is as a result of such encounters that he has come to harbour doubts about himself and his abilities. He feels highly anxious in his current interactions with others: he sees himself as inadequate and constantly worries that others will become aware and critical of his failings. He seeks to manage anxiety by trying to overcome perceived limitations through efforts to control and master his thoughts and behaviour; these efforts include perfectionist attitudes and compulsive habits, but he never achieves a sufficient level of comfort through such methods. Also, he seeks to accommodate others, trying to ensure that there is nothing he does or fails to do about which they could complain, but here too he never reaches a satisfying result, and, in fact, finds himself frequently ruminating about how he might have failed to please others or about how others might find fault with him. Due to the seeming ineffectiveness of his efforts he is often inclined to retreat or withdraw from social interaction and from other life endeavours in order to relieve his distress and minimize his risk of failure. One may see his various anxious attitudes and behaviours, as well as the conflictual nature of his internal ruminations, representations and object relations as features of self-defence.

Psychotherapeutic intervention, however, may help him to deepen his understanding of what is under threat and reveal that more than self is at risk: the source of his anxiety involves more than his inadequacies and perceived failings, and more than the potential or actual harshness of others, including the internalised representation of this harshness in the superego.[104] A reinterpretation of his anxiety in terms of the underlying threat to authentic relationship may encourage him to recognize his own contribution to such threat by virtue of his own rejection of relational commitment. He may come to realize that the greater threat is his own inclination to withdraw from relationship. Consequently, a genuine recovery would call for a renewal of his effort to engage with openness, trust, hope and initiative in such real relationship. In addition, he may come to see that the danger of which he is so acutely conscious is, in a way, actual: he could reject self and other; he could abandon relationship; and such inclinations do indeed pose a significant and real danger.[105] In other words, if he, as a subject of consciousness, approaches the other solely or primarily as an object of consciousness to be feared and/or repelled, our chronically anxious man will likely continue to experience himself as being in significant danger. Fortunately, it is a *danger from within* over which he may exercise some *healthy control*: this is a control that aims beyond subject and object of consciousness; the aim is towards engagement as subject of being with the other as subject of being. One's fear of the other as object of consciousness is to be converted into a concern for the other as subject of being. This may be particularly challenging for someone who has been a victim of serious injury perpetrated by another. We are not suggesting that the healing occurs solely or primarily through a concern for the perpetrator, but through a concern with one's relationship with the community of others more comprehensively.

One cannot undo the harm done to oneself in the past, but one may prevent the harm that one might in the future commit by continued withdrawal from, and rejection of relationship. This deepening or broadening of motivation results in a linking or transparent rather than a separating or opaque internal object. At this stage of working through or interpretation, the fear-for-self becomes fear-for-loss-of-self-and-other-in-relationship and begins to motivate our anxious individual in a positive or constructive direction: away from a circular defence of self and towards an openness to others and towards the defence of meaningful relationship. The *healthy control* that has been proposed in the above as a remedy to anxiety (aiming towards engagement as subject of being with another as subject of being) arises in the context of re-interpreting one's distress as an indication of a longing to base initiative and action on trust that there is opportunity for meaningful relationship. This belief in trusted connection extends especially to circumstances where one experiences one's security compromised by inadequacies, failings and criticisms (of self by others, or by self of others).

The circularity of the defence of self (i.e. the feeling of being stuck in a repetitive cycle of worry or rumination, common with anxiety conditions) is ultimately due, we believe, to the ontological gap between self and meaningful sources of relationship: a gap that prevents one from resolving anxiety, an anxiety whose resolution can only effectively occur through an increase of authentic engagement. We are emphasizing here the essential connection between the psychological experience of self in relation, and the ontological meaning of self in relation. Instead of truly moderating or resolving anxiety, the self-defensive mode involves both ontologically and psychologically avoidant strategies which ultimately maintain or reinforce anxiety. The reduction of the other to a merely self-referential object of consciousness is ontologically threatening (to both self and other) and, therefore, in some sense, psychologically distressing. By seeing and interpreting this distress as the experience of a need and desire for deeper connection, one then moves from the illusion of self-sufficiency to the stability implied in trusting and defending the depths of relationship. Of course, the process of reinterpreting anxiety to favour the ontological realignment of object relations (i.e. subject and object of consciousness with subjects of being; ego and internal object with external or real objects) may be rather challenging in so far as it requires a tolerance of vulnerability and the recognition of the other beyond one's control.

We have spoken of the *transparency* of the internal object when it is ontologically open, and of its *opacity* when it is ontologically closed. This notion of the open and closed object has wide application, beyond the confines of psychology. When, for example, *objects* such as technology, profit, power, and law are radically separated from their ontological and relational significance among subjects of being we are faced, not with authentic freedom or development, but with failure of meaningful engagement. On the other hand, when the object is open to, and integrated with ontological and relational meaning among subjects of being it has a transparent and linking purpose, and we may rely on it to favour participation in authentic encounter and development.

Normal psychological functioning and development depend on the *transparent*, relational, internal object, because this object remains open to subjects of being and their relations. In the abnormal situation, in which the object presents as *opaque*, one will experience a discomfort which is *ipso facto* an indication of the need to restore object transparency, in order to recover the solidarity among subjects of being. Consequently, because this *defensive* discomfort is based in an original and ultimate normality – i.e. the community of subjects of being – it becomes salutary as one interprets in it the call to address and challenge abnormality, that is, the call to address and challenge denial of relationship.[106] Therefore, the ontological priority of the comprehensive defence of commitment to actual relation[107] remains present, if hidden, within abnormality. Normal possibility or potential is always in a dynamic tension with abnormality.[108]

Moreover, we are proposing that it is a hermeneutics of belief which enables the search for the normal in the abnormal, and consequently a relational interpretation of psychopathological symptoms, a relational interpretation that seeks to restore and build the transparency of the internal object world.[109] Faith or trust in accord has to characterise this internal world, if that world is to be receptive of meaning.[110]

We may conclude from the above that the therapeutic process involves a continual effort to expand the confines of a self-defensive perspective, by broadening one's understanding of psychological experience to include a consideration of ontological dimensions. Accordingly, we are proposing that psychology be informed and transformed by ontology. We may expand Freud's dictum from "Where id was there ego shall be,"[111] to "Where the subject of being (open to other subjects of being) was there psyche (subject/object of consciousness; ego/internal object) shall be." To reflect what happens in the psychotherapeutic experience more comprehensively, however, we would also have to consider the reverse: "Where psyche was (troubled/symptomatic) there subject of being (open to other subjects of being) shall be." In the experience of abnormality the human psyche finds itself alienated from its ontological foundations, and to recover normality one has to explore and develop its connection to those foundations. Psychotherapeutic work takes place both at the level of the psyche *and* at the level of ontological foundations. Psyche does not depend on the (subject of) being in the way that ego depends on the id, however. The relation of subjects of being is the normalizing principle or influence for the psyche, whereas, for Freud, the id cannot be at the basis of normalization. Indeed, the id, as a primitive source may unleash abnormality.[112] We propose, instead, that normality arises only to the extent that psyche (the realm of subject and object of consciousness – and unconsciousness) expresses the openness (i.e. to distinction *and* relation, to freedom *and* commitment) that is given in the realm of subjects of being. And this happens only to the extent that the internal object *and* the subject of being find authentic expression (i.e. through their integration and compatibility) in the psychic sphere.[113]

We want to emphasize that psychological trouble is not simply the result of moral failure and that the cure or healing of psychopathology is not, therefore, simply an ethical cure. Yet the normality of which we speak does include – but is not limited to – the moral sphere. It is crucial to consider that moral and ethical considerations are frequently raised in association with psychological turmoil (e.g. problems with guilt, shame, unfairness, injustice, etc., are often implicated in psychopathological experiences). However, the main or central purpose of psychological treatment and interpretation is not to recommend better conduct or behaviour, but to seek the integration of the psychological and the ontological. Moreover, psychological treatment ought to involve some acknowledgement that the integration of the psychological and ontological is invariably present, if hidden, in the defence of self. When the defence of self is interpreted or deciphered in terms of this integration, the resolution of symptoms becomes manifest in a turning towards others and a reengagement in meaningful relationship. Accordingly, the therapeutic endeavour will involve exploring potential conflicts between the two modes of defence: defence of self and defence of relationship. It will also involve supporting the transformation of the internal object (and associated psychological experiences) from the opacity of *for-self* to the transparency of *for-complementarity* (of the distinction and relation of persons). When priority is given to one's availability and openness to being in relationship (over solely or primarily seeking to satisfy one's own needs and expectations),[114] then the intended solidarity with the other supports an authentic freedom and independence. This is a further manifestation of that to which we referred previously as the transformation of the meaningless into the meaningful, and the extraction of the normal from the abnormal.

D   *Conclusion*

We begin this essay by considering the ambiguity that arises in psychoanalytic theory with respect to the internal object: we note that psychoanalysts view this object as being a sign of linkage, yet also one of separation with respect to human relationship. We also note the tendency, in psychoanalytic thought, to resolve this ambiguity in a reductive manner, by which we mean that psychoanalysts tend to view the internal object as primarily a product of self-defensive withdrawal from real relationship. Moreover, the psychoanalytic explanation of the origin or basis of relational experience is often put in terms of non-relational principles or factors, such as the discharge of drives, primary narcissism, un-integrated or objectless stages.... If actual human relationship is something that is itself derived from the non-relational, self-oriented features of the human being, then the internal object will reflect those features. Nevertheless, an emphasis on relational influences is not lacking in psychoanalysis: the internal object is, paradoxically, itself a sign of the impact of interpersonal relations on interior psychological development. The development of Freud's own thought, as well as the development of the psychoanalytic movement more broadly, can be seen as an example of an increasing emphasis on relational factors.[115]

In an effort to address the philosophical underpinnings of this ambiguity and explore a possible resolution of it, we consider the systems of thought of three contemporary authors, Harman, Gergen and Schmitz. Harman and Gergen present views that appear to differ markedly from one another: for Harman objects withdraw from relation in order to be, and for Gergen relation is a source of constructed objects whose being is optional. Notwithstanding the fact that they do so for different reasons and with opposite outcomes, both Harman and Gergen, in our interpretation, propose a marked separation or disconnection between what it means to be and what it means to relate, and both in a way, restrict relationship to *knowing* rather than consider its foundation in *being*. This kind of disconnection and restriction, we indicate, is also implied, analogously, in Freud's tendency to offer reductive explanations of object relations. We have noted that in psychoanalytic theory object relations are viewed less as the result of actual relationship, and more as the result of an alienation from actual relationship; this is partly due to the tendency in psychoanalysis to understand the human organism as an essentially self-oriented entity. In an effort to find a non-reductive approach to address the ambiguity in question[116] we turn to the ideas of Schmitz, whose perspective allows one to consider that *to be* and *to relate* are complementary, and *to know* is compatible with such complementarity: one may affirm distinction (of being) without disconnection (proposed by Harman), relation without conflation (of being reduced to knowing, implied by Gergen), and internalisation of relationship (in the formation of internal objects) without assuming that such internalisation must disguise an essentially self-interested aim (as suggested by Freud). Furthermore, we apply Schmitz' differentiation between object of consciousness and subject of being (by analogy) to the differentiation between internal and external object relations in psychoanalysis, in order to propose a notion of the internal object that is essentially compatible with actual relationship.

Although we describe the internal object as having a structure that is fundamentally open to relationship, we also consider that it presents at times in an *opaque* rather than *transparent* fashion, closed in the context of self-defence rather than open in the support and defence of the relation of subjects of being. We do not view this opacity, however, as a sign of an inherently a-relational origin to the internal object. We emphasize that, even in its opacity, the internal object's link to the relation of subjects of being endures, even if this link becomes hidden or eclipsed.

In order to explicate how the internal object and the accord of subjects of being come together there are three factors to consider: 1) the epistemological level of the internal object, 2) the ontological level of the accord of subjects of being, and 3) the compatibility or integration between these two levels. The *epistemological* level of the internal object does not stand on its own but depends on the prior or underlying ontological accord of complements. If there is a breach of complements (i.e. breach between the distinction and relation of persons or subjects of being),[117] then the internal object is correspondingly opaque, and vice versa, if the internal object is opaque, then this implies a breach of complements. Moreover, the meaningfulness of ontological accord is not cancelled by disaccord; consequently, even in its most *opaque* expressions the internal object retains some transparency, that is, some connection to the meaningfulness of ontological accord. In any case, we do not view psychopathology as indicating an essentially unbridgeable division (or ultimate fusion) between the distinction and relation of persons, nor between such complementarity (i.e. accord of distinction and relation) and the internal object.

Psychopathology or abnormality may express the failure of (ontological) accord, but this does not cancel the influence of accord on psychological experience. Rather, it leads to a situation in which there is tension between accord and disaccord of complements. Indeed, the linking and separating (ambiguous) presentation of the internal object stems not from an essential division between being and relation, nor from an essential incompatibility between internal representation and the reality of actual relationship, but from the tension between normal and abnormal ways in which distinction and relation, and their internal representations, may find expression. In this tension, accord is not essentially dissolved by disaccord (and the internal object does not lose all of its *transparency*) because, as we will elaborate in the next essay, a healing influence is intrinsic to the way in which this tension unfolds. Indeed, sometimes it is those who are more troubled (i.e. under greater tension) who are more strongly driven by the salutary defence of the link between psychological experience and its ontological foundations. In this way one may approach troubled experience with faith or belief in its revelatory value, giving suspicion the important yet secondary role of noting the eclipsing features of that troubled experience. Accordingly, a hermeneutics of belief allows one to extract or recover the normal from the abnormal.

---

[1] This essay is a substantially revised version of an article, with the same title, originally published on the website, *hermeneuticsinpsychology.com*, in August 2013; that website is no longer being maintained, but may be re-established in the future.

[2] With respect to the importance of developing theoretical understanding in the clinical field we find the comments of Kazantzis, Reinecke and Freeman to be particularly relevant: "Theory provides undergirding to effective case formulation, clinical practice, and research. The art and science of psychotherapy without theory is like a stool, missing one of its supporting legs—shaky and unreliable" (p. xv). "Understanding the theoretical underpinnings of psychotherapy is a basis and context for competent therapeutic practice. Theoretical models help us to appreciate patients' belief systems, emotions, and behaviours as a gestalt rather than as a series of component parts. The capacity to develop cohesive formulations to explain the development and maintenance of patients' problems enables us to tailor and adjust therapy. Patients are likely to engage in those therapies that seem relevant and helpful to them, and to disengage from those that do not" (p. 363-364). Kazantzis, Nikolaos, Reinecke, Mark A., & Freeman, Arthur, (Eds.), *Cognitive and Behavioral Theories in Clinical Practice*, New York, The Guilford Press, 2010.

3 Our intent is not to exclude a consideration of empirical, subjective and socio-cultural/historical factors, but to insist that a consideration of their value calls for continual openness to their substantive underpinnings. We will be developing this argument over the course of this essay.

4 Our topic may appear to be somewhat anachronistic in view of the decline of the influence of psychoanalytic thought on the mental health field by the end of the twentieth century and the beginning of the twenty-first century. Despite this decline, however, there is general agreement that psychoanalysis remains influential. Also, in our view, as we will elaborate below, there continues to be value in recognizing the strengths, and in challenging the weaknesses of psychoanalysis. For various perspectives on the question of the current relevance and influence of psychoanalysis, see: Burnham, John (Ed.), *After Freud Left: A Century of Psychoanalysis in America*, Chicago, The University of Chicago Press, 2012, p. 8; Borch-Jacobsen, Mikkel, and Shamdasani, Sonu, *The Freud Files: An Inquiry into the History of Psychoanalysis*, Cambridge, Cambridge University Press, 2012, p. 307; Zaretsky, Eli, *Secrets of the Soul: A Social and Cultural History of Psychoanalysis*, New York, Vintage Books, 2004, p. 11; Safran, Jeremy, "Who's Afraid of Sigmund Freud: The Rise Fall and Possible Resurrection of Psychoanalysis in the United States," *Public Seminar*, Vol. 1, Issue 1, November 20, 2013,
http://www.publicseminar.org/2013/11/who-is-afraid-of-sigmund-freud/#.VOKlGvnF-Sq.

5 See Perlow, Meir, *Understanding Mental Objects*, New York, Routledge, 1995, for a history and discussion of the development of the concept of the internal or mental object in psychoanalytic theory.

6 Perlow, *Understanding Mental Objects*, p. 1, footnote 2, p. 9, p. 22.

7 Although the internal object has origins in the external object (e.g. the superego, which stands as a basic form of internal object development, is rooted in early relations with the actual parents), psychoanalysts generally understand the development and features of the internal object to be the result of ego-defensive factors. In psychoanalytic literature the establishment of the internal object is generally associated with some form of regressive withdrawal of energy (libido) from the other to the self or ego. For example, Perlow discusses the historical and conceptual significance of Freud's understanding of the role of withdrawal of libido from the external world in neurotic introversion vs. psychosis. With neurosis there is regression to internal object images; with psychosis there is regression to the ego as such, thus to a level of narcissism in which there is a more global loss of contact with the external world of real objects (Perlow, *Understanding Mental Objects*, p. 13). Perlow also contrasts Ferenczi's and Freud's differing views on identification or introjection (i.e.

these notions refer to processes which contribute to the establishment of the internal object). These differences reflect the ambiguity of which we speak: the introjected object is more a bridge to, than withdrawal from the other for Ferenczi and more withdrawal than bridge for Freud (Ibid., p. 25). Judith Hughes notes how Freud sees identification as a "'substitute for a libidinal [external] object tie'" and how this involves a "regression" or "introjection" of the object into the ego (Hughes, Judith M., *Reshaping the Psychoanalytic Domain*, Berkeley, University of California Press, 1989, p. 57). In discussing the development of the superego Freud speaks of how that which has been abandoned as object in the external world goes on to "become an integral part of the internal world" (Freud, Sigmund, *An Outline of Psychoanalysis*, translated by James Strachey, New York, W. W. Norton & Company, 1949, original published in 1940, p. 94-95).

[8] Consider, for example, Perlow's reference to the "shift [in recent years] from a drive-oriented approach to an interest in the role of an individual's interpersonal relationships in the formation and patterning of his mental organizations, processes and capacities." He also refers to the "growing interest in a 'relational model'" (Perlow, *Understanding Mental Objects*, p. 1).

[9] Consider Freud's understanding of the consolidation of the superego. Although Freud regards the child's earlier connections with the real parents as contributing to the formation of the superego, he understands its consolidation as involving the child's defensive and regressive withdrawal from, or abandonment of the parents as real objects at the time when the oedipal conflict intensifies. For Freud the rivalry associated with the oedipal conflict does not lend itself to *actual* resolution – i.e. the boy cannot eliminate the father to possess the mother and, therefore, resolves the conflict in terms of internal object creation through an identification with both parents (Hughes, *Reshaping the Psychoanalytic Domain*, p. 57). The ego withdraws its cathexis of or investment in the real objects (i.e. abandons a portion of the external world), and directs its energy or libido to the split off portion of itself that becomes the superego (Freud, *An Outline of Psychoanalysis*, p. 15, p. 94-95). Thus the ego both retreats from the external object and regresses narcissistically (the regression is *narcissistic* because the ego's involvement/interest/energy – cathexis – shifts from external to internal objects, the latter being part of the ego) (Hughes, *Reshaping the Psychoanalytic Domain*, p. 42-43).

[10] Yet here too we note some ambiguity in that Freud appears to consider that the mother's breast, as an external object, is an initial attachment *prior* to autoerotism; from this perspective, one might consider autoerotism as resulting from defensive withdrawal rather than constituting an original

stage of development. W. R. D. Fairbairn clearly understood autoerotism in this way (i.e. as the result of frustration in the relations with an external object) (see: Fairbairn, William Ronald Dodds, *Psychoanalytic Studies of the Personality*, London, Routledge, 1952, p. 33-34). Nevertheless, for Freud "object choice proper" develops later, and "autoerotic and narcissistic stages... [are] prior to object love" (Hughes, *Reshaping the Psychoanalytic Domain*, p. 42-43; p. 84).

[11] Freud, *An Outline of Psychoanalysis*, p. 69.

[12] See Perlow for a discussion of the development of the ego-ideal in Freud's thought and its "influence on later psychoanalytic thought – that interpersonal relationships (relationships with the external object) are transposed to the intrapsychic realm, leading to intrapsychic relationships between the different 'parts' of the ego" (Perlow, *Understanding Mental Objects*, p. 15). Despite such "transposition" Freud nevertheless seems to see the basis of idealisation in auto-orientation: see our discussion that follows.

[13] Freud, Sigmund, *Civilization and Its Discontents*, translated by J. Riviere, Mansfield Centre, CT, Martino Publishing, 2010 (original published: New York, Jonathan Cape & Harrison Smith, 1930), p. 57-58.

[14] We will be using terms such as *a-relational, non-relational* or *auto-orientation* to refer to modes of existing where there is 1) an implied lack of connection to the other, 2) withdrawal from, or striving to diminish connection, or 3) a merely functional, self-oriented, exploitative meaning to relation.

[15] Freud, *Civilization and Its Discontents*, p. 71, p. 80.

[16] For a critical exposition of the widespread influence of *individualism* in the field of psychology see: Fower, Blaine J., "Placing Virtue and the Human Good in Psychology," *Journal of Theoretical and Philosophical Psychology, 32*, 2012, p. 2-3.

[17] Freud, Sigmund, *New Introductory Lectures on Psychoanalysis*, translated by James Strachey, New York, W. W. Nortron & Company, 1965 (original published in 1933), p. 100.

[18] One may recall here Gordon Allport's proposal of the functional autonomy of motives as an attempt to free motivation from too strict a tie to instinctual drive (Allport, Gordon W., "The Functional Autonomy of Motives." *American Journal of Psychology*, 1937, 50, 141-156). The ego psychologists (Hartmann, Heinz, *Essays in Ego-Psychology: Selected Problems in Psychoanalytic Theory*, New York, International Universities Press, 1964, original published in 1939), and object-relations theorists (like Fairbairn, *Psychoanalytic Studies of the Personality*, and Winnicott, Donald Woods, *Through Paediatrics to Psycho-analysis: Collected Papers*, New York, Brunner-Routledge, 1998 – original published 1958)

also tended to emphasize motives that were independent of instinct or drive.

[19] Freud, *An Outline of Psychoanalysis*, p.84-85.

[20] Ibid., p. 20.

[21] Ricoeur identified Freud as one of three "Masters of Suspicion" (along with Marx and Nietzsche) (see: Ricoeur, Paul, *Freud and Philosophy*, translated by D. Savage, New Haven and London, Yale University Press, 1970, p. 28, p. 32-36). We will say more below about what we believe comes under suspicion in psychoanalysis.

[22] Yet, as we will discuss below, they appear to make some attempts to mitigate the emphasis on what we are calling non- or a-relational motives; indeed, in keeping with our theme of *ambiguity*, one may understand Freud's own theoretical development (of object-relations) as having had this direction – as we will also discuss below.

[23] Winnicott, *Through Paediatrics to Psycho-analysis*, p. 149.

[24] Hartmann, *Essays in Ego-Psychology*, p. 120, p. 166.

[25] Spitz, René A., *The First Year of Life: A Psychoanalytic Study of Normal and Deviant Development of Object Relations*, New York, International Universities Press, 1965, p. 35.

[26] Kernberg, Otto F., *Severe Personality Disorders: Psychotherapeutic Strategies*, Binghamton, New York, Vail-Ballou Press, 1984, p. 231.

[27] See: Sharpe, Matthew, "Jacques Lacan (1901-1981)," in *Internet Encyclopedia of Philosophy*, 2005, http://www.iep.utm.edu/lacweb/.

[28] For example, although Winnicott proposes a phase of un-integration at the beginning of psychic development, he nevertheless insists that there is "no id before ego" (Hughes, *Reshaping the Psychoanalytic Domain*, p. 136). Also, a marked exception to the view of an a-relational beginning to psychological development is found in Fairbairn's theory. He clearly saw the origin of psychological development in human relationship, albeit in an early form of dependence and identification. He famously said that "libido is not primarily pleasure-seeking, but object-seeking," and he dispensed with the id altogether by viewing it as essentially part of the ego. Unfortunately, in our view, he understood internal or mental object development as resulting primarily from ego-defence, and therefore did not resolve but accentuated the non-relational meaning and the basic alienating quality associated with the internal object world (Fairbairn, William Ronald Dodds, *Psychoanalytic Studies of the Personality*, p. 82, 95, p. 154-155, p. 163; see also: Hughes, *Reshaping the Psychoanalytic Domain*, p.102, p. 118-119). Perlow (in *Understanding Mental Objects*, p. 57) explains this ego-defensive origin by referring to "Fairbairn's basic view that the process of internalization, leading to the establishment of

internalized objects, occurs 'under the influence of situations of frustration during the early oral phase.'"

[29] As an example, Freud's elaborations of the role of object relations in the formation of the superego constitute significant developments of his theory. Perlow writes: "[A]s Freud progressed from a theory of the drives to a more general theory of the structure of the personality, especially in the structural model…, the concept of the 'object', especially as it is embedded in the concept of the superego as an 'internal object', became a major aspect of personality" (Perlow, *Understanding Mental Objects*, p. 15-16, p. 22). Consider as well the implicit emphasis on the importance of interpersonal relationship – in Freud's understanding of normality – noted by Erik Erikson. To a question asking "what a normal person should be able to do well," Erikson says that Freud answered, "Work and love" (Erikson, Erik H. *Childhood and Society*, New York, W. W. Norton & Co., 1963, original published in 1950, p. 264-265).

[30] Borch-Jacobsen and Shamdasani, *The Freud Files*, p. 47.

[31] Ibid.

[32] According to Borch-Jacobsen and Shamdasani, Jung proposed training analysis in 1912, but conflicts developed between Freud and Jung that same year, in part, over Freud's exemption from being analyzed (Ibid., p. 47, p. 49-51).

[33] Ibid., p. 47.

[34] Falzeder, Ernst, "A Fat Wad of Dirty Pieces of Paper: Freud on America, Freud in America, Freud and America." In Burnham, John (Ed.), *After Freud left: A Century of Psychoanalysis in America*, Chicago, The University of Chicago Press, 2012, p. 85-109, see: p. 106.

[35] Borch-Jamieson and Shamdasani, *The Freud Files*, p. 54.

[36] Ibid., p. 53; see also: p. 104-115, p. 119, p. 300-301. It is interesting that Freud seems to have remained somewhat ambivalent about this matter of the need for training analysis, suggesting at times, even after he had confirmed the need for training analysis, that a self-analysis might be sufficient for someone without too many psychological problems. Here too one senses some ambiguity with respect to the value and relevance of relation – in this case, as an aspect of, or requirement for professional development of the psychoanalyst (Ibid., p. 52).

[37] This a-relational origin seems to imply an equally a-relational *goal*, whether the latter is explicit (as, for example, with the death instinct – we will elaborate on this below) or stated implicitly in reductive understandings of the expressions of the life instinct or Eros (also to be elaborated below).

[38] See our discussion in a prior endtnote (# "28") of Fairbairn's counter: "libido is not primarily pleasure-seeking, but object-seeking" (Fairbairn, *Psychoanalytic Studies of the Personality*, p. 82).

[39] Freud, *Civilization and Its Discontents*, p. 71.

[40] Ibid., p. 102.

[41] Freud, *An Outline of Psycho-analysis*, p. 18; *Civilization and Its Discontents*, p.103.

[42] The ambiguity of the internal object (with respect to how it expresses linkage vs. separation) could be viewed as dependent on the contrasting roles of the life and death instincts: the life instinct connects and the death instinct disconnects, and the internal object reflects both of these inclinations. As we have argued, however, the *stronger* emphasis in psychoanalysis is on the reductive understanding of motivation, that is, on the primacy of auto-orientation as an explanatory framework. This implies the primacy of disconnection, from which it would follow that the death instinct has a stronger role than the life instinct in the explanation of human affairs. Indeed, we are suggesting that it is the linking role of Eros for which it is difficult to find support in psychoanalytic theory, or for which one finds what we refer to as only *weak/thin* support.

[43] Freud, *An Outline of Psychoanalysis*, p.18.

[44] One may consider here that there is some analogy between the attribution of Copernican features to the system of thought of Freud and to that of Kant. Kant's claim of producing a Copernican revolution in philosophy also presents a paradox, in that his philosophy displays a marked anthropocentrism. Graham Harman (whose work we will be discussing below) writes in this respect: "Both Latour and Meillassoux have justly objected to Kant's analogy: whereas Copernicus drove the earth from the center of the cosmos and put it into motion, Kant restores humans in the center in a manner more reminiscent of Ptolemy" (Harman, Graham, *The Quadruple Object*, Alresford, Hants U.K., Zero Books, 2011, p. 45; original published in 2010 in French: *L'objet quadruple: Une métaphysique des choses d'après Heidegger*). Even with many of those who broke away from psychoanalysis or developed psychological theories partly as a critical response to it we see the centrality of the human self (i.e. giving priority to auto-orientation or self-reference) not diminished but maintained or even increased. Although they use the term in diverse ways, consider, for example, the centrality of the notion of *self* in perspectives like those of Carl Jung, Roberto Assagioli, Carl Rogers, Abraham Maslow and Heinz Kohut. In their systems of thought one may note some emphasis on the relational (and perhaps – as within psychoanalysis – some ambiguity regarding orientation to self vs. orientation to other), but we

would have to say, as Harman indicates with respect to Kant above, that there is more of Ptolemy than Copernicus in these approaches.

Alison Scott-Baumann summarizes the decentring associated with Copernicus, Darwin and Freud: "Copernicus denied our centrality in the universe, Darwin denied our centrality in the animal kingdom and Freud denied our centrality even in our own mind" (Scott-Baumann, Alison, *Ricoeur and the Hermeneutics of Suspicion*, London, Continuum International Publishing Group, 2009, p. 44). See also Borch-Jacobsen and Shamdasani for a discussion of the historical context within which parallels were drawn between Freud, Darwin and Copernicus (*The Freud Files*, p. 1-16). One may understand Ricoeur's depiction of Freud as one of the three Masters of Suspicion (Ricoeur, *Freud and Philosophy*, p. 32) as related, more or less, to this notion of the decentring of the human mind or consciousness. Scott-Baumann explains Ricoeur's view: "It seems to Ricoeur that Marx, Nietzsche and Freud begin their work with the premise that conscious thought should be regarded with suspicion and as an illusion that requires demystification. Guile must be used to approach the guile of the conscious mind: it conceals its complex and often amoral workings from itself and from others" (*Ricoeur and the Hermeneutics of Suspicion*, p. 45). Despite some form of decentring and challenge (suspicion) regarding mind, consciousness, and the place of the human in the cosmos, we see the approaches of the Masters of Suspicion (and one may also include here some features of Darwinian thought) as contributing to an understanding of human affairs that is, on the whole, as self-referential, if not more self-referential, than the one allegedly being replaced. As we will go on to explain, this is because we put greater emphasis on being, relationship and co-operation than on consciousness, ideation and competitive striving (see "Appendix C" for further discussion on this matter).

[45] Harman, Graham, "On Vicarious Causation," in Robin Mackay (Ed.), *Collapse Vol. II: Speculative Realism*, Falmouth, Urbanomic, 2007, p. 187-221; Harman, Graham, *Circus Philosophicus*, Winchester, U.K., Zero Books, 2010; Harman, *The Quadruple Object*.

[46] Gergen, Kenneth J., *An Invitation to Social Construction*, London, Sage Publications Ltd., 2009 (First Edition, 1999); Gergen, Kenneth J., *Relational Being: Beyond Self and Community*, Oxford, Oxford University Press, 2009.

[47] Schmitz, Kenneth L., *The Recovery of Wonder: The New Freedom and the Asceticism of Power*, Montreal, McGill-Queens University Press, 2005; Schmitz, Kenneth L., "The Solidarity of Personalism and the Metaphysics of Existential Act," in P. O'Herron (Ed.), *The Texture of Being, Essays in First Philosophy*, Washington, The Catholic University of America Press,

2007, (pp. 133-145), Vol. 46 in Jude P. Dougherty (General Ed.), *Studies in Philosophy and the History of Philosophy*; Schmitz, Kenneth L., *Person and Psyche*, Ashton, Virginia, The Institute for the Psychological Sciences Press, 2009.

[48] Harman, *The Quadruple Object*, p. 6, p. 8-11.

[49] Harman, "On Vicarious Causation," p. 189.

[50] This quote is taken from comments made during the question period following a lecture given by Graham Harman at Purdue, on January 14, 2013. Only the lecture part is now available at the following website: http://figureground.ca/2013/01/17/video-graham-harman-purdue-jan-14-2013/.

[51] Harman, *The Quadruple Object*, p. 44. Harman approaches relation with a critical stance. He seems to take the relation involved in human knowing as a prototype (of all relation) and goes on to propose that this kind of relation occurs with all manner of entities. He then applies a Kantian-like framework to such *relation* or *knowledge* (or its analogous equivalents across the spectrum of objects, including, for example, the relations among rocks and specks of dirt). For Harman the knower (in Kantian vein) only *indirectly* or *obliquely* accesses the real through *allure* and metaphor, while *direct* access is limited to the sensual object (which is Harman's term for Husserl's intentional object). This allure is involved in the calling of a name: "names call out to objects deeper than any of their features." There is a sense here in which one comes close to knowing the thing-in-itself (by calling out to what is deeper than features or phenomena, one goes beyond a Kantian framework). Yet, any relation between things remains forever indirect and the chasm or gap between the knower and the thing-in-itself seems similar in Harman and Kant, except that for Harman, as we noted, it is universalized to cover relations between or among all kinds of objects, not just the relations of the human mind and the noumenal world (Harman, "On Vicarious Causation," p. 188-189, p. 215-216). As we will further address below (and in "Appendix C"), we see an ontological basis to relationship among objects that gives rise to a compatibility – not a chasm or separation – between being and thought (for remarks on this *chasm* see introductory comments by Harman in "On Vicarious Causation," p. 187-188). Harman says, "What is real cannot be mastered by vision or knowledge and therefore always remains disconnected from us" (Harman, "Purdue Talk, January 14, 2013"). We can agree, to some extent, with the first part of that statement, with respect to how knowledge is in some sense restricted by the limits of the human knower (or in Harman's expansion of the field of knowing, by the limits of any object's *apprehension* of another), but we cannot agree with the second part: that such limits to

human knowing imply a radical disconnection between knower and known, or more to the point, between knowing and what exists beyond that knowing in the thing itself. Harman argues for this disconnection by indicating that "*no* sensual objects 'correspond' to real ones," and he explains that, therefore, no conceptual model becomes the reality conceived (Harman, Graham, "The Road to Objects," *Continent, 3.1*, 2011, p. 179; originally given as a lecture at the CREA club, Amsterdam, on March 10, 2011). But, in our view, distinction and connection co-exist ontologically, and the conceptual model of the known by the knower arises in the context of the ontological complementarity of knower (as subject of being – i.e. more than subject of consciousness) and known (as subject of being – i.e. more than object of consciousness). For Harman (whose position is consistent with an occasionalist view of relation and causality) the reality that exists is independent of its being conceived, and must *flee* from the conceptual model the knower forms of it. Yet, if the relations of an entity and its being co-occur, then even the relations brought about in the process of one thing knowing another do not have to involve the dissolution of being into knowing, or knowing into being. Knowing and being co-occur and truly relate without dissolution of one into the other (and without flight of one from the other) because co-occurrence is a feature of being more fundamentally. Where Harman sees disconnection as the feature of the object that permits it to be – despite relation, as it were – we see distinction (and not disconnection) as a feature of the object that both has it be, and allows it to be compatible with and open to relation, including the relation of knowing. Where Harman sees relation as necessarily leaving the depth of the object untouched, we see openness to relation as inherent to and not essentially threatening to such depth of being. We will elaborate on these points when considering Schmitz below.

[52] He does make room for what seems like more than surface interaction in appealing to the role of *allure*. (Harman, "On Vicarious Causation," p. 188-189, p. 215-216).

[53] Gergen, *Relational Being*, p, xv; Gergen, *An Invitation to Social Construction*, p. 4.

[54] Gergen, *Relational Being*, xvi.

[55] His unbounded being bears some resemblance to the lack of differentiation associated with the notion of origins in psychoanalysis, which we have considered to be *a-relational*.

[56] Ibid., p. xv.

[57] Ibid., p. xx-xxi.

[58] Ibid., p.5.

[59] Ibid., p. xxvi.

[60] Gergen, Kenneth J., "Response to Book Reviews: Relating to My Reviewers," *Journal of Theoretical and Philosophical Psychology, 31*, 2011, p. 69.

[61] Gergen, *An Invitation to Social Construction*, p. 6.

[62] Gergen, *Relational Being*, p. xv.

[63] However, truth that exceeds such power will be essential, as we will discuss below, in assessing what "more promising outcomes" might be.

[64] Consider how Robert Sokolowski, in his *Phenomenology of the Human Person*, speaks of an entry into truthfulness when one begins to speak with others; this is related to his notion of the human person as *agent of truth*. See: Sokolowski, Robert, *Phenomenology of the Human Person*, New York, Cambridge University Press, 2008, p. 4.

[65] Gergen, "Response to Book Reviews," p. 69.

[66] William James famously spoke about "truth's cash value" in "Lecture VI" of *Pragmatism*, 1907: http://www.authorama.com/pragmatism-1.html.

[67] Gergen, *Relational Being*, p. 396-397.

[68] We should add that we completely agree with the notion that we actively participate in the construction of our lives and futures, but we cannot see that as a justification for believing in constructionism; we cannot meaningfully construct if not accompanied by truth, nor can we meaningfully construct from a position that excludes encounter with being (i.e. ontology). See "Appendix C" for a further discussion of the roles of creativity, freedom and truth as features of human experience.

[69] We are applying the concept of hermeneutics of suspicion, echoing Ricoeur's use of the term (Ricoeur, *Freud & Philosophy*, p. 32-36). We will be elaborating on this below.

[70] Perlow, *Understanding Mental Objects*, p. 1, p. 7-8.

[71] He does, however, as we have discussed (in previous endnote, # "51" and will discuss further in endnote # "86"), speak of the connection between objects through allure. (Harman, "On Vicarious Causation," p. 188-189, p. 215-216).

[72] In the "Solidarity of Personalism and Existential Act," Schmitz speaks to how the relational meaning of person *and* the realism associated with the metaphysics of existential act come together. We will consider the implications of some aspects of this perspective below.

For an excellent overview/exposition and discussion of the personalist perspective, see the article: Williams, Thomas D. and Bengtsson, Jan Olof, "Personalism," *The Stanford Encyclopedia of Philosophy* (Spring 2014 Edition), Edward N. Zalta (Ed.), URL = http://plato.stanford.edu/archives/spr2014/entries/personalism/

[73] Schmitz explains this distinction:

In the metaphysics of the high Middle Ages, the term *object* stood for the way in which something other than the knower made itself present to the knower. The actual tree in the garden was not in itself an object; but it became an object insofar as it made its presence seen, heard, or understood by the confirmation of the visual, auditory, or intellectual power to the tree's causal action. The actual tree as it stood there in the garden in its own being was not as such an object; on the contrary, it was a subject. So that the relation of knower to known was a relation of subject to subject, that is, a relation between two subjects of being. This observation places us at the great shift, one might even say the decisive reversal, that differentiates the modern outlook from the ancient and medieval understanding. The shift can be seen in the altered role of the term *subject*. According to the traditional metaphysics the tree in the garden was a subject of being (*suppositum entis*), whereas in the modern outlook the term subject came to mean the subject of consciousness (*subjectum mentis*) (Schmitz, Kenneth L., "The First Principle of Personal Becoming," *Review of Metaphysics, 47-4*, 1994, p. 761-762).

Schmitz also writes: "The modern concept of subject [...] confined as it is to human thought, sensibility, or feeling – that is, to Descartes-Kant, Hume, and Rousseau, respectively – is too restricted to provide an ample enough horizon for the accommodation of all of reality. It is inescapably reductive" (Schmitz, *The Recovery of Wonder*, p. 95).

[74] Schmitz, "The First Principle of Personal Becoming," p. 761-762.
[75] Schmitz, Kenneth L., "Transcendentalism or Transcendentals? A Critical Reflection on the Transcendental Turn," *The Review of Metaphysics, 58*, 2005, p. 560.
[76] Ibid., p. 543.
[77] Schmitz, *The Recovery of Wonder*, p. 102-103.
[78] Schmitz, "The Solidarity of Personalism and the Metaphysics of Existential Act," p. 143.
[79] Michael Hanby refers to a passage by Hans Urs von Balthasar that makes a similar point. Hanby writes that von Balthasar "warns about the conflation of the orders of being and knowledge." With such conflation von Balthasar says that, "[t]he object's whole essence would consist in being an object for a subject; there could be no more question of a free self-revelation on its part." It is interesting to see that, whereas Harman seems to affirm the independence of the object as requiring some form of ultimate inaccessibility to protect it from assimilation by the subject (an assimilation which he calls *overmining* – see previous discussion of this term), von Balthasar sees the independence of the object as setting the

stage for genuine encounter: a "free self-revelation on its part" (Hanby, Michael, "Reconceiving the Organism: Why American Catholic Bioethics Needs a Better Theory of Human Life," *Communio*, 41, Fall 2014, p. 615-653; see p. 650 for reference to von Balthasar; passage from von Balthasar taken from the following: von Balthasar, Hans Urs, *Theo-Logic I: The Truth of the World*, translated by Adrian J. Walker, San Francisco, Ignatius Press, 2000, p, 81).

[80] This means that the relation of knowledge (epistemology) rests on, or presupposes a way of being (ontology).

[81] Gergen, *An Invitation to Social Construction*, p. 4.

[82] Indeed, we believe that by relying on pertinent aspects of Schmitz' philosophy we may share and affirm *both* Harman's emphasis on the autonomy of the object and Gergen's (implicit) emphasis on the relational meaning of being.

[83] See Stratford Caldecott's discussion of *Evangelii Gaudium* (November 2013) by Pope Francis, in *Not as the World Gives, The Way of Creative Justice*, Kettering, Angelico Press, 2014, p. 223.

[84] Schmitz, "Transcendentalism or Transcendentals?" p. 542. The passage continues, "for this is to elevate subjective fear to a primal force, whereas in accord with the classical metaphysics of Plato and Aristotle wonder was quite enough." We will explore this subjective (i.e. self-oriented), fear-or-threat-based (therefore defensive) attitude in terms of its analogous role in psychological theory and seek to provide an approach that is based on a different point of departure, especially in the area of psychopathology: faith before suspicion, granting the latter a secondary rather than primary role.

[85] In using the term, hermeneutics of suspicion, we allude in part, to Ricoeur's distinction between the hermeneutics of belief or faith (recovery, restoration, reconstruction, recollection...) and the hermeneutics of suspicion (Ricoeur, *Freud & Philosophy*, p.28; Itao, Alexis Deodato S., "Paul Ricoeur Hermeneutics of Symbols: A Critical Dialectic of Suspicion and Faith," *Kritique*, vol. four, number two, 2010, p. 4, p. 7-8; Scott-Baumann, *Ricoeur and the Hermeneutics of Suspicion*, p. 69, p. 153; Kaplan, David M., *Ricoeur's Critical Theory*, Albany, New York, State University of New York Press, 2003, p. 21). We will be elaborating on some of the similarities and differences between our proposal and Ricoeur's position below.

[86] Schmitz, Kenneth L., "Enriching the Copula," *The Review of Metaphysics: A Commemorative Issue. Thomas Aquinas, 1224-1247, 27,* 1974, p. 492-512; see: p. 511-512. Note that in this passage by Schmitz, the "possibility of cognition" is rooted in the "vicariosity" or relation of

one being with another. By analogy we will speak of the internal object as rooted in the actual relationship between self and other.

   Harman (see: "On Vicarious Causation") speaks of "vicarious causation" in explaining relation, and this has some similarity to what Schmitz alludes to here. With Schmitz, however, there is less suspicion, less need to protect things from one another, as it were. We could say that, from the perspective which Schmitz offers, relation is not alien to being; on the contrary, it is rupture from relation that is alien to being. He writes that "[e]ach being *in-sists, re-sists,* and *ex-ists* in relation to others" and enjoys "the 'freedom' to be itself *(ens per se)*" but "[t]his does not close beings into themselves" and "*reçevoir*...[extends] to non-personal things as well as to personal beings" (Schmitz, "The Solidarity of Personalism and the Metaphysics of Existential Act," p. 143). We could say that where Harman is suspicious of relation Schmitz seeks its salutary meaning. Yet Harman himself echoes this salutary trust where he starts his "Introduction" to *The Quadruple Object* (p. 5) with the words: "Instead of beginning with radical doubt we start with naiveté." There will be more on *naïveté* in further discussion of Ricoeur below (see, in particular, endnote # "109").

[87] Caldecott, *Not as the World Gives* p. 242; original quote from Chesterton, G. K., *A Short History of England*, London, Chatto & Windus, 1917, p. 59.

[88] Schmitz, Kenneth L., "A Not Uncritical Harmony," Catholic Social Science Review, Volume V, 2000, p. 17-22, see p. 20.

[89] If objects of knowledge were only or mere objects of knowledge, Gergen would be correct, but if objects of knowledge have an intrinsic relation to subjects of being, then he is mistaken.

[90] Schmitz, "A Not Uncritical Harmony," p. 20.

[91] We will consider several aspects: 1) the ontological *equality* between the complements of being and relation, 2) the priority of this ontological equality over hierarchical expressions of being, 3) the way in which this ontological equality influences hierarchical reality, providing a norm that penetrates the inner workings of the (hierarchical) *distribution* of power and thought. In this context, human ideation or thinking is not viewed as something that necessarily alienates one from reality nor keeps one from its depth (as Harman proposes), nor is it a process that is intrinsically alien from the independent realities it may recognise or affirm (as Gergen proposes). Rather human ideation is viewed as compatible with being because being "makes a gift of itself to thought" (Schmitz, "Enriching the Copula," p. 511-512).

[92] This differentiation of the *subject of consciousness* from the *subject of being* has some analogy to Martin Buber's differentiation of the *I* who

participates in an *I-it* relation from the *I* who participates in an *I-Thou* relation (Buber, Martin, *I and Thou*, translated by Walter Kaufmann, New York, Touchstone, 1996, first published in German in 1923).

[93] In other words, the *psychological* relation of internal to external object bears some analogy to the *philosophical* relation of object of consciousness to subject of being.

[94] There is priority of subject of being over object of consciousness, but compatibility as well, because the object of consciousness has its basis in the depth of relationship, that is, in the solidarity between or among subjects of being. As we have seen and will continue to consider, however, the object of consciousness, and its analogue, the internal object – in view of their potential to become ambiguous – may function to divide or obstruct rather than connect and facilitate meaningful relationship.

One could argue, from a subjectivist, solipsistic or social constructionist perspective, that all relations are limited to subject-object of consciousness, and that there cannot be (or one cannot know, in Kantian vein) anything underlying or transcending the realm of knowledge; however, this would involve giving priority to a hermeneutics of suspicion, and it would involve concluding that the ontological cannot or does not unfold into or towards the epistemological, that "being" does not make "a gift of itself to thought" (Schmitz, "Enriching the Copula," p. 511-512).

[95] Ibid.

[96] Chesterton, *A Short History of England*, p. 59.

[97] Freud, Anna, *The Ego and the Mechanisms of Defence*, London, Hogarth Press, 1968 (original published in English in 1937, in German in 1936).

[98] There is a double meaning to the word *from* in this context, both of which are intended here: 1) as a human person one originates *from* others, in that one did not generate oneself, and 2) one is to be distinguished *from* the other, as in being an independent and free entity. Thus an essential dependence *and* an essential independence – as co-occurring – are already indicated in defining the distinction of being, even *before* considering unity or relation as such.

[99] We will develop this theme of a healing purpose or aim to the tension associated with the mix of accord and disaccord in the second essay in this book.

[100] As previously noted, we are viewing the object of consciousness and the internal or mental object with some degree of equivalence despite differences (i.e. analogously). The object of consciousness and subject of being distinction refers to epistemological and ontological realms, whereas the internal or mental object of psychoanalysis refers to the psychic realm. We may therefore draw a further analogy between the *philosophical* need

to connect the object of consciousness with the subject of being and the *psychotherapeutic* need to connect the psychic realm with the ontological realm; the latter connection speaks to connecting internal and external objects.

[101] Harman too emphasizes a disconnection between the thing as it is and the way it may enter into relation; however, whereas Gergen disconnects in order to essentially conflate (being and relation), Harman uses the disconnection implied by Kantian-like construction to protect the *in-itself* status of the object.

[102] Harman draws a distinction between real and sensuous objects, which has some analogy to the way we have distinguished subject of being and subject/object of consciousness (and the analogous psychic realm of ego/internal object). Also, he identifies the psychic realm with the sensuous object. He notes that there is a psychic aspect to all objects, not in so far as they exist, but in so far as they relate (Harman, *The Quadruple Object*, p. 70). It is beyond our scope here to address the intricacies or subtleties of Harman's thought and argument on these matters. We would suggest, however, that relation is not only psychic; rather, the relational features of the psyche are based in a deeper relation that ontologically exceeds the psyche, in the same way as the real object for Harman exceeds its (sensuous) appearance. Consequently, we would have to disagree with Harman's claim that we are most ourselves in sleep and dream: that is, that it is in "freedom from relation in which we are most ourselves" (Ibid., p. 71). We would argue, instead, that we are most ourselves when we are *and* relate, even if such may happen by times in sleep. Relation does not only occur at the surfaces of objects, in our view; it calls to, and comes from the depths of objects as subjects of being, something to which Harman himself alludes when he speaks of how "names call out to objects deeper than any of their features" (Harman, "On Vicarious Causation," p. 216).

[103] Hughes, *Reshaping the Psychoanalytic Domain*, p. 62.

[104] We elaborate on the harshness of the superego in the second essay in this book, in the section "M" titled, "An Alternative Explanation for the Harshness of the Superego."

[105] The approach we offer here differs from perspectives, associated with CBT (cognitive behavioural therapy), in which there is the tendency to understand anxiety and other dysphoric states as the consequences of distortions of cognition. In contrast to such perspectives, we are more interested in how one may interpret anxiety and other dysphoric states (and the thoughts associated with them) in terms of how they reveal rather than simply conceal or distort one's exercise of reason or one's experience of reality. We recognize that there may be deviations of thinking contributing to psychological disturbance, but we seek to understand the ways in which

an underlying *person-in-relation-based* fidelity to meaning may be influencing such deviations and disturbance. Thus, beyond unmasking the *virtual* threat, we seek the *actual* threat that cognitive-affective disorder may contain. CBT (including some third wave approaches such as mindfulness meditation), on the other hand, often seems to imply that one ought to give primary attention to *virtual* rather than *actual* threat as the source of psychopathology. For a detailed exposition of several CBT approaches including the presentation of some third wave perspectives, see: Kazantzis, Reinecke and Freeman, *Cognitive and Behavioral Theories in Clinical Practice.*

[106] In the situation which is normal or harmonious in an uncomplicated way – without tension towards or from the abnormal – we would not speak of *defence* but simply of support/enhancement of, or deferral to relationship.

[107] We mean here a defence of freedom/independence that is supportive of commitment/solidarity and vice-versa.

[108] And this tension towards the norm may be manifest or hidden, explicit or implicit, conscious or unconscious.... In keeping, broadly speaking, with the psychoanalytic emphasis on the unconscious one may consider that the human subject is not always conscious, yet still participates in some way with objects, such that both subject and object may be wholly or partly unconscious, as in dreams. One may speak, therefore, not only of subjects and objects of consciousness, but also subjects and objects of unconsciousness.

[109] When applying hermeneutics to psychopathology and healing we propose giving priority to belief or faith over suspicion, and we generally employ the terms, *belief* and *suspicion*, in the sense developed by Ricoeur. We also follow Ricoeur's approach in so far as he affirms the importance of both distinction and relation between various complements such as freedom and nature, self and other, dissymmetry and mutuality, and we share his concern to avoid totalizing tendencies in which one simply fuses one term with the other (Scott-Baumann, *Ricoeur and the Hermeneutics of Suspicion*, p. 115-116, p. 170-171). In particular, we see some applicability of the Ricœurian hermeneutics of suspicion to the breach and fusion we have identified as features of abnormality. Differences between our perspective and that of Ricoeur arise, however, when we consider our view of normality. We do not believe that our own understanding of normality is compatible with what Ricoeur calls his (paradoxical) post-Hegelian Kantian position. In approaching complements or *opposites* Ricoeur adopts a standpoint that goes beyond the polarities involved – thus he is Hegelian – but without resolving the separation or tension by a fusion

of opposites – thus he remains Kantian or returns to Kant. Ricoeur retains the (Kantian) sense of a gap that is unbridgeable, while also affirming that connection is tentatively possible by adopting a position within/beyond the gap that lies between the complementary/opposing terms (see: Scott-Baumann, *Ricoeur and the Hermeneutics of Suspicion*, p. 115-116, 118-120, 126, 133, 170, and Kaplan, *Ricoeur's Critical Theory*, p. 12-13). As we will elaborate below, in our understanding of normality we do not see gaps that are unbridgeable, nor do we consider connections to be tentative. For Ricoeur the hermeneutic circle is comprised of a first naïveté that is to be deconstructed via suspicion and this may lead ("if we are lucky") to a second naïveté (Scott-Baumann, *Ricoeur and the Hermeneutics of Suspicion*, p. 132). We propose, however, that if the first naïveté is to be subject to suspicion, then there must be an implied prior naïveté to this *first naïveté*. Our understanding of normality implies such an *original naïveté* (*prior to Ricoeur's first naïveté*) rooted in the inherent complementarity between distinction and relation. In our view, suspicion and critique have a role only when there is a deformation of the distinction-relation complementarity, that is, only if the latter *becomes* an anti-complementarity (involving division or fusion of complements). Ricoeur might agree with this in so far as he proposes that suspicion be applied only proportionate to the degree of false consciousness, but, we would suggest that he leaves what we are calling *original naïveté* insufficiently articulated (Scott-Baumann, *Ricoeur and the Hermeneutics of Suspicion*, p. 75). As intimated above, however, we do share Ricoeur's view that a second naïveté may result from applying the hermeneutic arc of suspicion. For example, with respect to psychotherapeutic process, this would occur as a consequence of working through what we have called abnormality (Ricoeur's notion of first naïveté and our notion of abnormality appear analogous), but, from our perspective, this second naïveté would be anchored in an *original* naïveté, not just in the negation of Ricœurian *first* naïveté (i.e. *original* naïveté implies a faith that is prior to suspicion and that is not *merely* naïve). Our *original naïveté* clearly differs from what Ricoeur calls *first naïveté*, in that first naïveté involves false consciousness and calls for remedy or healing, whereas original naïveté speaks to something that is not in jeopardy. Thus, we differ from Ricoeur with respect to the way we understand the origin and basis of polarities encountered in reality, and with respect to the stance one is to adopt towards them. As noted above, Ricoeur takes a position beyond or within the gap that he identifies between the poles of opposites, in a dialectical tension that is not to be ultimately resolved. From our viewpoint, the problematic status is not in the *opposites* or complements that configure normality, rather, it is between the normal and the abnormal expressions of

such *oppositions* or complementarities. We, therefore, focus on the
discord between (abnormal) breach and (normal) distinction or between
(normal) relation and (abnormal) fusion, or, more comprehensively,
between the (normal) complementarity of distinction and relation, on the
one hand, and the (abnormal) anti-complementarity of breach and fusion,
on the other. Consequently, in psychotherapeutic process, we are not
seeing inherent conflict between independence and relationship, freedom
and commitment, self and other; we do not see an inherent contradiction,
incompatibility or tension in these terms: we see distinction and relation as
co-occurring and in accord. (We may also recall here our differences with
Gergen – re: distinction – and Harman – re: relation). The tension is not
between the poles as such, but between the normal and abnormal
expressions of the complementarities which they express. And our goal,
with respect to the healing of psychopathology, is not to maintain some
form of dialectical third position as is Ricoeur's approach (see: Scott-
Baumann, *Ricoeur and the Hermeneutics of Suspicion*, p. 115-116, 118;
Itao, "Paul Ricoeur's Hermeneutics of Symbols," p. 11-13; Kaplan,
Ricoeur's Critical Theory, p. 41-45; Ricoeur, Paul, "Hermeneutics and
Critique of Ideology," in J. B. Thompson, Ed. And Trans., *Paul Ricoeur:
Hermeneutics and the Human* Sciences, Cambridge, Cambridge University
Press, 1981, original published, 1973," p. 100) but to detect the tension
towards the normal in the abnormal, and to seek, therefore, the original and
ultimate meaning hidden within the abnormal. It is the original that is to
be restored and developed through the struggle with the abnormal (or *first
naïveté*). In this way the innocence of what we are calling *original naïveté*
(that which is prior to, and therefore more fundamental than Ricoeur's *first
naïveté*) may find expression, development and fulfillment in the maturity
of the *second naïveté*.

[110] Our approach here would be consistent with Luigi Giussani's
elaboration of a "suitable attitude in *the dynamic of knowing* an object."
He says, "We want to describe what morality consists of in so far as the
dynamic of knowing is concerned." His "moral rule" is: "*Love the truth of
an object more than your attachment to the opinions you have already
formed about it.* More concisely, one could say, 'love the truth more than
yourself.'" Giussani is not speaking of the internal object but of actual
objects (including the other). In his approach we see a similar emphasis to
that which we have proposed above on the priority of actual connection
(our notion of actual connection would correspond to what Giussani calls
the "truth of the object"). Giussani, Luigi, *The Religious Sense*, translated
by John Zucchi, Montreal, McGill-Queen's University Press, 1997, p. 30;
p. 33.

---

[111] Freud, *New Introductory Lectures on Psychoanalysis*, p. 100.

[112] Freud, *An Outline of Psychoanalysis*, p. 38.

[113] We would suggest that Freud, in a way, proposes the id as a sort of ontological substratum of the psyche, but, as we have seen, this involves a reductive paradigm that contributes to the ambiguity we have described with respect to the meaning of internal and external object relations. In some of the early developments of psychoanalysis, however, there were attempts to challenge this reductionist paradigm and the implicit assumption that the id forms the foundation of psychic life. For example, as we have previously noted, W. R. D. Fairbairn emphasizes relational rather than instinctual origins of psychic development, and sets aside the id altogether; instead of seeing the foundation or origin to psychic life in the id, he sees it in human relationship (Fairbairn, *Psychoanalytic Studies of the Personality*, p. 88-90).

[114] This kind of priority is not an abandonment of self-interest, but an insertion or integration of the latter into a relational context; it is an overcoming of circumscribed or abstracted (i.e. *abnormal*) forms of self-interest.

[115] Perlow, *Understanding Mental Objects*, p. 1.

[116] The ambiguity has to do with whether relation has an ontological foundation or basis. The questions one may consider include the following: Is relation simply a surface phenomenon (in keeping with Harman's perspective) or an arbitrary construction (in keeping with Gergen's perspective)? Is relation something that essentially alienates one from an assumed a-relational, self-oriented individual nature (as suggested in Freud's perspective)? Is relation ontologically based (as Schmitz implies)?

[117] The complementarity or accord of subjects of being is a complementarity of distinction and relation because a subject of being both remains itself and enters into relation.

II

THE HERMENEUTICS OF PSYCHOTHERAPY:
HEALING THROUGH BELIEF[1]

A *Introduction:*
   (i) *The Priority of Belief*
   (ii) *Time as Healer*

(A-i) *The Priority of Belief:* We base this essay on the premise or understanding that all wounds tend towards healing,[2] and propose, therefore, that the work of the psychotherapist, as a healer of wounds, is that of a participant in a healing process that has always already begun, that is always, in some sense, already a given. This formulation might apply analogously to various kinds of biological, communal, political or spiritual healing, but our own focus will be on the psychological – and on the philosophical underpinnings of psychological healing. We further propose that to appreciate and foster the healing tendencies of which we speak calls for the application of a hermeneutics of belief to the understanding and treatment of psychological symptoms. By this we mean that we are to give priority to belief over suspicion, trust over mistrust,[3] in order to consider and favour what we may call the *revelatory value* of troubled psychological experience. We will elaborate on this revelatory value below. To start with, however, let us briefly consider how the position we are proposing differs from psychoanalytic, cognitive-behavioural and humanistic (including positive psychology) approaches.

From a psychoanalytic perspective one views symptoms or troubled feelings as potentially revelatory of unconscious conflict. One approaches symptoms with suspicion in order to reveal what is hidden in them (i.e. there is suspicion, as it were, of the manifest and conscious in order to reveal the hidden and unconscious). From cognitive-behavioural approaches one tends to view symptoms or troubled feelings as resulting from distorted or disordered thoughts (or schemas). Consequently, one is inclined to understand disordered thoughts and the troubled feelings that accompany them as essentially lacking revelatory value. In that perspective value is found more in correction or dismissal of the symptom than in the consideration of how a symptom might be linked with something meaningful. The emphasis in humanistic psychology is on a holistic understanding of the human self, and on that self's inherent inclination towards its own actualisation; there is, as well, a tendency to view symptoms as a failure of self-actualisation. Such failure is usually understood as the result of restrictions on the expression of the self, often attributed to factors and influences external to the individual (e.g. social influences). In positive psychology, which is, in some ways, a current and further development of the humanistic school, one continues to see the latter's focus on the positive or adaptive inclinations in human functioning, albeit in a broadened manner that includes, among other things, a consideration of character strengths and virtues.[4]   In addition, positive psychology places greater emphasis on empirical evidence, and is critical of what are deemed to be unscientific claims and approaches within humanistic psychology. Like the humanistic school with which it is associated, however, positive psychology shows a tendency to view symptomatic experience as essentially detracting from the positive agenda of human flourishing. Indeed, positive psychology defines itself essentially in opposition to a psychology that focuses primarily on psychopathology.[5]

We share with psychoanalysis the view that symptoms are revelatory, although we do not see them as only revelatory of the unconscious; rather we focus how they reveal the influence of complementarity (to be elaborated below). With respect to the cognitive-behavioural school of psychotherapy we agree with its emphasis on the correction of distortions of thought that might underlie symptoms, but also believe that symptomatic experience involves more than mere distortion, because we see in such experience an inherent link with meaning. We also agree with the importance which the humanistic school places on the positive and holistic basis of human development and flourishing; however, we believe that we will find these positive meanings, not simply by setting aside troubled human experience and making the positive our focus (as appears to be the general tendency in positive psychology); rather we believe that such meanings are to be found by exploring the very heart of human suffering.   Where positive, humanistic psychology sees the need to withdraw from psychopathology to emphasise the normal and healthy parts of human experience, we see the need to engage the tensions and conflicts in the psychopathological to discover therein the seeds of longing for normal and positive human flourishing.[6]

By speaking of the *revelatory* value of symptomatic experience, therefore, we are proposing that meaning or normality discloses itself within the context of the experience of difficulty or abnormality. We define meaning or normality in terms of the complementarity of distinction and relation (between self and other), and abnormality as the breach of this complementarity. Moreover, we are proposing that abnormality cannot be radically circumscribed. In other words, the suffering of abnormality is never essentially or simply meaningless, and we will argue that this is the case because the injury, pain and discord involved in suffering are intrinsically oriented by the normality and meaning associated with healing.[7] We will also focus, in expounding this theory, on how normality or complementarity finds expression in the context of a *hierarchy of being*: in a higher and a lower that call for integration. For example, one may face circumstances in which one is to balance and integrate the *lower* desire to competitively assert oneself with the *higher* desire to co-operatively support the other in relationship.[8] By proposing that co-operative engagement is higher than competitive assertion, we are not dismissing the value of various potentially constructive expressions that one might associate with assertion, such as innovation, creativity or self-affirmation. We are saying, rather, that the meaningfulness of such initiatives ultimately depends on the norm of complementarity, and that the very possibility of taking such initiative depends on an underlying co-operative context.

To recognise or appreciate this *norm of complementarity* we propose that it is necessary to give belief[9] priority over suspicion. Our intent is not, however, to exclude suspicion, but to have it exercise a secondary, if necessary, role. Consequently, in our approach, a hermeneutics of suspicion – along with its corollaries of doubt and negative critique – still has a place alongside a hermeneutics of belief. In our view, there are times when the experience of psychological struggle requires suspicion to unmask and challenge the sense of ultimate despair or meaninglessness that may lurk within or behind the troubled feelings associated with such struggle. However, from a perspective that gives the hermeneutics of belief primacy, feelings that involve a sense of despair and meaninglessness are first of all approached as protests, and it is the values or principles for which they protest that are given priority. The primary effort of the interpretive process or hermeneutics ought to be to endorse those values or principles. Only *secondarily* ought one to apply suspicion to the nihilism, despair and meaninglessness that may be implied by troubled feelings. Thus the hermeneutics we propose, while giving priority to belief, nevertheless involves a *sifting process* of separating meaning from meaninglessness, hope from hopelessness.[10]

Paul Ricoeur speaks of the three Masters of Suspicion, Marx, Nietzsche and Freud, and sees them as unmasking false consciousness.[11] The latter notion refers to how manifest ideas, found, respectively, in ideology, conventions of morality, and consciousness, are, purportedly, couched in disguised or deceptive form with respect to their actual meaning. These manifest ideas, which one may generally characterise as supporting *false consciousness*, are said to hide the economic or power advantages involved in class struggle (Marx), the weakness or slavish conformity of conventional (and ultimately relative and arbitrary) moral claims (Nietzsche), and the instinctual meanings and conflicts behind conscious human experience (Freud). In contradistinction, we see nihilism or despair (as a feature of the experience of psychological turmoil), and not ideology, moral beliefs or consciousness, as the main object towards which one ought to direct suspicion.

(A-ii) *Time as Healer:* It is said that time is a healer and, indeed, in the tendency and tension towards healing – which we are proposing as an essential or inherent feature associated with the presence of a wound – one may recognise a form of time that heals. Yet, there are psychological states or experiences in which such *healing time* seems inaccessible. For example, there is the sense of being stuck in a static or stagnant situation: the *no light at the end of the tunnel* found in the experience of irretrievable loss in depression; the intransigence of holding a grudge in anger; the perpetual or recurring sense of uncertainty and disconnection in the experience of anxious anticipation; the continual sense of depletion, worry and discouragement associated with chronic pain. These all involve negative circumstances that one tends to experience as impossible to overcome; they all imply some sense of permanent breach in the complementarity or harmony that, we have proposed, essentially characterises normal or meaningful existence. In contradistinction to this sense of being stuck in a static or a-temporal state with permanently negative features, however, one may have the experience of *healing time*, which favours openness to repair or recovery. To counter depression there is *light at the end of the tunnel* or hope. To address the intransigence associated with some forms of anger, there is apology, making amends and forgiveness (thus healing the offence created by injustice through the application of both justice and mercy). And to permit one to work through and beyond the experience of perpetual anxious anticipation, or unavoidable pain, there are forms of openness, acceptance and receptivity that allow one to reengage in, and develop trusted connection. These examples suggest how the experience of static (and stagnant) timelessness may yield to the experience of reparative or healing time.

One may also consider, however, another form of timelessness that is not statically negative, a timelessness that conveys the sense of an eternal abundance and closeness, a permanent reconciliation both in justice and love, and an endless security. This timelessness has eschatological features that, in a fairy tale, for example, are conveyed in the prototypical ending "And they lived happily ever after." We will consider later in this essay how time *always* implies this positive sense of timelessness (or permanence) – as opposed to the negative, stagnant timelessness (or permanence) noted above – and that this *always* finds expression through the human experience of hope.

B   *Freedom that Unites & Unity that Liberates vs. Failed Freedom that Divides & Pseudo Unity that Dominates*

As noted, we propose that normality or meaning is rooted in a complementarity of distinction and relation. This implies, on the one hand, that an authentic distinction (associated with freedom, uniqueness and independence) intrinsically favours relation, while, on the other hand, an authentic relation (associated with commitment, solidarity and unity) intrinsically favours distinction. We may best understand this harmony of distinction and relation in terms of the distinction and relation of persons – we would say that this is its eminent and prototypical expression.[12]   As an example of the distinction and relation of persons, consider how each member in a family may contribute in his or her own unique (*distinct*) way to the bonds that form that family, and those bonds (*relation*) in turn may support the flourishing and freedom of each unique member.

We further propose that if normality or meaning is conveyed by the complementarity of distinction and relation, then abnormality involves the failure of this complementarity or accord. With respect to this breach of complementarity, abnormality may present in two ways. Instead of an authentic distinction (i.e. independence, freedom, uniqueness) that favours relation, we have an inauthentic distinction that *dissents* from relation; and instead of an authentic relation (i.e. communion, commitment or closeness between or among persons) that favours distinction, we have an inauthentic relation (characterised by rupture, fusion or domination)[13] that *offends* distinction. As noted above, normality, on the other hand, favours complementarity (or accord). It presents as an authentic, independent and free *assent* that gives rise to and supports communion, commitment or relation, and it presents as an authentic *relation* (i.e. communion, commitment or closeness) that gives rise to and supports independence or freedom.

If, as Ricoeur proposes, hermeneutics is the theory of the rules that preside over an interpretive process,[14] then the theory we offer is one that starts with and gives precedence to the complementarity or accord of distinction (of being) *and* relation (of persons), and of analogous complements such as independence *and* connection, freedom *and* commitment, multiplicity *and* unity, uniqueness *and* solidarity, singularity *and* universality, to be *and* to relate....

This is what we intend by a hermeneutics of belief: an interpretive process open to, and rooted in a given ontological-relational accord.[15] It is this accord or connection that *merits* belief or trust. Thus, for example, loyalty or friendship would merit one's belief or trust. We recognise, however, that in human experience one also faces the disaccord between complements, that is, the failure of complementarity. One could say that failures, such as disloyalty or betrayal, do not *merit* belief or trust (thus the need for the hermeneutic moment of suspicion). Consequently, one faces a struggle between the complementary and the anti-complementary expressions of persons in relation: this struggle occurs in those human experiences that involve an opposition between the accord and disaccord of complements. For example, one may find oneself, in response to the experience of betrayal, reacting in ways that aggravate division and distrust (disaccord) vs. responding in ways that demonstrate one's belief in the value of relationship (accord), even if there may be limitations to reconciling with the party in question. Moreover, this ontological opposition (between accord and disaccord) finds expression, in our view, in the opposition between giving priority to the hermeneutics of belief vs. giving priority to the hermeneutics of suspicion.

We see troubled feelings, including psychopathological expressions of such feelings, as involving and reflecting this struggle between accord and disaccord. One may thus witness, in troubled human experience, the struggle of a freedom that assents to relation in contradistinction to a failed freedom that dissents from relationship (e.g. Do I engage in or choose conduct that allows me to stay true to my promises and commitments or do I react primarily out of a misguided understanding of self-interest in order to gain some momentary advantage?). On the other hand, one may note relation that supports freedom of distinction in contradistinction to pseudo-relation that offends against the freedom of distinction (e.g. Does a friendship, family group, or social institution support the opportunity for the parties that constitute them to express their uniqueness, and discover what they have to offer one another, or do these relational ties stifle and threaten such freedom?).

Note, in all this, the paradox of normality: in the normality of complementarity the purpose of freedom is to bind oneself, via assent, to relational commitment, and the purpose of relational commitment is to support freedom. The one occurs *with* or *in* the other; thus, do we speak of normality and meaning as involving a complementarity, accord or harmony of distinction and relation, of freedom and commitment, of diversity and unity. [16]

The hermeneutics of belief has one consider distinction and relation (freedom and commitment, diversity and unity) as an ontological accord.[17] Consequently, by *failed*-freedom or *pseudo*-relation we intend respectively: 1) a quasi or not-quite freedom that fails *to be* freedom, or 2) a quasi or not-quite relation that fails to express *authentic* or *true* relation. This lack of *being* and *truth* speaks to more than merely mistaken actions and thoughts; the lack is ontological. In this context one may consider that there is an intrinsic priority of being over non-being, which supports the basic priority of belief over suspicion in the interpretive process or hermeneutics. This interpretive process starts and ends with this normality (ontologically and relationally based) even as it addresses the mixed reality of accord and disaccord (we will say more about the notion of *mixed reality* and how hermeneutics applies to it in a later section).[18]

C *Horizontal Relation and Vertical Integration: The Complementary and the Hierarchical*
    (i) *The Characteristics of Vertical Hier-archy*
    (ii) *The Characteristics and Influence of Horizontal An-archy*
        (a) *Priority of the Horizontal*
        (b) *Accord, Transcendence and Equality of Complements*
        (c) *Compatibility of the Horizontal with the Vertical*

(C-i) *The Characteristics of Vertical Hier-archy:* We believe that the complementarity that defines normality finds expression by analogy across a spectrum or hierarchy of being, such that the distinction and relation of persons express the higher levels of being, while the distinction and relation of non- or im-personal aspects of reality express the lower levels of being. We ought to emphasise that we do not see the impersonal realm of being as radically apart or separate from the personal, even if the two realms differ substantially. In addition, the impersonal realm includes a wide range of things including the world of principles and abstractions (e.g. mathematics, ideas), and the world of non-personal animate things (such as plants, insects and birds). In a sense, all that is not personal belongs to the category of the non- or im-personal. Our point is that there is a hierarchy of being with the person as the higher expression and the non- or im-personal as the lower expression.

Furthermore, human persons do not simply exist at the top end of this spectrum, but contain, express and experience within their lives the full range of this hierarchy. However, the personal is an intrinsically inclusive realm in which one finds both the personal and the impersonal, whereas there is a tendency to approach the impersonal as an exclusive realm that lacks a connection to the personal. One could say that the personal carries the sense of the *whole*, the impersonal carries the sense of the *part*.

Consider, by analogy, how a mechanistic view of reality never allows for an appreciation of the more comprehensive reality of the intentions of living entities, or how a strict pragmatism excludes a-priori any meaning beyond reductive explanations. For example, one might consider that a particular throw of a baseball is based in the muscular structure of the arm of the pitcher, the neurological factors influencing the arm, the physics of motion, etc. These factors of determination, definition and explanation may provide vital and relevant data, but a focus on the comprehensive meaning of the action is not captured in the analysis of those factors. On the other hand, recognising, for example, that the pitcher threw the ball to get another player out as part of a baseball game, allows one to consider the comprehensive meaning and goal of the action. The comprehensive assumes the parts or particulars (i.e. structure, neurology, physics), even if not explicitly; yet the parts or particulars, in so far as they are deliberately circumscribed (according to method) do not refer to the comprehensive or whole. Moreover, with respect to a pragmatic or functional explanation, one would consider the action of throwing the baseball solely in terms of winning the game, and gaining advantage for the player's team (i.e. competition), and omit the more comprehensive goal and purpose expressed in playing (i.e. co-operation). We will say more below about how competition and co-operation are ordered in human experience.

Complementarity, as we have defined it, involves a form of *generosity* (of being)[19] that speaks to how both distinction and relation *co-exist* or are *co-extensive* in what one may call an *equality* of ontological status.[20] In speaking of hierarchy, however, we are introducing a notion of ontological *inequality*: of a higher and a lower, of a greater and a lesser, of a more and a less....

This reference to hierarchy raises questions about what might determine that something is higher or lower, and about what the power relations among these levels of being might be. We have indicated an initial basis for differentiation by speaking of the higher as personal and the lower as impersonal. In this context one may consider, for example, the basic hierarchical differences one observes in nature among stones, blades of grass, insects, fish, mammals, human beings, etc.[21] We have also noted that hierarchy not only applies to the world of nature but also to the world of knowing and ideas. In this respect, one may distinguish personal (higher, deeper, more comprehensive) from impersonal (lower, more surface, narrower) subject matter to which knowing is directed – even if all forms of human knowledge are essentially personal in that personal subjects are involved in the experience and generation of knowledge.

To further address the differentiation of levels of hierarchy we believe it necessary to distinguish two types of power or influence that one may associate with hierarchical structure: 1) controlling or competitive exercise of power, and 2) supportive or co-operative exercise of power. In other words, one may consider: 1) a hierarchy in which the higher refers to the relatively more dominant or controlling manifestations of power, and the lower to the subordinate levels subject to such power, and 2) a hierarchy in which the higher refers to the relatively more service-oriented or collaborative manifestations of power, and the lower to the levels that are open to, benefit from, and participate in such collaboration and service.[22] In addition, we would emphasise that human experience tends to include both types or aspects of hierarchy: that is, life experience will involve an admixture of dominance and service, control and support, competition and collaboration (and regarding the hierarchy in thought or knowledge one may speak, analogously, of limited and comprehensive, narrow and broad, superficial and deep aspects of thinking).[23]

For example, consider the role of parents in a family. They have, at one and the same time, both a form of authority or power that indicates their dominance and control over their children, and a form of authority or power that indicates that they are to serve and support their children. Moreover, in a way that perhaps further adds to the complexity of hierarchy, we would say that service-oriented or co-operative expressions of power have, ontologically (and ought to have, morally),[24] a fundamental and ultimate priority over controlling or competitive ones (we will develop this principle below).[25] In other words, there is a *hierarchy within hierarchy,*[26] such that service has priority over domination, co-operation over competition, even if one cannot completely disentangle one aspect of hierarchy from the other – as we see in the example of the family relations of parents and children.

Another example of how these two aspects of hierarchy manifest themselves within human experience may be noted in friendships (i.e. expressions of *co-operation*) that may also involve *competitive* engagement. One plays chess or tennis with one's friend and strives to win the game, but winning or competitive striving remains secondary to the valuing of friendship or companionship as expressed, in part, in the conventional wisdom, "It's not whether you win or lose that counts, but how you play the game." That which urges one to compete remains secondary to that which calls one to co-operative, mutual interaction; after all, the parties need to *willingly come together* in order to compete. In this example of the chess or tennis game between friends, the quest for *winning* and for the impersonal or *less-than-personal*[27] gain (e.g. involving competitive values such as possession, status, achievement, conquest, mastery…) appears to take priority over personal or inter-personal gain (e.g. involving co-operative values such as generosity, engagement, contribution, participation, service…), but this appearance of priority, is precisely an *appearance*, that is, a *play* or *fiction*.[28] Note, for example, how children's play might involve seemingly violent events – for example, a chase or a sword fight – but the child knows it is a game, that is, that co-operation has priority over the seeming violence.

With respect to how hierarchy influences forms of knowledge one may similarly consider how some forms of knowledge allow one to dominate and control a situation (e.g. conducting a chemistry experiment), while others call for an attitude of receptivity and wonder (e.g. admiring a beautiful sunset).[29] One may consider, as well, that by giving priority to the hermeneutics of belief over the hermeneutics of suspicion, we are, in fact, proposing that hermeneutics itself involves a hierarchical structure. We say more about this aspect of hierarchy in "Appendix C."

To summarise, hierarchical expressions of being introduce a notion of inequality. This inequality has two main or broad expressions: 1) *competition* (higher against lower) or *dominance* (higher over lower), on the one hand, and 2) *co-operation* (higher with lower) or *service* (higher of lower), on the other. Both are features of human experience, yet, in a fundamental and ultimate sense, co-operation and service have priority over competition and dominance. In the above, we refer to this pattern of priority as *hierarchy within hierarchy*. We will discuss below how this nesting of one form of hierarchy within the other (i.e. a hierarchy of meaning within a hierarchy of power), along with the priority of a co-operative/service form of hierarchy over a competitive/dominance form of hierarchy, ultimately depends on what we refer to as an *an-archic* equality of complements.

(C-ii) *The Characteristics and Influence of Horizontal An-archy:*
(C-ii-a) *Priority of the Horizontal:* The *hierarchy within hierarchy*, referred to above, presupposes an ontological and moral priority that, we understand, arises from the complementarity of distinction and relation. By this we mean that hierarchy depends on, and is informed by a norm that *transcends* it: a norm that comes from the non-hierarchical – one could even say *an-archical* – *equality* of complementarity (we will elaborate on the notion of *equality* in section "C-ii-c" below). By "an-archical" we do not mean something without order or principle to it, or something that is its own principle;[30] rather, by anarchical we mean the mutual deferral (between distinction and relation of persons) that one sees in acts of authentic love (a deferral fundamental to complementarity). Moreover, we consider that such deferral has essential priority over any hierarchy or power-differential: that is, love is the ever fuller meaning of being. We will develop in what follows the notion that complementarity thereby imparts or transfers, as it were, its equality (or non-hierarchy or *an-archy*) onto the inequality of hierarchy. We will refer to this association between complementarity and hierarchy in terms of *compatibility*.

(C-ii-b) *Accord, Transcendence and Equality of Complements:* Before exploring this question of compatibility between complementarity and hierarchy, however, let us consider that the *equality* of the complements in complementarity (i.e. the equality between distinction and relation of persons), like the *normalising* of hierarchy, is itself achieved through a transcendence:[31] that is, the equality of complementarity does not refer to a mere equality of entities that stand *immanently* next to one another.   With complementarity there is more than an abstract equality of entities: there is the mutual transcendence of distinction and relation, such that each term goes beyond itself, in its openness to, and connection with the other.

There are two aspects to this transcendence: 1) as a person one transcends one's distinct and unique identity in order to consent to, and share in the common ground or common identity of relationship; 2) those in relationship transcend that which unites them (i.e. their relational or common identity) in order to affirm that which distinguishes them (i.e. the uniqueness of each member), and to affirm other persons or groups they may encounter from beyond the immediate boundaries of the relational identity in question, persons or groups who, therefore, also present as *distinct*.[32]

As an example of how relationship transcends itself to affirm its complement – i.e. the distinct or unique person – consider how the parents of a family with several children, in which financial resources are limited, may decide to make sacrifices that limit the availability of funds for the family as a whole in order to support sending one of their children on to higher education. The needs of the whole are to some degree frustrated in order to support the one. One sees a similar sacrifice in a family with a handicapped child who may require more attention and assistance than siblings with more normal capacities. Indeed, setting aside the exceptionality of these cases, or even the essential role of family support, there is a sense in which each and every person, in his or her own uniqueness and freedom, is fundamentally the *recipient* of that uniqueness and freedom. The existence of each one of us has an essentially *given* quality that originates in the relational bonds on which one's life is based. Conversely, one may consider that as a receiver of one's own existence, one is also a responder: it is as a responder who reciprocates (on the basis of the existence one has received from relationship) that one goes beyond self to support (i.e. to give back to) relationship. The child favoured with a higher education goes on to transcend self by supporting the family that made that education possible, or indeed, goes on to contribute to the larger community. The handicapped child transcends self to affirm others by offering gratitude to his or her caregivers, and making his or her unique contributions to family and community.

In any case, we have noted in the above, not only that hierarchy transcends itself in taking its norm from complementarity,[33] but that there is a transcendence inherent within the expression of complementarity itself. Moreover, this latter notion of transcendence, which we may characterise as *horizontal transcendence*,[34] allows us to expand our understanding of normality. We have previously defined normality as the accord of complements (and abnormality as a breach of that accord). We may now, in view of the role of transcendence, consider that normality calls not only for an accord, but for a *transcendent* accord (of complements). Therefore, the sole immanence of distinction or relation would indicate abnormality: with sole immanence, distinction would not go beyond itself to affirm relation (in the above example, the child, for whom the family made sacrifices, would not go on to support family or community), and relation would likewise remain closed within itself and not affirm distinction (again, in the above example, the family would not support the child to go on to higher education).[35] In contradistinction, the normality of complementarity calls for the person to move beyond sole self-interest, and for those in relation to move beyond sole group-interest. This transcendence within complementarity, however, involves neither a diminution of self (or person) nor a diminution of relation (or group). The distinction of self is *affirmed* by its sharing in relation, and relation is *deepened* by its affirmation of distinction. This form of transcendence, therefore, does not extinguish but rather affirms and deepens the terms of complementarity.

Since the equality of complementarity expresses the mutual transcendence of distinction and relation, complementarity favours personal uniqueness *and* interpersonal connection. Moreover, as implied above, this *equality* through transcendence has comprehensiveness and depth, such that it refers to more than the sole equality of entity to entity.[36] An equality that speaks only to the immanent comparison of entities tends too easily, in our view, towards an individualist position, where one risks reducing distinction to a solipsistic notion of arbitrary freedom, or where one risks reducing relation to a nominal array of solitudes that do not share in a real connection with one another (or if they do interact, do so only competitively).[37]   A collectivist perspective, in contradistinction to an individualist one, may speak to the importance of relation. The tendency with collectivist notions, however, is to give relation priority over distinction: that is, collectivism tends to emphasise unity by diminishing the value of distinction, and by reducing the meaning of (relational) unity to mere homogeneity. Despite the differences between individualism and collectivism, one sees in both, the tendency to force a certain hierarchical, unequal structure onto the equality of complementarity: that is, with individualism the *distinct* individual is to have priority over the *relational* collective, and with collectivism the *relational* collective is to have priority over the *distinct* individual.[38]

(C-ii-c) *Compatibility of the Horizontal with the Vertical:* Having indicated, in the above, how complementarity itself involves a transcendence between equal terms, let us now return to the question of how the hierarchical and complementary dimensions, when ordered – within themselves and mutually – manifest *compatibility*, while when disordered they manifest *incompatibility*.

We have proposed that it is appropriate for hierarchy to take its norm from complementarity, and, therefore, for the former to defer to the latter. We are now considering (as indicated above with the examples of individualism and collectivism) that the converse is inappropriate. It would be inappropriate, in other words, to impose the inequality of hierarchy onto the equality of complementarity. Let us elaborate.

If hierarchy takes its norm from complementarity, then one may conclude that the vertical order within hierarchy that results from this influence is not based solely on power or advantage, but on the meaningfulness of relationship. It is in view of the influence of this meaningfulness that one comes to recognise and appreciate the priority of co-operative service over competitive dominance. We could say that, in keeping with this priority, *power* defers, or is subordinated to *meaning*. A hierarchy that is not open to the norm of complementarity, however, tends to be a hierarchy where mere power or advantage is identified as the higher or ruling factor: *meaning* defers, or is subordinated to *power*. If one views complementary relationships from a perspective emphasising this latter kind of hierarchy, there will be a tendency to establish inequality where one ought to have equality. This is what we noted, for example, with individualism and collectivism. The *distinct* individual and the *relational* collective vie for power over one another, instead of being *equal* complements: that is, the dynamic becomes one of power rather than one involving an equality of accord in which each term transcends itself towards the other. When influenced by the transcendent equality of accord any power or hierarchical relation involving the individual and the collective is to be subject to the norms of service and co-operation; this shows the normative influence of complementarity on hierarchy.

In the above we have identified three basic features of the normality of complementarity: 1) the *accord* of complements, 2) the mutual *transcendence* of complements, and 3) the *equality* of complements. Conversely, one may characterise abnormality by 1) the *breach* of complements (failure of accord), 2) the *sole immanence* of distinction or relation (absence of transcendence), and 3) *imposition* of a power-based hierarchy onto complementarity (lack of equality).

We are emphasising that the equality of complementarity does not simply refer to an equality of distinct individuals, nor simply to an equality based on the homogeneity of the collective, but to an equality that allows for both the distinction of individuals and the common ground (universality) of the collective: an equality, we therefore say, of the distinction and relation of *persons*. Furthermore, we are proposing that, in contradistinction to forms of individualism and collectivism that tend to emphasise the breach, sole immanence and/or inequality of complements, the emphasis on the distinction and relation of persons refers to accord, transcendence and equality of complements.[39]   It is this accord, equality and transcendence of complements (i.e. normality), that provides the inner norm of hierarchy, and allows one to see, as previously considered, that the order of hierarchy is subject to meaning and not to *sole* or *mere power*.

One may designate this emphasis – that allows for distinct persons *and* relations among them to be (to fully co-exist), and for power to defer to, and be informed by meaning – as a form of personalism.[40] With this proposed personalism the *distinction* of the person (analogous to the individual) has an *equal* ontological status to the *relation* of persons (analogous to the collective) through an accord or complementarity of mutual transcendence.[41]   In addition, the nature of hierarchy, under the influence of this complementarity, finds its essential order in the priority of service and co-operation over dominance and competition, a priority that itself depends on transcendence: hierarchy's deferral to complementarity's influence.

In view of this transcendence and equality one may understand the sacrifices that human beings make for one another. Consider, for example, the following exchange, which speaks to both the value of the sacrifice of a single person for a group of persons, and the value of the sacrifice of a group of persons for a single person. This *complementarity* is captured in this conversation between the characters of Spock and Kirk (played by Leonard Nimoy and William Shatner) in two Star Trek movies, *The Wrath of Khan* and *The Search for Spock*. In the first movie Spock gives up his life in saving the crew of the starship; in the second several members of the crew risk their lives to save a *revived* Spock. The *argument* is made for how the *one serves the many* (i.e. transcending self-interest through service of the many), yet the *argument* is also made for how *the many serve the one* (i.e. transcending group-interest through service of the one):

> *Spock* (dying): Don't grieve Admiral. It is logical. The needs of the many outweigh…
> *Kirk*: …the needs of the few…

Spock: ...or the one. *Star Trek II: The Wrath of Khan* (1982)

Spock (who has been brought back to life and rescued): My father says that you have been my friend. You came back for me.
Kirk: You would have done the same for me.
Spock: Why would you do this?
Kirk: Because the needs of the one... outweigh the needs of the many. *Star Trek III: The Search for Spock* (1984)

Although it is largely implicit in the above example, the events unfold within a context of hierarchy: i.e. admiral, captain, first officer, members of the crew.... One may note that it is a spirit of service and co-operation that influences this hierarchy in that they all set out to rescue Spock at great risk to themselves. The order of command defers entirely to the order of the service of the person. In other words, transcendent complementarity informs the order of hierarchy, in that it imparts to the latter a deeper or more comprehensive meaning than it would have when considered solely within *its own terms*. By *its own terms* we mean a *mere* hierarchy, that is, one not informed by an-archic complementarity as the normative basis for its integration. Such *mere* hierarchy tends to be determined solely by the pragmatics of power. In contradistinction, the relative priority of co-operation and service over competition and dominance (i.e. *hierarchy of meaning within a hierarchy of power*) applies the generosity and transcendence of the co-existence of distinction and relation to assertions of power, turning what might be a *mere* exercise of power into a *meaningful* or *authentic* exercise of power. In a hierarchical arrangement of power that is informed by the *co-existence* of distinction and relation of persons found in complementarity, the higher is not that which is simply stronger or which has the advantage of brute force; rather, the higher is that which is more distinct *and* related, more free *and* collaborative. Consequently the reign of the higher over the lower becomes essentially a reign of service.

We noted earlier that human persons do not simply exist at the top of the vertical range of hierarchy, but instead contain, express and experience, within their lives, the full spectrum of hierarchy. We have also indicated that it is appropriate for the norm of complementarity to inform the order of hierarchy, while it is inappropriate for *mere hierarchy* to dominate or rule complementarity. One may consider, therefore, that there are compatible and incompatible ways for the vertical (hierarchical) and the horizontal (non- or an-archical) to find expression in human experience. [42]

Compatibility between these vertical and horizontal dimensions depends, to some extent, on a way of ordering hierarchy both within itself and with respect to complementarity. The higher is higher in terms of service or *descent* to the lower, and the lower (competition) defers or *ascends* to this higher (co-operative service). Moreover, this deferral within the hierarchical results from the more fundamental deferral of hierarchy itself to the non-hierarchy (or an-archy) of complementarity, that is, a deferral to the co-existence of distinction and relation, freedom and love, independence and unity, one and many. With respect to this compatibility between the an-archic and the hierarchic, an-archic complementarity *serves* hierarchic order (by providing it with a meaningful point of reference), and hierarchic order *defers* to an-archic complementarity (by preserving the priority of co-operation and service over competition and dominance). Note the paradoxical quality of the ascent (or deferral) of hierarchy into the non- or an-archic realm. Hierarchy moves out of inequality into equality, out of relations of competitive, immanent power into relations of collaborative, transcendent meaning; however, as we will discuss in sections that follow, in its auto-transcendence, hierarchy is not thereby cancelled (i.e. does not cease to be hierarchy); rather, in its becoming compatible with an-archy, it is transformed while remaining hierarchical.[43]

Healing of wounds occurs along the two dimensions we have identified (and *between* them): the horizontal, complementary, an-archic one, and the vertical, co-operative/competitive, hierarchical one. Indeed, healing is necessary along and between these two dimensions because wounds involve breaches that occur in and affect both dimensions (and their *compatibility*).

We have considered how complementarity is breached – or one may say, wounded – when distinction fails to support relation, or when relation offends distinction. We have also considered how the integration of hierarchy fails – one may again say, wounded – when dominance or competition gains priority over service or co-operation. Thus, each dimension expresses the normal or meaningful, but, each is also subject to wounding through abnormality. In addition, we are proposing that the fullness of normality and healing in human affairs involves the compatibility of these two dimensions, a compatibility that finds support when the complementary informs/serves the hierarchical, and when the hierarchical defers to the complementary. This compatibility is disrupted, however, when the hierarchical dominates the complementary (we should clarify that when hierarchy is *integrated*, it takes its norm from complementarity and, therefore, would not disrupt the latter: that is, only a reduced hierarchy of *sole* or *mere* power would dominate complementarity). The compatibility is also disrupted if complementarity (due to an internal breach in which, for example, distinction rejects relation or relation rejects distinction) fails to serve or inform hierarchy. Thus, the fullness of normality calls for a compatibility between complements that are in accord,[44] on the one hand, and hierarchy that is integrated, on the other.[45]

D *The Metaphysics of Complementarity and Hierarchy: The Analogy between the Accord of Complements and the Integration of Hierarchy*

Complementarity involves, as we have said, distinction that opens to relation and relation that opens to distinction. Distinction refers in some ways to the notion of existential affirmation (i.e. the power or energy to exist): independence, freedom, actuality, *to be*, etc. Relation, on the other hand, refers to the notion of connection between or among entities: sharing, closeness, interdependence, mutuality, solidarity, common ground, *to relate*, etc. With hierarchy, we have noted two kinds of order: competitive dominance and co-operative service. One may consider that there is some analogy between the two aspects of complementarity and the two kinds of order in hierarchy: that is, distinction is to relation (in the case of complementarity) as competition is to co-operation (in the case of hierarchy). Therefore, just as one sees, with complementarity, that the affirmative (distinct) and associative (relational) aspects of being are in a fundamental accord, so too, with hierarchy, does one see that the competitive and co-operative degrees of being are oriented towards integration. However, despite some analogy, it is important to note the significant differences between the accord of complements and the integration of the orders of hierarchy.[46]

With complementarity, as previously noted, one has an equality of ontological status: distinction *equals* relation, freedom *equals* communion.[47]   With hierarchy, on the other hand, we have an inequality, expressed in a scale of meaning,[48] such that, for example, competitive dominance does not equal – and, indeed, ought to have less priority than – co-operative service.[49]   However, just as distinction is not lost in its transcendent accord with relation, and relation is not lost in its transcendent accord with distinction, so too does the inequality in the orders of hierarchy not simply disappear through the integration of these orders. The hierarchical adopts and adapts the *equalising* influence of complementarity within its own *unequal* structure. Through the priority of co-operative engagement over competitive striving, hierarchy does not cancel itself, but deepens the very meaning of higher and lower: i.e. the higher is not that which is able merely to exert greater force, but becomes that which is able to inspire greater conviction regarding the meaningfulness of collaboration; the lower is not that which is limited to passivity and reactivity, but becomes itself a participant in and contributor to the order of meaning.

Consider, for example, the way in which competition and co-operation express themselves in the human and the natural world. With competition the emphasis is on how the more powerful or higher reign over the less powerful or weaker.[50] In a framework in which one considers only the hierarchy of competition or power, the greater or higher is that with the winning advantage or capacity for control. As we have argued, however, with a fuller or deeper notion of hierarchy, one considers that hierarchy depends on complementarity for its norm.[51] It is this norm that introduces co-operation and service into hierarchical order (we have called this introduction and influence of complementarity into hierarchy, *hierarchy within hierarchy*).[52] Therefore, to define hierarchy solely in terms of competitive power fails to consider the integral potential of hierarchy and the ontological basis of that potential (in and from complementarity). Furthermore, in a hierarchical framework, in which collaborative power has priority over competitive power, the *informing* by the higher is never a mere domination; rather this informing involves supportive service. In keeping with the spirit of supportive service, the *conforming* or *deferral* of the lower (to the higher), on the other hand, is not mere submission to a greater power, but an involvement or engagement that may itself display affirmative and creative power. In other words, the lower orders of being are not merely passive and chaotic. This not only implies a relative autonomy for competitive striving (and lower levels of being), but it also indicates that competitive striving (and lower levels of being) enjoys *only* a relative autonomy: relative to the normative influence of complementarity on hierarchy, that is, to the priority of collaboration over competition.[53]

Moreover, one could say that it is this normative influence of complementarity and the ontological priority of collaboration to which it gives rise that support the priority of belief (which orients one to consider the trusted connection that underlies collaboration) over suspicion (which orients one to consider the failure of trusted connection, that is, *dis-accord* and *dis-integration* – to be elaborated below).[54]

E   *Permanence, Impermanence and Healing Time: Factors in the Healing of the Wound*

We have suggested that in the wound there is a tendency towards healing, but how, indeed, does a person experience this *normalising*, healing tendency, when the wound is also a sign of the experience of harm or damage associated with abnormality?

One may note that there is a dual meaning to troubled experience or psychological disturbance that corresponds to a dual meaning of the wound: the troubled person finds himself or herself both subject to distress and in search of a remedy. Consider, for example, how thoughts and feelings associated with depression – when explored in depth – not only indicate a sense of loss, but also involve a protest against loss, and express a longing for the restoration or recovery of connection and wholeness. This indicates that the abnormality of breach and disintegration does not completely eclipse nor abolish the normality of complementarity and integration. On the contrary, normalisation appears to be an intrinsic feature of the person's experience of abnormality. It makes its appearance in and through such experience in various forms: as a tension, a promise, a longing, a desire, a protest....

Moreover, this influence of the normal in and through the abnormal indicates that normality does not simply refer to a circumscribed ideal state: in troubled human experience the normality of complementarity, in some sense, combines with and finds expression in and through abnormality in order to transform the latter. One notes, for example, that part of the purpose of discomfort or pain is to draw attention to the wound so that one may seek its healing.

What happens in the experience of the wound that allows one, not only to recognise a breach and feel distressed about it, but also to hope in, desire, and move towards its healing? We propose that this expression of normality or meaning, in and through one's involvement with or exposure to abnormality, involves a shift in the experience of *permanence*. We have previously referred to how a sense of static timelessness comes to be associated with troubled feelings, and also referred to how healing time involves an opening, through hope, to a positive kind of timelessness. But often, in human experience, it is the *negative* sense of permanence, associated with being or feeling wounded, that seems dominant. Consider these various expressions of dysphoric affect: "There is no hope for me, no light at the end of the tunnel"; "I will always remain angry and can never forgive others for what they have done to me"; "I will always remain in my guilt and can never be forgiven for what I have done"; "There is no excuse or remedy for one as incorrigible as I".... Consider, as well, the poetic description of such static, dysphoric timelessness in the words of the Mariner from Samuel Taylor Coleridge's *The Rime of the Ancient Mariner*,

> Day after day, day after day,
> We stuck, nor breath nor motion;
> As idle as a painted ship
> Upon a painted ocean.

Note, in these examples, how the breach between self and meaning is felt to be permanent and irreversible. Should one, however, turn one's attention to the healing aspect of dysphoric experience (and, therefore, to the healing aspect of the wound), then the permanent negation of meaning is *temporalized* or *historicised*, as it were. Hopelessness, fault and incorrigibility lose their permanent status and become *impermanent*. Thus, my feeling of hopelessness becomes temporary and there *is* light at the end of the tunnel; my anger does not herald a permanent rupture with the other but a longing for justice and mercy that might heal the rupture; my guilt is temporalized if I seek forgiveness and find a forgiver; my admission of incorrigibility may not indicate that I am at the end of my rope but at the beginning of acceptance that can lead to a positive self-transformation (consider, in this respect the meaning of the AA admission of one's alcoholism: to say, "I am an alcoholic" is not a statement of hopelessness but of hope and trust that sobriety is *always* on offer). In *The Rime of the Ancient Mariner*, we also see this hopeful orientation to relationship towards the end of the poem where the Mariner says:

> O sweeter than the marriage-feast,
> 'Tis sweeter far to me,
> To walk together to the kirk
> With a goodly company!

This temporalizing of what at first seemed like a permanent negation of meaning allows for time to become a healing time, and brings to the fore a *new* sense of permanence, one that affirms rather than negates life and meaning. At the heart of healing time is a hope that orients to this new permanence. In this process one is not healed *of* time, in some form of escape from it; rather one is healed *through* time, and, moreover, one's experience of hope indicates the openness of (healing) time to *permanent* meaning. There appears, as it were, a co-extensiveness between healing time and permanent meaning.

Furthermore, for this healing to proceed, we propose that one requires an *authentic* or *true* acceptance of the abnormal: an acceptance of the abnormal is authentic or true when it occurs in the light of the normal. One may speak, in this context, of an acceptance of the co-existence of the normal and the abnormal that calls for an unconditional acceptance of the whole person. Yet *unconditional* does not imply neutrality, because acceptance itself is not neutral but rooted in the hermeneutics of faith: acceptance involves the affirmation of permanent meaningfulness (and of trust that one has access to that meaning through *healing time*). It is a normalising – not a neutral – perspective that orients one to have trust and hope in the complementarity of distinction and relation, freedom and commitment: and this normalising perspective is especially required when one confronts the rupture of these complements. Indeed, a true acknowledgment and acceptance can occur only within a framework of such hope; otherwise, without hope one does not have a genuine acceptance, but only a seeming or superficial acceptance that contains, perhaps, an attitude of indifference, or some form of resignation or cynicism. Instead, a true acceptance challenges meaninglessness and opens one to healing.

As noted above, in the context of this healing, a different sense of *always* – than that of permanent meaninglessness – makes its appearance and gains priority. The therapist has the task of sharing in and encouraging the patient's movement from the *permanence* associated with hopelessness to the *permanence* associated with hope. This sharing and encouragement on the part of the therapist involves both empathising with the patient's experience of the threat of permanent meaninglessness, and being sensitive to various ways in which the patient expresses *doubt* regarding this negative permanence – and, therefore, this sharing and encouragement by the therapist demonstrate that the patient is, in some sense, already in possession of *faith* in the permanence of meaning. There are various ways in which a person may express a doubt or protest regarding meaninglessness, and it is crucial that a therapist remain sensitive to those ways and not adopt a one-sided approach that either ignores the patient's sense of desperation or fails to consider that the patient is struggling to hope.

Moreover, such doubt or protest regarding meaninglessness is in line with what we have considered to be the appropriate, *secondary* application of the hermeneutics of suspicion. To doubt, suspect and protest meaninglessness, gives priority to belief.

As noted, the presence of normality in the experience of abnormality orients this experience towards healing and meaning. Thus one might say, "I am depressed (and face abnormality), not only because I have lost my sense of meaning and wholeness, but *in order to* recover my sense of meaning and wholeness." Or one might say, "I am anxious, not only because I lack a secure attachment and have avoidant habits, but *in order to* find secure and engaging modes of relationship in my life." In this context, the *acceptance* of the abnormal (i.e. despair, insecurity, fragility, vulnerability) is also the affirmation of normalisation (i.e. hope in recovery of meaningful relationship in the face of rupture and meaninglessness).

Consequently, the feelings of the depressed or anxious person are never solely indicative or warning of breach and disintegration; in some measure those feelings also signify a normalising and healing tendency. Indeed, in terms of what we have said previously about the priority of the accord of complements over the disaccord of complements, one may conclude that troubled feelings are in some fundamental way expressive of this priority: that is, even in the most troubling of circumstances, there is a sense in which the permanence of meaning comes *before* the apparent permanence of meaninglessness. Indeed, there is a paradox in the human experience of meaning: it is ever being newly discovered, and yet, in its permanence, it is ancient.

To summarise the above, one may highlight three aspects of the experience of healing time in the person who is working through dysphoric affect. Firstly, there is the realisation that the seeming permanence of meaninglessness becomes temporalized or impermanent. Secondly, time becomes healing or transformative in the context of a hope based in the permanent priority of meaning over meaninglessness. Thirdly, this healing time speaks to a dramatic development in which one encounters a mix of meaning and meaninglessness, accord and disaccord. Healing initiates a sifting process in which one accepts that meaning and meaninglessness (or accord and disaccord) occur together, while one also realises that one is to distinguish and sort through them.

Essentially, it is complementarity that supplies the actual *permanent* norm to the drama of dealing with troubled feelings, and that provides the basis for trust and faith (i.e. hermeneutics of belief).[55] Suspicion or doubt retains a secondary role in contributing to the discernment and separation of the sifting process, yet suspicion or doubt does this only if it allows the priority of faith or belief to exercise the salutary and authentic acceptance of the abnormal (the abnormal approached and understood as continually influenced by a normalising influence).

As noted above, the patient's suspicion or doubt regarding the negative permanence of meaninglessness is to open the way for further development of faith and trust in the positive permanence of meaning. Consider the humble and normalising acceptance of the abnormal expressed in the AA admission, "I am an alcoholic." This is not a fatalistic kind of acceptance, nor is it a passive, resigned submission to meaninglessness and disaccord. Indeed, the deeper the authentic acceptance of the harm caused by meaninglessness, the deeper the discernment of the difference or separation between the normal and the abnormal. "I am an alcoholic" does not mean that I am doomed to a life of drunkenness, nor does it mean that I condone drunkenness; on the contrary, it is an affirmation that a path of sobriety opens before me, and drunkenness is something I want to reject. Moreover, this path of sobriety, not without paradox, relativizes the drunkenness that appeared absolute, and shows the sober path as one that is open to an authentic permanence or a true absolute.[56] It is the light of faith and trust that permits the acknowledgement or disclosure of the experience of difficulty, and that allows the healing process to take hold. The hermeneutics of belief, as an essential feature of this healing process, favours the deepening of this acknowledgement or disclosure.

F   *The Lesser Mysteries of Dissent and Breach; the Greater Mysteries of Complementarity and Integration: Recovering the Normal from the Abnormal*

One is not only confronted by wounds that result from the world of nature (e.g. natural disasters, diseases) but also by those that result from human agency. This is apparent, for example, when in considering the harm that results from one's personal faults, one realises that one knows better, but, as an agent of wrongdoing, somehow fails to do better. In light of what was discussed above regarding complementarity and hierarchy, one may describe the cause of the harm or wound that results from human agency in terms of various possible failures: freedom fails to assent to relationship; relationship takes on an offensive or oppressive form to which one consents; one makes decisions that favour reductive (i.e. solely competitive) rather than constructive (primarily co-operative) *descent* (and corresponding *ascent*) along the hierarchy of being. Nevertheless, the ultimate reason as to why such failures occur remains somewhat mysterious, that is, without final or complete explanation.

This mystery arises, we believe, because an ultimate explanation regarding human failure inevitably touches on the question of meaning: that is, human failure is ultimately a sign that one has despaired regarding meaning with respect to self and/or with respect to others, and that one is subject, in some sense, to the effect or impact of this endorsement of meaninglessness. Meaninglessness, which speaks to the failure of complementarity and integrity, has some association to emptiness, lack or nothingness, and, as such, does not lend itself to full explanation.[57]   In contradistinction to meaninglessness, meaning, which speaks to the normal and normalising expression or influence associated with complementarity and integrity, refers not to emptiness or lack, but to the fullness and presence of being.

Both the emptiness and the fullness present one with mystery, however. With emptiness there is an ultimate lack of explanation, reason, or sense: a *negative* mystery.[58] With fullness, on the other hand, there is something that exceeds our capacity for sensing, reasoning or explaining: a *positive* mystery that reveals a mark of excess or generosity in being (as one might experience in falling in love, or in a parent's love of a child).[59] We propose, furthermore, that, because of its inherent emptiness, the meaninglessness of dis-accord and dis-integrity refers to a *lesser mystery* and, because of its inherent fullness, the meaningfulness of accord and integrity refers to a *greater mystery*.

It is on this *greater mystery* that one may base the hermeneutics of belief: that is, belief is rooted in the meaningfulness of the complementarity of distinction and relation, freedom and commitment, uniqueness and solidarity, and on the integrity of descent and ascent of hierarchy.[60] The *lesser mystery* involves the breach of complementarity and the breakdown of hierarchy, and thus presents one with something one is to ultimately negate, reject, doubt, critique.... It calls, therefore, for the hermeneutics of suspicion, which, as we have argued, retains legitimacy only if it defers to and depends upon the priority of belief. This priority of belief is ontologically based: that is, it is rooted in the priority of fullness of being over lack of being.

In the wound, healing and breach do not exist in separate realms. Rather, the wound combines healing and breach in a dynamic that involves the normalisation of the abnormal (i.e. a healing disposition or tendency in tension *against* abnormality): in the dynamic of normalisation, complementarity and integrity combine with disaccord and dis-integrity, in a manner that overshadows and transforms these breaches of meaning. In other words, the greater mystery overshadows the lesser mystery. This does not diminish the sense of personal or communal fault associated with human agency to which we referred above. In fact, recognising fault in the context of discovering an offer of, or inclination towards healing contributes both to the intensity of that sense of fault and to the placement of that intensity (i.e. guilt, regret) into a reparative, healing or normalising context.

Therefore, this overshadowing of lesser by greater is not without tension; indeed, it often presents as a dramatic battle, conflict or struggle, as we saw in our previous discussion of the transformation that has one pass from the hopelessness associated with the experience of *negative permanence* into the hopefulness associated with the experience of *positive permanence*. In addition, the overshadowing of lesser by greater does not prevent the moments of eclipse of greater by lesser. As we saw, and will develop further below, this happens because the overshadowing of lesser by greater is not simply a matter of necessity or given nature, but involves an invitation to (and in) freedom to respond to what is given, and the possible experience of that freedom's failure. Furthermore, this means that one confronts the possibility of actual or real loss (i.e. the failure of freedom to support unity or commitment, and of unity or commitment to support freedom; the failure of the higher – via its reduction to mere power – to serve the lower, and the failure of the lower to open itself to authentic support from the higher). One may speak, therefore, of healing vs. non-healing (i.e. reparative vs. destructive) aspects to the tension and temporal unfolding that affects the wound. Thus, in the course of time, life hangs in a dramatic balance, its fate undecided, even if the priority of complementarity (and hierarchical integrity) is, in principle (ontologically and metaphysically), not in doubt.

The hermeneutics of belief is the appropriate way to approach the wound (i.e. belief provides the interpretive key) because the suffering that results from the tension between complementarity and anti-complementarity (i.e. breach of complements) is inherently meaningful; the wound is a wound of the living body (and, by extension, of the living community), and it is this *living context* that allows it to be intelligible as a wound that tends – despite the harm it indicates – towards healing. Thus the wound, never desirable in itself (in view of the meaninglessness that is involved in its inception), becomes, when oriented by the living context in which it occurs, a striving to repair, a way to express meaning that overcomes meaninglessness; it becomes a locus of healing.

In view of the inflicted damage that is a feature of the wound, one may note that a certain powerlessness characterises it. A wound may result from my own failings or from those of others, or from untoward circumstances. Yet, regardless of origin, I normally cannot simply remedy the problem by a *mere* exercise of effort, will or power. I experience some degree of helplessness or powerlessness (limits on what I can do) as a feature of confronting or facing a wounded state; this applies even (or perhaps especially)[61] if the wound with which I am dealing is one I have inflicted upon myself.

The apparent powerlessness associated with the experience of the wound is not, however, an ultimate powerlessness. In the experience of the wound, I may lack the power of sheer force but I have available other *powers* (to be elaborated in the next section) that may find expression as the wound becomes a feature of unity and service, unity in the context of complementarity, and service in the context of hierarchy. Unity and service at first seem compromised by the attacks of dis-accord and dis-integration, attacks which are, as already noted, real attacks. But the condition of being under such attack and threat is not the final word, even if the possibility of an ultimate self-destruction cannot be eliminated – because such a final status will depend on my decision to accept or refuse the invitation or call to exercise freedom in a meaningful manner.[62] We should clarify that an experience of unwillingness, resistance, or difficulty in accepting such an invitation does not, in itself, constitute a definitive refusal. On the contrary, the acknowledgement of difficulty and weakness may be a sign of bourgeoning faith. Recall that the alcoholic's humble acknowledgement, "I am an alcoholic," is not a statement of despair or giving up, but, on the contrary, it is rooted in belief that there are reasons to trust and hope in recovery. It is not an end but a *continuous* beginning.

We have emphasised that the wound, despite being an indication of damage, is at the same time oriented towards healing. As we have seen, this healing depends on the normalisation of abnormality: an offer or grant of normality in the experience of abnormality. Moreover, we have indicated that this normality does not simply refer to a circumscribed domain, but to a dynamic influence that involves the dramatic confrontation of the seeming permanence of meaninglessness with hope in the permanence of meaning. It is on the basis of this dynamic *normalising* normality that coexists with, and challenges abnormality that one sees the sense of hope being *always* available and credible, through the hermeneutics of faith, throughout time and history. This availability, over the course of time, of the normalising influence of complementarity, makes of time a healer, and we propose that this reparative potential or possibility is the meaning or heart of history: that is, at the heart of history is the offer of this *healing* as *always* available in the dimension of time.[63]

To put all this in terms of the experience of psychological symptoms, one could say, for example, that a person's experience of depression, anxiety or anger cannot be the *last word*. A deeper look at the temporality within which troubled experience occurs shows us that hopelessness is to be understood as temporal – despite its initial appearance as statically timeless or as negatively permanent. Healing flows from the fact that the *wound* – e.g. expressed through depression, anxiety, anger – finds itself in a *time* that is open to and dependent on an *always* that justifies one's hope in the permanence of meaning: depression contains the desire to overcome loss; anxiety contains the desire to find security and peace; anger contains the desire for justice, and, ultimately, mercy.[64]

In the above we speak of the greater mystery, with reference to complementarity and integration, vs. the lesser mystery, with reference to dissent, breach and dis-integrity. We may consider at this point a further differentiation – of the greater mystery – between *original* accord or harmony, and accord or harmony that comes about as a result of the healing or reparative inclinations associated with the wound. Original accord exists, in principle, *before* one is wounded, while reparative accord is achieved through the healing process *after* one is wounded. Moreover, healing or repair is not just a restoration or recovery of an original harmony. It is a surpassing of that original good: that is, there is potentially greater good that unfolds in the healing of the wound than in the original, healthy, unwounded state of human life. This does not mean that one is ever justified in simply wounding in order to repair: the greater good of the healing state over the unwounded state cannot be reduced to pragmatic manipulation; such reduction would itself be a perpetuation of wounding.[65] Rather, the greater meaning or normality that is achieved through healing (i.e. greater than *original* normality) is a sign of hope for those who suffer.[66]

The greater good of the wholeness established through healing over original human wholeness becomes apparent, for example, when one considers the generosity of spirit required to care for someone who has behaved in a faulty or offensive manner (fault or breach being an antecedent to the experience of the need for reconciliation among persons). On the whole, the generosity required to forgive the one who has wronged you is greater than the generosity required to care for someone who has always remained loyal. Moreover, one may appreciate, in this context, that, in order for the new wholeness that results from healing to be a greater good than original wholeness, it must fulfill and not contradict that original wholeness. In view of the basic continuity between the wholeness that results from healing and the wholeness that is original, one may see that both are, in some sense, fundamentally tied to the *always* associated with the normality of complementarity. As we have said in the previous section of this essay, one experiences this *always* or *permanence* of meaning in a paradoxical manner: as both ever new (new healing) and yet ancient (consistent with original wholeness).

One may also consider that the relation between the hermeneutics of belief and the hermeneutics of suspicion will depend on the three moments – implicitly noted above – in the unfolding of complementarity: 1) original accord, 2) rupture or disaccord, and finally 3) repair and renewal of accord. If one applies the priority of the hermeneutics of belief over the hermeneutics of suspicion to these three moments, one might initially propose that the hermeneutics of belief applies to the original accord and to the ultimate repair or renewal of accord, while the hermeneutics of suspicion applies to the intermediary phase, in which rupture or disaccord has occurred. Although this has some validity, one would have to add that even the hermeneutics applied to rupture involves an exploration of the *mix of reality*[67] (i.e. meaning *and* meaninglessness, accord *and* disaccord) and not an exploration of pure rupture. This is the case because rupture that exists in time cannot be radically circumscribed (i.e. separated from the healing influence of *permanent* meaning). Therefore, the hermeneutics applied to rupture ought not to remain simply a hermeneutics of suspicion, but ought to become a mixed one (of belief and suspicion) that matches, as it were, the mixed reality to which it applies. It is in view of the original and ultimate accord that the intermediary phase of disaccord is not pure *dis-accord*. Note, therefore, how suspicion ought to always find itself nestled between two bookends of belief, as it were. Suspicion is thus to be informed on one side by belief in an *original* accord, and on the other side by a belief in a *healing* accord.

G *Strength through Weakness: Wounds of Love*

We began this essay with an emphasis on how, in human experience, the wound expresses, not only breach or harm, but also healing. In other words, wherever one finds a wounding of life one also finds a tendency towards healing. One could say that expressions of such a healing tendency – for example, the mother comforting the child who is hurt, the dog licking the wound of its pup, the authentic reconciliation of warring factions – involve some form of transformation rooted in love. One may speak, therefore, of wounds as *wounds of love*. Let us elaborate on this notion of *wounds of love?*[68]   We propose that there are three factors to consider with respect to how love comes to be closely associated with the wound.

Firstly, we have noted that the wound involves a healing tendency which, in psychological and personal terms, one may associate with love: that is, the tendency towards healing is a form or expression of caring impulse and caring relation.[69] *Secondly*, the wound indicates the effects of dis-accord and dis-integration (i.e. the harm and damage of wounding). These indications of breakdown not only suggest a weakness in terms of one's lack of *power* to overcome or avoid harm, but also a potential weakening of and threat to *love* (i.e. in the sense that – at first sight – a diminution of power suggests a diminished capacity for loving, and, as well perhaps, a diminished sense of, or of openness to being loved). One might say, however, that love is made *strong in weakness*: that is, love may be strengthened, paradoxically, despite or even due to the experience of lack of power. For example, the love of my partner is wounded in the experience of betrayal, but strengthened in the experience of forgiveness. Moreover, this paradox of *strength through/in weakness* refers, *thirdly*, to how the healing tendency in the wound, speaks to more than the strength of power alone.

As we will elaborate, this paradox – of being made strong in weakness – refers, in our view, to the *strength* of complementarity, where the power or freedom *to be* relinquishes itself, as it were, in a transcendence towards the meaningfulness of relationship. It is as though the person acknowledges and accepts weakness, but does so trusting that such weakness is not an ultimate obstacle to relationship. For example, after being wounded I may feel lost and disconnected, but in reaching out to the others, I experience solidarity, and thus become stronger. In this way relationship to the other confers its *equality* onto my weakness;[70] consequently my weakness *enables* my strength.[71]

Recall our earlier discussion of accord, transcendence and equality as basic characteristics of normal complementarity – and of the normalising or healing impact of complementarity in the experience of abnormality. A consideration of the unity of complementarity, as a *transcendent, equalising accord*, allows one some insight into how one may love in and through weakness or lack of power. The strength in weakness lies in the potential one has, even in weakness, to favour relationship and share in it. Indeed, the meaningful, complementary exercise of freedom involves a continual surrender (i.e. transcendence) of power towards the relationship of love: one may speak of such a freedom – that consents and conforms to love – as a *loving freedom*.

When the power of freedom becomes divorced from love, however, even dramatic exercises of one's power are for naught. Consider:

> If I speak in the tongues of men and of angels, but have not love, I am only a resounding gong or a clanging cymbal. If I have the gift of prophecy and can fathom all mysteries and all knowledge, and if I have a faith that can move mountains, but have not love, I am nothing. If I give all I possess to the poor and surrender my body to the flames, but have not love, I gain nothing (1 Corinthians 13:1-3).

The power of freedom *and* the communion of relationship form a unity that demonstrates the priority of complementarity (i.e. greater mystery) over the failure associated with the breach of complementarity (i.e. lesser mystery). This is the case because the *strength in weakness* of the wound is not a strength of power alone, that is, of a circumscribed freedom in which one simply exercises control or simply does as one pleases; we are emphasising that *strength in weakness* refers, on the contrary, to a strength rooted in a transcendent accord of the equal complements of freedom and love.[72] A self-serving, radically circumscribed freedom would express breach rather than accord, immanence rather than transcendence, inequality rather than equality.[73]

As we have seen, however, there is an ontological priority (i.e. a priority given in the nature of being, given in principle) of complementarity over anti-complementarity, of fullness over emptiness. This priority speaks to a normalising or healing tendency that seeks to overcome the disaccord, sole immanence and inequity associated with breach. In this way the weakness that is a consequence of breach comes to be (through the normalising, healing process) a weakness raised to equality via a transcendent accord – and therefore strengthened: an *empowered powerlessness*. The power *taken* (i.e. weakened through a form of taking that wounds) becomes a power *given up* or *surrendered* (i.e. strengthened through a form of giving – through trust in relationship – that heals).[74] It is thus that powerlessness is not the last word on, or final destination of life, but has the potential to become a passage through which an authentic freedom, a *loving freedom*, may be expressed. The *wound against love* becomes a *wound for love*, a *wound of love*.

One ought to clarify that this *wound of/for love* does not in any way justify or suggest the endorsement or promotion of the injustice (e.g. cruelty, violence, cynicism, self-indulgence...) that may cause the wound or contribute to it. There is to be no praise for wounding. One may indeed speak of the acceptance of suffering and struggle, and even propose that the sharing of suffering is not without inherent joy; however, this joy cannot stem from the suffering as such, but only becomes possible as a consequence of the belief, trust and hope that there is *always* a meaningful or good way to live through a meaningless or bad situation. For example, one may be *happy* to set out to rescue a person caught in a fire, notwithstanding the risk to one's own life, a risk of suffering and even dying through such an action. Like Sydney Carton in Dickens' *A Tale of Two Cities*[75] one might even say, "It is a far, far better thing that I do, than I have ever done; it is a far, far better rest that I go to than I have ever known." It is only, however, in view of the offer of, and engagement with the meaning of relationship that one may speak of an appropriate attitude of acceptance and letting be towards suffering. In addition, one ought to be cautious about facile generalities or abstractions about suffering; when applied to concrete circumstances, an authentic joy of acceptance cannot involve a dismissal of sorrowful reality, but must instead be rooted in an acute appreciation and deep acknowledgement of sorrow. Thus, the embrace of the situation in which one confronts meaninglessness one is powerless to change[76] is not to become an endorsement, approval or condoning of the meaninglessness nor of the powerlessness. We will be elaborating on the characteristics of appropriate acceptance below in section "O."

H *Freedom as Power and Freedom as Right*

To better understand this *strength in weakness* of the wound, we propose a particular way of differentiating two aspects of freedom. There is freedom of choice, control, or to do as one wishes: this refers – somewhat abstractly – to the ability to decide among possibilities or directions without qualification of the context or quality of such decision. On the other hand, there is freedom as commitment and engagement: in this case the emphasis is not only on circumscribed freedom or freedom *per se*, but also on the relational quality and meaning that orients that freedom, and to which that freedom orients itself. For the purposes of the discussion that follows, we further propose to designate the first kind of freedom as one of *power*, and the second kind of freedom as one of *right*. By power we intend the characteristic in a person which allows an action or decision to be simply un-coerced, whereas by right we intend the characteristic in a person which not only qualifies an action or decision to be un-coerced, but further qualifies it as oriented towards (i.e. in accord with) the meaning of relationship.

One may see here an analogy to the hierarchical distinction we made between competitive and co-operative power: that is, co-operation is to competition as right is to power.[77] Just as co-operation is to have priority over competition, so too is right to have priority over power. Indeed, one could say that the goal of hierarchical integration would be to have power defer to and, as it were, *become* right. Or we could put this another way: there are two kinds of freedom, the unfulfilled freedom of power and the fulfilled freedom of right, and the unfulfilled is ever to seek its fulfillment. We propose this differentiation of levels of power to draw attention to the risk of reducing right to power (see later discussion of Nietzsche), and to draw attention to the internal hierarchical structure of freedom.

The exercise of power and the exercise of right both involve expressions of freedom and assertions of being; however, we are suggesting that power and right exist on a hierarchical continuum, such that power is the surface or lower expression of right, and right is the deeper or higher meaning of power. One may further consider that in the exercise of *surface* or *outer* power one does not necessarily realise *inner* right and virtue. Freedom fails to be itself if it expresses (surface) power in a manner that contradicts right. Such a contradiction constitutes a wound, because the failure to integrate power with right involves the failure to receive into hierarchy the norm of complementarity; this would be the failure of compatibility between hierarchy and complementarity.[78]

Indeed, recognising a hierarchical difference in the exercise of power and right allows one to begin to distinguish between appropriate and inappropriate expressions of power. Consider the following example of abusive power that threatens human right. If, from a position of authority, I take advantage of subordinates for private gain, then my exercise of power and freedom fails to realise the deeper purpose of such power and freedom; I am doing what I have the power to do (i.e. what I am able to choose to do), but I am failing to apply my freedom meaningfully or *right*-fully.

Note that one would normally speak, in this example, of my failure to respect the *rights* of my subordinates. But respect for the right of the other depends clearly on the *rightful* exercise of my power or freedom. When my power or freedom is not in accordance with the right of the other, then my power itself fails to be right or virtuous; I fail in my obligation or responsibility to relationship. The freedom of right is not unilateral but the result of right matched with obligation, as Simone Weil has indicated.[79] Indeed, unless the respect for, and obligation to the person has priority over the abstracted (in the sense of circumscribed) notion of choice, then such an abstracted notion (of such central importance to modern democracy) loses the basis of its own support. If the reality and dignity of the person is not the basis for the respect of freedom, then one tends to approach the power of freedom as a circumscribed, self-enclosed reality, and relationship no longer has *equality* with freedom. This inevitably threatens the equality of individuals.[80]

In the framework we propose (where we differentiate right from power hierarchically) right flourishes when its hierarchical relationship with power is integrated, that is, when hierarchy is oriented by the norm of complementarity. Conversely there is a failure of right when power or freedom remains unconcerned, as it were, with *right*-ful direction; that is, when one fails to integrate the freedom of power with the freedom of right, one fails to follow the norm that complementarity provides for meaningful integration.[81] One may infer, therefore, that normality or meaning, as we have been defining it, calls for right to *inform* power and power to *conform* or *defer* to right.[82]

Moreover, returning to the above example of the abusive expression of freedom, one could say that where one exercises power in an abusive manner, there is an implicit call, if not a cry, for healing. This is a call to respect right: the norm of complementarity (person in relation) is to inform the hierarchical arrangement of powers such that the freedom of right (to which obligation to the other is integral) has priority over the freedom of power (which is exercised abusively if it remains abstracted or separated from considerations of relational meaning). Moreover, one should speak of the exercise of power and right not only in some ideal, original state of harmony, but – as implied in the previous section where we spoke of the greater good of healing over original wholeness – in circumstances where there has been failure of hierarchy and complementarity.

Note, however, that we are not dismissing the value of the assertive power of a human being (i.e. the power to choose): we are only saying that it is crucial for such assertive power to respect the norm of complementarity, and where necessary, participate in healing by becoming a healing power, a *loving freedom*. In this way the exercise or assertion of freedom becomes an expression in accord with right, and not a mere expression of force.

There is perhaps no question that more greatly divides and troubles us in modernity (and *post-modernity*) than that of how to integrate power and right.[83] By giving priority to power, Nietzsche, it may be said, announced a fusion between power and right, or, perhaps, more to the point, the reduction of right to power (as we have defined these terms). He was, perhaps, less providing an original vision than reflecting the zeitgeist by declaring the will to power as the supreme value. Furthermore, with his rejection of the so-called slave morality, he seemed to distance himself from that which could keep this idolatry of power in check. And this lack of a principle of restraint is consistent with the lack of support for the priority of right over power. This idolatry of power found particularly strong expression through such movements as the significant promotion of eugenics in the early 20th century and the dictatorial regimes of that same century, but continues in current times to manifest itself in the emphasis on individual power.[84] By virtue of an inversion of hierarchy, power has usurped the place of right. The problem is a crisis of faith that we see implied in Nietzsche: with the loss of belief in the priority of right, only arbitrary power, stripped of meaning, remains. We could speak here of power that creates its own meaning, an idea that finds some resonance in Nietzsche's thought. However, as David Bentley Hart points out, Nietzsche was not cavalier about the implications of such a shift, and had a keen awareness of the consequences of what he was saying, an awareness that contemporary believers in the arbitrary creation of values seem to lack.[85]

As noted above, Simone Weil proposed that human right requires social obligation to sustain it.[86] She points out that a right unsupported by the obligation and solidarity required to sustain it loses its viability, although we would argue that, when considered in the context of complementarity, it retains its truth, and its paradoxical *strength* (i.e. via what we have referred to as the on-going offer of *equality* inherent to complementarity). I may have limited powers to exercise rights; however, the rights themselves stand or fall depending, not on the power of their exercise, but on whether they are true. Nevertheless, as Weil implies, human attitudes, conduct and laws may support or negate the power to exercise right. If one jeopardises the accord between the distinct, unique life of the human person, and the relational context of support and commitment that is to favour that life, one compromises right. This severance of accord implies an abuse of power: that is, it implies giving power priority over right, and disconnecting the exercise of power from the social obligation that could secure, support and favour right. A genuine equality, rooted in the transcendent accord of equal complements, seems to be a challenge to a modernity and post-modernity that has discovered great value in the power of individual freedom, but is less attentive to the need to co-ordinate that value with the *equal, complementary value* of communion or solidarity (of persons).

From the perspective we are proposing, a right is something one can neither destroy nor create: it is a given. People do not gain new rights; rather, they may gain new powers to exercise the rights they always essentially or intrinsically *have had*. Conversely, one may sometimes witness (in oneself as well as others) the exercise of powers that bear no real relation to actual rights. Actual rights may be denied or eclipsed but they cannot be destroyed, no more than one can destroy the law of gravity by declaring it does not exist.[87]

If powers are related to rights as the lower is related to the higher, then all power is ultimately dependent on right. This is the case even though the modern zeitgeist might not readily accommodate such a notion, because, in the suspicious temper of our times, the tendency is to give priority to power (both with respect to explanatory systems of thought and the actual ordering of social relationships).[88] However, because right and power exist on a (hierarchical) continuum, and in view of what we have said about the service of the lower by the higher, it is perhaps understandable that some confusion arises with respect to the meaning of the differences between power and right.

For example, we must consider, in view of what we said about the role of service in hierarchy, that right places itself, as it were, in the hands of power, in a form of respectful condescension (i.e. service of the lower by the higher), and that the person exercising power may then remain true to what he or she holds in his or her hands, or not: one may exercise power in a way that is faithful to right or without faith in regard to right. One may, through the *dis-integrated* exercise of power, unleash destructive force over right, and though this is clearly a failure of justice and trust, it does not erase the truth of the (ontological) priority of right over power.

Furthermore, one could say that right (despite, or indeed because of its higher position) takes on powerlessness and thus *submits* to (i.e. serves) power. This powerlessness refers to the transcendence and surrender that are features of service. The intent of this submission to powerlessness – in the context of service – is not capitulation of right to power, however; the purpose of this submission is to win over power to right, in order to grant to power itself a share in what is higher than itself, to transform it.

One has in one's humanity both power and right, and these call for a balance and an integration that involve a recognition of the higher service orientation of right over the lower competitive function of power. Power is not thereby to be suppressed; rather, it is to be applied and find expression within the normative influence of complementarity. In this way the competitive, assertive aspect of power, via deferral, may actually further the co-operative and relational aspect of power.

In any case, our concern is specifically in the area of mental health or psychopathology, where it is often one's own exercise of power that eclipses one's right. One may note this, for example, in the excesses associated with anxious control, paranoid attitudes, and compulsive habits. With these three forms of psychopathology, one may consider the respective exercise of *powers* vs. *rights*. With anxiety one may see the *power* of excessive self-protection and avoidance vs. the *right* (and obligation) of appropriate trust and engagement. With paranoid attitudes one may see the *power* of rejecting others vs. the *right* of the other to one's solidarity. With compulsive habits one may see the *power* to dominate or control *relation with reality* vs. the *right* to share and act as a participant (and not sole controller) in the *reality of relation*. In each of these examples the inordinate exercise of power interferes with the expression of the fuller meaning of one's humanity.

Conversely, by embracing right, power is elevated; action is filled from within with the truth of right. All exercise of power ought to be informed by this truth. This *informing* allows power to express right, and it is ultimately right that confers power; this allows power to be *true* or *authentic*. All power exercised outside of right is inauthentic and unjustified. It is clear that the power to do something does not, in itself, confer the right. Right rests on the complementarity of distinction and relation, on the (ontological) generosity which permits both the power of freedom and the meaningfulness of relationship to be. Right depends on what we have called normality or meaning. Right depends on a freedom conformed to solidarity and on a solidarity that supports freedom. But, we know that right can be transgressed by power. Power can divorce itself from right and lord over right, a capitulation Nietzsche seems at times to prescribe. This is the perpetration of an abnormality, a wounding, whereas Nietzsche and others of like mind would have it become the norm for the super-man.

One may note that right does not lord over power, but only *invites* power to co-operate in the process of integration. This is the *weakness* of right. It is of interest to consider that Nietzsche seems to have had little patience or tolerance for weakness; perhaps, he wanted to secure control over right by reducing right to power (one of the problematic ideas with which modernity has to contend).[89] A hermeneutics of belief would have us search Nietzsche's ideas for how his ultimate interest might have been, in some sense, to protect right from being thwarted. Bernard Williams, for example, discusses the ways in which Nietzsche remained committed to truth and indicates that he preached neither a utilitarianism with respect to morality nor a relativism with respect to truth.[90] In our view, however, Nietzsche's hermeneutics of suspicion compromises the quest for both morality and truth. Nietzsche writes in *Antichrist*: "'Faith' means not *wanting* to know what is true."[91] If, however, Nietzsche is wrong regarding his indictment of faith, if our quest for truth, even via reason, is not hindered but assisted by faith, then the exclusion of faith becomes a prejudice that limits openness to truth (and openness to the role of truth in determining morality).

One may give priority to healing and trust over damage and breach in the experience of the weakness of the wound. This expresses a *hopeful acceptance*[92] in which there is the refusal to turn right into power, or to reduce truth to brute force – a reduction we see in the saying "Might makes right." To simply *force* people to behave in accordance with right is to offend right, because right depends on freedom, not force or coercion. But this implies that the freedom on which right depends cannot itself be reduced to mere force or the mere exercise of power. "Might makes right" is the corruption of freedom *and* truth. One may speak here of a complementarity of freedom and truth where "truth is integral to freedom," but "freedom is also integral to truth."[93] Note the personalist dimension of truth that is implied. Truth not only refers to an adequation of mind and reality, but, in view of (person-based) freedom's reciprocal relation with truth, truth refers, as well, to the relation between freedom and the (authentic or true) good of relationship. In other words, truth is not simply the adequation of mind and reality (in the abstract) but refers to and includes (more concretely) the union, relation or *adequation* of freedom and the good of relationship, freedom and the good of the other.[94]

Furthermore, in view of the priority of this relation between freedom and good, it follows that it is not the way of right to lord over (i.e. to reduce freedom to sole power); it is the way of right to persuade and invite, to gently call. The weakness of right is its strength, for the invitation that radiates from right is the invitation to love in freedom; and love may be commanded, but it cannot be forced. Moreover, freedom itself, in the human experience, is not simply a *fait accompli*, but calls for continual development through one's response to the invitation or calling of sharing, communion, commitment and solidarity.

In the above, we are not, however, proposing an anarchy with respect to power (e.g. no government, laws or law enforcement), on the one hand, nor excessive coercion (e.g. undue restriction on the individual's exercise of power to force compliance with obligation to collective interests), on the other: rather, we propose that one recognise the limits of the mere power or freedom of choice, while appreciating how relational bonds (friendship, marriage, family, community, nation...) favour and support the authentic freedom of the members involved in those bonds. It is only when power accepts its limits, as it were, that it remains rooted in, or open to right, as it is only when relational entities favour personal life or freedom that the expression of right may flourish: the consideration and application of these principles should help prevent both anarchic and relativist forms of individualism, on the one hand, and totalitarian forms of collectivism, on the other. The priority of right over power is a principle that could help one to keep the ever-present threat of the idolatry of power in check (in the collectivist and/or individualist forms such threat may take).

I   *Some Ethical Implications of 'Healing through Belief'*

In this context, one may further reflect on the ethical or moral implications of the priority of right over power. We propose that an *ethical moment* occurs precisely when there is consent by the person – or the community of persons – to have *mere* power give way or defer to the meaningfulness of right. In our view, this deferral to meaning speaks, by analogy, to the priority of the complementary over the hierarchical. Thus, a failed ethical *moment* is one where one's conduct or behaviour involves a decision to grant power dominance over meaning, that is, to allow *mere* hierarchy to dominate complementarity.

If complementarity provides the norm for hierarchy, then ethical questions will always involve more than a consideration of power. There has been a tendency in both individualist and collectivist currents of thought, however, to reduce questions regarding rights to terms of power (e.g. the individual ought to have the right/power to do what he or she wants without coercion or interference by society, and even the right/power to have society do his or her bidding; or the collectivity ought to have the *right* not only to have its interests protected from threats posed by self-interested individuals, but to directly shape individuals so that they can serve collective interests). Whether couched in individualist or collectivist terms the emphasis has been on control, and the language of power dominates the discourse: the individual is to dominate the social, or the social is to dominate the individual.

What seems missing is a deeper ethic that takes complementarity into account, an ethic that does not start with the politicisation of ethics or morals, but sees questions of power as subsidiary to questions of good. We cannot ignore questions of power, but, if we too readily politicise morality, we will move increasingly away from ethical thought. Our emphasis on complementarity as a normative influence on deliberations regarding the use of powers – communal and/or individual – leads us precisely to consider that which transcends and ought to inform power (i.e. the meaning of relationship). We then understand the ethical or moral moment as the assent and consent to this deferral of power to meaning (i.e. the informing of power by meaning), and the unethical as the dissent from such deferral (i.e. the rejection of meaning).

Our challenge, therefore, is not simply to balance collective and individual interests, even if prudential considerations will no doubt call for such balancing. The more fundamental challenge is to favour a society in which both the personal and social are permitted to make their respective contributions in a complementarity: thus, child and family, student and school, citizen and nation, individual and community are to be mutual participants, complementary to one another. One may realise, therefore, that the problem with the effacement of complementarity is not simply a question of the distribution of individual and social powers of control, as though questions of morality and justice were to be determined primarily on the basis of balancing the individual's domination of the social with the social domination of the individual (i.e. reaching some sort of midpoint between collectivist and individualist ideologies). To reduce the *personal* and the *relational* to a matter of mere power struggle undermines the ability of person and society to exert a mutually humanising influence on one another.[95] Conscience, as the memory and recognition of the other, is stifled. Power is an essential yet subsidiary component of human experience. As we will explore in the next section, even in powerlessness, the meaning of complementarity need not be forfeited.

J *Recovering the Meaning of Power from Powerlessness*

In human life one is inevitably confronted with the problematic experience of various kinds of powerlessness (personal, social, political, economic). One may consider that the experience of human powerlessness is not only the result of natural limitations (e.g. the consequence of natural disaster or disease) but is also imposed, socially, politically, economically, etc., through human agency and practice. Furthermore, one sees in the experience of human powerlessness, not only a restriction of power, but also a threat to meaning. Still, powerlessness cannot be equated with meaninglessness. One may consider, for example, how the experience of powerlessness, although undesirable in itself, can actually become the locus where meaningful forms of relationship, such as conviction, commitment and solidarity, flourish.

I cannot deny that the powerlessness caused by nature or the other's oppression harms me, and yet *my consent* to the meaninglessness expressed in the oppression may pose the greater threat to me. In other words, beyond the harm that I experience in my oppression, I may even more seriously injure myself through my own abandonment of meaning, through my own failing in my freedom to assert truth and meaning. For example, even though my heart might be broken by the rejection of my lover I more grievously injure myself (and my relationships with others) by giving up on love altogether. Consider what Jacques Philippe writes in *Interior Freedom*: "We are not always masters of the unfolding of our lives, but we can always be masters of the meaning we give them." He also quotes Christiane Singer: "What ruins our souls is not what happens outside, but the echo it awakes within us." [96] Consider as well, Viktor Frankl, who writes that human freedom "is not freedom from conditions, but it *is* freedom to take a stand toward the conditions." [97] These references further emphasise that one ought to understand one's distress not only as the consequence of circumstances that inflict frustration, pain, or harm, but also in terms of how, in such circumstances, one orders one's consent or freedom.

If I consent to the divorce of freedom from meaning, I am seeing myself and/or others condemned not only to powerlessness but to meaninglessness. In order to engage powerlessness meaningfully I have to affirm the factors that promote meaning and negate those that threaten meaning. Such threatening factors are likely to include my own inclination towards cynicism, vengeful hostility and despair. These are factors that tend to negate a meaningful exercise of freedom and cancel or eclipse an openness to the value of relationship and solidarity (with the other as person). It is on the values of relationship that an authentic power of freedom can be based, developed and renewed.

Doubt, critique and suspicion are appropriate responses to such negative influences and inclinations as cynicism, vengeful hostility and despair. This application of suspicion is a negation of negation, and, as previously argued, it is oriented by belief in a *prior* (*original*) and *subsequent* (*ultimate*) trusted connection. This connection may be weakly outlined, barely visible or even seem completely eclipsed, forgotten and unattainable. However, the only way to make sense of the negation of negation of which we speak is to see that it involves more than a reversal of powerlessness. It cannot be a mere restoration of control, a mere thirst for power, a mere pragmatic conquest. It calls one to give priority to the meaningfulness of connection with the other.

Indeed, the mere quest for control, power and conquest reminds one of psychoanalytic explanations of how fantasies of omnipotent-like power may function as ego-defensive manoeuvres. Consider, for example, the manic triad of defences as proposed by Melanie Klein: *control, contempt* and *triumph*. These defences are said to protect the ego from "guilt, risk of loss and dependence," that is, from difficulties and vulnerabilities arising in one's experience of relationship. *Control* involves denial that the other or *object* has an independent reality, *contempt* diminishes the worth of the other, and *triumph* "triumphantly reverses the situation of who is small and who is big."[98] Through the application of these *manic* defences one avoids or diminishes the painfulness associated with the reality of dependence and separation, the guilt associated with aggression, and the fears associated with the unpredictability of interpersonal interaction. Such defensiveness, however, also prevents a real bond or connection to the other, and thus frustrates possibilities of real caring.[99]

If the defensively *omnipotent* exercise of power essentially compromises and threatens relationship – even while it indicates an attempt to protect the ego – then it follows that the appropriate exercise of power would involve a response that somehow supports relationship. Where one is dealing with significant threat or damage to relationship, an appropriate exercise of power would call for the expression of a *healing freedom*. Such freedom suggests a notion of integrated power that is not arbitrary: in applying *healing freedom* one gives priority to meaning over power; in defensive omnipotence one gives priority to power over meaning.

At this point we may raise a further question with respect to what the ultimate or omnipotent expressions of power might mean. We have noted two divergent notions of power: an integrated or authentic power, on the one hand, and a dis-integrated, inauthentic power, on the other. We believe that these two notions speak to two corresponding notions of omnipotent power. In the above, we have considered an *inauthentic* omnipotence which compromises and threatens relationship, by basically denying the other in order to protect the ego. An *authentic* omnipotence, on the other hand, would involve an ultimate expression of power that does not separate itself from the meaningfulness of relationship. Consider, in this respect, Antonio Lopez' explication of Divine omnipotence and its influence in terms of "the gift of oneself to the end for the sake of another."[100] In this conception, ultimate power or freedom does not refer to mere domination and control that stands in opposition to powerlessness, but to a fullness of being based in a maximum engagement in the meaningfulness of relationship: the "gift of oneself to the end."[101] Moreover, in view of the distinctions we have drawn between different expressions of power (such as co-operation and competition, or right and power), and in view of the impact of *healing freedom*, such maximum engagement may not be incompatible with the experience of powerlessness.

These divergent ways of characterising ultimate power or omnipotence (i.e. mere control vs. fullness of being) bear some analogy, therefore, to our prior distinctions between competitive and co-operative forms of relating, and between power and right. We have argued that these varying expressions of power can only be understood appropriately in the context of hierarchical integration. An integrated vision of power may provide the positive sense in Nietzsche's reflections on power: he sought, perhaps, a true or even meaningful power. In our view, however, he failed to see that authentic power is not necessarily cancelled in powerlessness.[102] Powerlessness is not incommensurable with right and obligation, and not incommensurable with what we are calling authentic power (i.e. by authentic power we mean any power that is a reflection or image of a true omnipotence, a fullness of being: the "gift of oneself to the end"). The abundance of right and obligation can take root in powerlessness, and, therefore, meaning may be found in the midst of such lack. Though paradoxical, one may conclude that the concrete experience of powerlessness may not be incompatible with authentic power and, as well, may not be incompatible with authentic omnipotence.[103]

Without the priority of right (as the authentic meaning of power) over mere power (as the sheer force of control) any established right to exercise power will lose its meaning and legitimacy as it becomes reduced to power alone. In fact, blind power (power emptied of meaning) and empty powerlessness (powerlessness that lacks meaning) are two sides of the same coin, corollary to one another: indeed, in some sense, identical. The more *mere* power becomes dominant, the more one witnesses an end to the meanings associated with rights and obligations, and an end to the priority of co-operation and service over competition and dominance. Without the compass of meaning, the rudder of power lacks true direction. Without meaningful direction power becomes *mere power* and eclipses right, obligation, co-operation, service, and the complementarity in relationship; such mere power may be equated, therefore, with empty powerlessness.[104]

With respect to mental health we are not saying that power *per se* is abnormal, but we are saying that disintegrated power (i.e. a radicalised *per se*) is, indeed, abnormal. Disintegrated power is essentially the result of the abandonment of the norm of complementarity. This dis-integration is ultimately an expression of disbelief and despair. In *consent*[105] to hopelessness, distinction withdraws from relation: the faith, generosity and liberality that favour complementarity disintegrate into the disbelief, miserliness and narrowness of anti-complementarity. But right and obligation do not cease to exist. The wound is not fatal. The promise of healing begins even as the wound is inflicted. The turmoil of psychological distress both conceals and expresses this promise. The turmoil may be a sign that one has been stung with the venom of despair, but at the same time it is a sign of a protest that seeks the antidote of hope.[106]

K *The Paradox of Inner (Individual) Origins to Psychological Problems and Outer (Relational) Solutions*

Although psychological problems may have origins that arise from within (e.g. in a failure of freedom) they do not necessarily have solutions that come solely or primarily from within. Consider the paradigmatic or prototypical breach of relationship resulting from a failure of freedom to support another person whom one is called to support. For example, I may be fully responsible for offending a friend, but I alone cannot provide the solution to this breach. A remedy will require my apology (i.e. being sorry) and my friend's forgiveness, in other words, our co-operation. How often do we see in the guilt associated with severe depression a sort of solitary and therefore ineffective struggle with painful feelings that avoids this co-operative route to a solution? The person experiences an intense sense of responsibility for a failure, and seeks from within the self alone the solution to the guilt. But such a solution does not arise, neither from denial of fault nor from self-reproach: a true and healing remedy comes only from engaging in relationship through a willingness to make amends, based in *being sorry*, and from openness to, and hope in forgiveness by the other. Without this *being sorry in hope of forgiveness* all efforts to repair are provisional, incomplete, tentative....

Consider the following allegory of how I may be responsible for my difficulties, yet unable to effectively address them on my own. I fall off a cliff due to my own carelessness, and then find myself precariously perched on a ledge, unable to reach up to the place from which I fell. Someone, however, comes along and extends a hand. By accepting the other's help I am able to solve what I could not solve on my own. I was the main cause of my predicament, but I could not, on my own, without a *helping hand*, provide the solution to my predicament.

It is on the basis of a misguided application of my independence and power that I fail, but the remedy to breach of relationship cannot arise simply from my further exercise of independence and power. I have to enter the sphere of dependence and *powerlessness* to seek and find forgiveness. I may, however, have to be careful not to turn this acknowledgement of dependence and powerlessness into an attitude that exonerates me from responsibility. In any case, when power fails right, relationship is breached, but only the generosity that favours the co-existence of right (as the authentic power of freedom) and obligation (as the renewal of relationship) can heal the breach.

Power thus finds its own legitimate expression and becomes channeled into service when it defers to right and obligation. How many traditions, on the one hand, and revolutions or reforms, on the other, have sought to apply a notion of right, but then reduce that notion to one of sole power, thereby losing the significance of right? Such a reduction not only tends towards the loss of right, but, as well, to the loss of the utility of power itself.

To recapitulate the above, when I exercise power in a manner that alienates from right and obligation, I am the cause of my troubles. Not all psychological problems may begin with this abuse of power, but many psychological problems that linger involve this kind of failure. Yet the solution or remedy to this kind of failure involves a relational principle which requires more than an *inner* – in the sense of solely self-based – change. In other words, although I may be the cause of my troubles (i.e. they come from within), I cannot be the sole solution to my troubles.[107] An essential part of the solution or remedy to my problem comes, not from *within* me (meaning, from me alone) but from *without/beyond* me (meaning, from more than me, from openness to relationship). As noted above, a paradigmatic or prototypical example of this is the guilt I feel when I offend another. I feel guilty for my offence, for which I am responsible, but I cannot, on my own, remedy the problem. I need to be sorry and make my apologies and amends to the other, and I depend on the other's forgiveness for healing and reconciliation.

Here one may see a further manifestation of the priority of right (and obligation) over power. My own power may keep me stuck in psychological difficulty, but to find a remedy I have to allow power to be mixed with obligation, right and meaning, so that power may be transformed and become true, and, therefore, *truly* effective. One could say that power is to *ascend* by accepting the condescension of right: power lets itself be transformed into right, surrenders to right, and right *serves* power, raising it up to itself. This condescension of right does not annihilate or distort right, because it happens in freedom and in truth. This truth is a truth of love (i.e. love expressed as service) that is also a love of truth (a love that supports the authentic power or freedom of being). [108] Only in this way may we effectively address the so-called false consciousness that past and current masters of suspicion critique. In other words, the truth and falsity of consciousness (Freud), conventional morality (Nietzsche) or ideology (Marx) can only be determined on the basis of the healing impulse that is active in the accord of complements and the integration of hierarchy.

L *Freedom and Defence*

From the perspective we offer, symptomatic experience already contains within itself the tendency towards healing. Before we even begin to reflect upon and attempt to address them, troubled thoughts and feelings already have an inner orientation towards complementarity or normality. The wound is a sign of abnormality, but it is also already in a dynamic tension with and towards normality; we noted earlier that the wound exists within a living body, which, we could say, *conspires* to heal it. Fatal wounds may appear to erase any hope of healing, but, as also noted, the human experience of suffering contains an inherent reference to an *always*, a hope that points beyond even the finality of the fatal wound (for example, consider the human practices associated with mourning and commemorating the dead).

It follows from these considerations that, by applying a hermeneutics of belief, one would approach and interpret troubled feelings (arising in connection with being wounded) in terms of how such feelings might express the promotion and defence of complementarity. Notwithstanding the tendency towards complementarity, however, the behavioural strategies that people often use when experiencing troubled feelings would seem, paradoxically, to promote anti-complementarity. Recall our discussion of manic defences as outlined by Melanie Klein. Attitudes that involve the defences of *control, contempt* and *triumph* indicate attempts to protect the ego from threat in a manner that often involves significant rejection of, or withdrawal from relationship. One could say that this type of defensive response defends or promotes anti-complementarity, because the response interferes with achieving the trust and closeness required to form and maintain a caring relationship. On the other hand, one may work through the threat and vulnerability associated with anxious, aggressive or depressive feelings in a manner that not only promotes the protection of self or ego, but also builds and restores relationship, thus maintaining or enhancing complementarity.[109]

It is of interest to consider that one may characterise the main object of the suspicion of the Masters of Suspicion as some form of human defensiveness. For example, Marx, Nietzsche and Freud respectively refer to bourgeois ideology, conventional (slave) morality, and Victorian attitudes to sexuality, and one may see in each of these an expression of false consciousness. This false consciousness involves a defensiveness in which the underlying, actual goals that motivate people's attitudes and actions are said to be disguised. It seems implicit to their approach that exposing such human defensiveness would contribute to liberation. In our view, however, this liberating effect would depend on whether belief is granted priority over suspicion.

It could be liberating to realise that economic interest (Marx), power (Nietzsche) or sexual or aggressive instinct (Freud) is behind our conscious ways of thinking, if there were something to liberate: that is, if there were some principle beyond those forces that could offer a new and deeper orientation, and that would confer meaning. If, however, suspicion extends to the point that one considers greed, power and instinctual release to be the essential forces underlying human experience, how is insight into their influence supposed to effect a liberation? In that case, there would be nothing to liberate. If suspicion has and retains priority in the interpretive process, then actual liberation would appear to be compromised.

We have proposed that there is an appropriate role for the hermeneutics of suspicion; however, we have also emphasised that there is a problem if suspicion gains priority. When suspicion becomes the pervasive or fundamental feature of the interpretive process, the explanation of human behaviour is reduced to some form of self-interest, and consequently human relationship is reduced to power struggle. Moreover, the interpretive paradigm that gives primacy to suspicion places the one who uses this paradigm into the role of the *suspicious knower* who gazes upon subject matter (e.g. false consciousness) that is *suspect*. Note, as well, that the primacy of suspicion does not leave much room for a *mixed reality*: that is, one does not tend to view the other (and, perhaps, the self) as *both* self-interested *and* altruistic, *both* driven by economic interest *and* human interest, *both* oriented by sexual instinct *and* familial affiliation. No, from the perspective of suspicion only one-sided conclusions tend to follow: altruism is *really* a form of self-interest; the claim of human interest is *only* a disguise for economic interest; familial affiliation is *only* a result of inhibited sexual instinct.

In each of the Masters of Suspicion there is, in our view, the tendency to fall short of providing a perspective that allows one to move towards an authentic emancipation. It is not necessarily their critique of a (*defensive*) false consciousness that we question. Rather, as noted above, we raise concern about the *reduction* in approach (one becomes a *suspicious knower*) and in subject matter (one attends to that which is *suspect*). For Marx there is the tendency to reduce the explanation of human historical development to the warring of social classes, even if the eventual goal is to establish a classless society. For Nietzsche morality is reduced to an exercise of power, even if such a reduction is meant to establish a greater authenticity. For Freud human consciousness arises from the influence of unconscious instinctual (sexual and aggressive) forces, even if the discovery or awareness of these influences is meant to free one from neurotic dependence on their unconscious effects. The problem is not with the partial validity of their critiques nor with the positive aims they might have (i.e. with respect to creating a more equitable society, a more authentic or noble expression of self, a greater insight into unconscious influences). The problem is not with what their suspicion uncovers (when it does uncover something significant); the problem is with the way their suspicion limits the scope of their subject matter, and the scope of their own approach to that subject matter.

One could say that, when the critique of *idealism* becomes too strong or pervasive, as we believe it does with the Masters of Suspicion, one limits or threatens *realism*. Consider Viktor Frankl's comment, delivered at a lecture he gave in 1972, on how one's approach to human nature is affected by the question of *idealism* vs. *realism*:

> If we take man as he really is we make him worse. But if we overestimate him...If we seem to be idealist and are overestimating, overrating man...we promote him to what he really can be. So we have to be idealists in a way, so that then we wind up at the true, the real realist. And you know who has said this? –

*If we take man as he is, we make him worse, but if we take him as he should be, we make him capable of what he can be. – ...*This was Goethe. He said this verbally [literally]. And now you will understand why in one of my writings, I once said, "This is the most apt maxim and motto for any psychotherapeutic activity."[110]

Although Marx, Nietzsche and Freud may have supported the ideals of equality, freedom, and truth, respectively, the primacy of suspicion in their hermeneutics tended, in our view, to compromise their quest. A hermeneutics of suspicion (i.e. where suspicion has primacy in one's method of interpretation) will tend towards the eclipse of the ideals one may have wished to affirm, even if it was the desire to defend those ideals that may have prompted one to become suspicious in the first place. Suspicion fosters a lack of trust in one's connection to the other, in favour of placing a greater "trust" (and certitude) in what one possesses in oneself. This, as proposed above, tends to reduce relationship to a matter of power struggle. When one is primarily suspicious, one imagines that one has discovered the conspiring of the other; however, one may be seeing less of the other and more the projection of oneself.

With a hermeneutics of belief one is not to ignore the insights that arise from a suspicious attitude; the intent, rather, is to make room for the mix of reality (i.e. not reduce everything to an object of suspicion). Furthermore, with trust as primary, one need not fall into naïveté, because belief or trust is not oriented to assuming that reality unfolds as it should, that all will turn out well, that positive attitudes will lead to positive results, nor that human beings always act on the basis of lofty and virtuous motives. The belief and trust that is a feature of the hermeneutics of belief indicates something more fundamental than positive thinking. It does not depend, primarily, on good outcome – neither in terms of fortuitous circumstance, nor in terms of others' or one's own virtuous conduct. It does not assume a harmonious past, a happy present nor a good future. On the contrary, the purpose of belief and trust, as we have outlined these principles, is to give primacy to the healing influence associated with complementarity, and this clearly implies that one is also aware of the damage (to complementarity and hierarchical order) that needs healing. To trust and believe in a healing remedy requires an intimate awareness and knowledge – not naïveté – with regards to the wound that needs healing.

In our view, the hermeneutics of belief, when applied to the understanding of psychopathology and psychotherapeutic treatment, permits one to develop a comprehensive and inclusive understanding of defensive features of human experience, such that even what appears to be an example of auto-oriented ego-defence will be viewed in the context of complementarity. Thus, one will be seeking, in defensive reactions, not only the features of defence that indicate a reinforcement of breach, but also those features of defence that indicate a tendency/tension towards the accord of complementarity. The defensive reactions arising in association with troubled feelings (e.g. withdrawal associated with depression, compulsive behaviour associated with anxiety) may variously reveal and conceal the underlying complementarity to which they are essentially oriented, and in the course of psychotherapy, therapist and patient are to work together to recognise, in these defensive features of symptomatic experience, both the offer of, and threat against complementarity. One could say that in the work of therapy one is, on the one hand, to apply a hermeneutics of belief to promote the discernment of complementarity; this serves to renew complementarity after it has been breached. One is, on the other hand, to apply a hermeneutics of suspicion, in order to identify the way that narrowly defensive manoeuvres contribute to breach, and thereby one also may promote the renewal of complementarity.

We are saying that to approach the negation of complementarity with suspicion is appropriate, and we have previously spoken, in this respect, of a *negation of negation*. We should add, however, that this negation of negation is not simply an example of producing a positive by negating a negative. The primacy of belief is implicit, in our view, even in suspicion itself, in that to make sense of suspicion one must recognise that its purpose is ultimately to find *that in which one can believe and trust*. For example, the jealous lover attacks the beloved, ostensibly, to turn that person into someone trustworthy. One often sees, however, that the willingness to even consider trusting the other may be lacking in the jealous lover. Similarly, the conspiracy theorist wants to unmask the ways in which the government tells lies and manipulates in order, ostensibly, to have government conduct itself in a responsible fashion. In Kafkaesque style, however, the belief that there is a way for relationship with the other to be or become trustworthy may be lacking or absent in the conspiracy theorist. As noted previously, an excessive, pervasive suspicion seems to defeat the very reason or purpose that initially prompts one to become suspicious. In any case, giving primacy to belief is not, in the end, a dismissal of suspicion: the priority of belief over suspicion is an affirmation of the belief contained in suspicion itself. Paradoxically, to develop an authentic understanding of suspicion I must give priority to belief. And when I do apply the hermeneutics of suspicion to my experiences of the breach of relationship in the *secondary* manner we have proposed, I am, in a sense, paradoxically searching for belief or trust in and through suspicion: only when I uncover the belief in suspicion, am I remaining true to suspicion!

One may thus have, from a position that gives priority to belief, some alliance with those who give priority to suspicion. And one may even agree that, in some ways, belief may display, at times, some degree of naïveté. At the same time, however, one must realise that to strongly endorse a given suspicious perspective can itself be rather naïve. Also, we would argue that suspicion, as an attitude, has the psychological quality of closing the horizon of what we may investigate, whilst belief can have the quality of keeping that horizon open. Suspicion is rooted in defence of the self or of *one's own*, whereas belief is rooted in the receptivity to, and defence of more than self. We could add, that belief loses its openness and becomes more like suspicion as it becomes more self-referential and defensive, and this surely happens. It is with this sort of critical perspective that the Masters of Suspicion and those who share their viewpoint have understood belief: they have reduced belief to a self-referential, defensive position. Consider, for example, how Marx saw religious belief as the "opium of the people," Nietzsche as an expression of "not wanting to know the truth," (*The Antichrist*, Section 52, 1988) and Freud as the neurotic manifestation of an infantile wish. One may have to continually reform belief to keep it from adopting the limitations or restrictions that we are associating with suspicion, but a primary suspicion tends to undermine belief rather than restore it.

Freud viewed the ego as vulnerable to the instincts of the id, the demands of reality, and the threats of a punitive superego.[111] In this conception, the ego has much against which to defend itself, and – as argued in the first essay in this book – the psychoanalytic notion of defence speaks largely to the auto-oriented, self-protective stance of the ego. We propose, in contradistinction, an expanded notion of defence that goes beyond ego-defence as such, and includes the orientation to protect relationship. Moreover, we are proposing that *to be* is *to be in relation*. This casts the power of ego (i.e. ego as affirming being: "I am") into a relational context: what we have called *complementarity*. Thus, we do not view self-orientation as primary: what is primary is the complementarity of person and relationship, the complementarity of *to be* and *to relate*. In this context one arrives at a more comprehensive understanding of defence, one that includes the defence, not only of the sole ego, but of the complementarity between ego and relationship. Despite the (ontological) primacy of the accord of complementarity, however, one readily recognises that the breach of complementarity is not an uncommon feature of human experience. It is expected, therefore, that defences will at times present as auto-oriented. As previously noted, however, even these auto-oriented defences may reveal some tendency towards complementarity: that is, they are not likely to be solely auto-oriented but to display to some extent a mix of anti-relational auto-orientation and pro-relational other-orientation (i.e. orientation towards complementarity). Note how this approach is opposite to that of the hermeneutics of suspicion: instead of suspecting, for example, that a self-oriented motive lurks behind an altruistic motive, one considers how the self-oriented motive, even as it contributes to the breach of complementarity, still contains, in some sense, tendencies towards the accord of complementarity. Therefore, ego-defence is likely to express more than the mere defence of the ego, even when it seems to be primarily auto-oriented and contributes to the wound of breach. The hermeneutics of suspicion seems to allow for the consideration of only one basic aspect to human motivation: auto-orientation. The hermeneutics of belief, on the other hand, allows for the consideration of two aspects to motivation: auto-orientation and orientation to the other.

A hermeneutics of belief allows one to acknowledge a *mixed reality* in which *auto-orientation* may harmfully separate itself from *other-orientation*, that is, a mixed reality where the terms of complementarity lose what we have called their accord, equality and transcendence (to one another), and where the delicate balance of being and relationship is wounded. Still, the reality is *mixed*: the wound itself is oriented towards healing. It is due to this healing orientation that the hermeneutics of belief allows one to achieve an inclusive grasp of both breach and remedy, harm and repair, division and reconciliation....

It is this inclusiveness that a hermeneutics of belief brings to the understanding of ego-defence and to other forms of defence (including, for example, collective forms of auto-oriented defensiveness expressed in various ideologies). It is interesting to note that within psychoanalysis, as within the other systems of thought marked by a primary suspicion, there is a sense in which an excessive auto-orientation *is* viewed as problematic.[112] The unmasking of false consciousness involves the unmasking of the unjust, excessive or rigid self-interest that underlies such consciousness. To the extent that the aim of interpretation is to suspect that which diminishes meaningful contact with reality and meaningful forms of relationship, such an approach would be consistent with a hermeneutics of belief. Furthermore, this unmasking would presumably have the objective of promoting meaningful contact and relationship.

This assumes, however, that the meaningful goals are in the sights of the psychoanalyst and patient. It assumes, for example, that *work and love* are the goals of psychoanalytic practice. To a question regarding what a normal person should be able to do well, Erik

Erikson reports Freud to have answered, "Work and love."[113] It also seems, however, that Freud was ambivalent about a meaningful core to human existence (see our first essay in this book for a discussion of Freud's understanding of the life and death instincts, and the ambiguity in psychoanalytic theory regarding the reality of meaningful relationship). Furthermore, in our view, the interpretive analysis of ego-defence (as conceived in psychoanalysis), which is a central feature of psychoanalytic practice,[114] only brings one to the *threshold of freedom.*

Psychoanalysts tend to view defences as basically directed to protecting the ego from the threat of anxiety, and they proceed to interpret or analyse defences in order to free patients from the excessive or rigid hold that these defences may have on them. Within the hermeneutics of belief, it is insufficient to promote emancipation without also seeking the accord that makes such emancipation meaningful. In other words, to discover the fuller meaning of freedom one has to also take into account the accord of freedom with relation. If one stops at the uncovering of the unconscious expressions of ego-defence, at what we are calling the *threshold of freedom*, one only has *freedom from*, a kind of negative liberty. Without further qualification and development this may even become the (non- or failed-) *freedom* of relativism or arbitrariness.[115] As noted earlier, for the unmasking of self-oriented forces through suspicion to have a meaningful purpose requires the belief in some principle beyond those self-oriented forces. Freedom requires an orientation to relation (in truth) if its expression is to be salutary.[116]

We have emphasised that freedom has its origin and goal in relationship and that to radically separate freedom from the good found in relationship is a failure of freedom. In this requirement of complementarity,[117] it is not enough to unmask ego-defence and lay bare the motives and conflicts of which one is not conscious. When one is challenging ego-defence, one has to ask what one is actually and ultimately seeking to defend. If, in analysing defence, one simply promotes a *mere* or *circumscribed* freedom, one has not effectively interpreted or challenged ego-defence. Indeed, if one promotes *sole* or *abstracted* freedom one may be reinforcing ego-defensiveness rather than challenging it. This is because, by emphasising such freedom, one does not leave the sphere of the ego. Rather, to deal meaningfully with freedom one has to recognise, via an application of the hermeneutics of belief that (excessive) ego-defence is a wound, and that, as a wound, it is a sign of both the *rupture* of complementarity and the *healing influence* of complementarity. Therapist and patient are to work together to uncover both the rupture and the healing. The excessive and rigid defence of the ego is almost never devoid of some sign or indication of the longing for complementarity. As noted earlier, a hermeneutics of belief allows one to see that the human being experiences a mix of self-interest and altruism, insularity and solidarity, acquisitiveness and generosity.... By recognising this mix it becomes possible to seek the salutary balance of complementarity. We have argued that when the hermeneutics of suspicion has primacy, it is more difficult to find meaningful connection in the *mix of reality*. To authentically unmask meaninglessness one requires an anchor in meaning; however, primary suspicion tends to eclipse the meaningful aspect of the *mix of reality*. Alternatively, with the priority of a hermeneutics of belief, one may consider both meaning and meaninglessness (and *sift through them*).

Consequently, we would say that a belief in trusted connection between self and other does not render one naïve about the faults and failings associated with human beings and human nature, but it does grant a greater opportunity to apply (*secondary*) suspicion to self – that is, to see fault in self and not *only* in the other. It is of interest to note that the Masters of Suspicion seem to begin with suspicion of relation (to others), and this tends to close their own systems of thought in a largely auto-defensive posture. We argue, on the other hand, that one must begin with belief or trust, and only apply suspicion in a secondary way, such that one does not dismiss belief, but continually reforms and renews it. Moreover, this positon allows one to remain open, in a qualified way, to expressions of primary suspicion, because one may recognise that suspicion and auto-defensiveness conceal – and therefore potentially reveal – reasons to renew belief.

M *An Alternative Explanation for the Harshness of the Superego*

The question regarding how to explain superego harshness was an important one in the early development of psychoanalysis. Psychoanalysts noted that the superego was often harsher than what one might expect or predict on the basis of actual early childhood experiences and influences. Freud wrote in *Civilizations and Its Discontents*, "Experience has shown…that the severity which a child's superego develops in no way corresponds to the severity of the treatment which it has itself experienced."[118] It is of interest to consider that, on the basis of reflections in the prior section of this essay, we can offer an alternative explanation for the problem of the severity of the superego to that proposed by Freud and other analysts such as Melanie Klein. As we will discuss below, Freud and Klein would appeal to the influence of the death instinct to explain superego severity.

It is of note that the topic of superego harshness is of importance not only with respect to the history of psychoanalysis, but also with respect to the understanding of psychopathology more generally. Consider that superego harshness is implicated in a variety of mental health problems such as depressive reactions, obsessive worry, excessive guilt, mistrustful attitudes… – all of which in some way involve the harshness of excessively punitive internal object relations. In addition, superego harshness has implications for the understanding of some forms of problematic social phenomena. Consider the excessive harshness associated with divisive oppositions found at various levels of social structure (familial, communal, political, international, etc.) and their at times harmful and even violent manifestations (e.g. racism, terrorism, long-standing feuds). These are examples where excessively punitive inclinations of the superego are directed against others (perhaps through some form of projection), and these aggressive inclinations contribute to harmful divisions between factions in conflict with one another.

As mentioned above, Freud and other analysts such as Melanie Klein, came to explain the harshness of the superego, along with other forms of extreme aggression, as a consequence of the death instinct. In our first essay in this book, we propose that Freud's conception of the death instinct arises as a consequence of – what we interpret as – his reductive, a-relational understanding of the basic foundations of human motivation. We discuss that Freud posits a fundamentally auto-oriented human organism, characterised by factors such as primary narcissism and autoerotism – factors which one may yet interpret as life-oriented in so far as they involve an aim to enhance self and pleasure: that is, with narcissism and autoerotism one is still dealing with matters that are in some sense consistent with a *positive* drive for life and survival. We see this emphasis on the primacy of auto-orientation, however, as leading Freud to posit a *negative* drive or desire to return to ever earlier or anterior stages of life. This drive to return to earlier stages leads eventually to pre-life – thus, ultimately to a non-living state or *death*.

One could explain the logic of our interpretation of Freud as follows: if *return* to autoerotism and narcissism is an essential feature (if not foundation) of human motivation, then why stop at stages that are still associated with life? Why not see the *return* as aiming farther back still, as it were? In other words, if auto-orientation is the essential, motivating characteristic of a living organism, then one might well expect that the orientation towards life itself is but a detour from a drive towards a more radical *self-sufficiency* than that which the drive to live (i.e. Eros) can provide. Thus, we are suggesting, Freud concludes that there must be a drive to die: a drive to return to the *nothingness* prior to the organism's coming to be.[119]

In our view, the proposal of a drive to die is, therefore, the consequence of viewing the living organism as fundamentally auto-oriented. This fails to consider the living organism's essential participation in relationship or complementarity. Consequently, we see the Freud's proposal of death instinct as a mistaken notion that does not describe an essential drive of living organisms nor an essential aspect of human motivation. Furthermore, if we recognise the notions of primary auto-orientation and death instinct as mistaken, then we may propose an alternative explanation for phenomena associated with the apparent severity or harshness of the superego.

For us, the explanation of superego harshness lies not in the drive to return to an a-relational origin (including pre-life or death), but in the failure to maintain and develop the essentially relational origin inherent to human life and existence. As one's attempt to resolve a breach of relationship becomes more solipsistic, so to speak, one may expect to see an increase in the severity of judgement towards either self or other; or, as the features of relationship fail to support the members of that relationship in their uniqueness and freedom, one may expect a similar severity. The cause of harshness is not, therefore, intrinsic aggression, sadism, nor a death instinct. The cause is, rather, the breach of complementarity, in which the freedom of distinction is exercised without regard to, or support for relationship, or in which relationship expresses itself in a manner that jeopardises the freedom of distinction.[120]

Moreover, the experience of harshness – which will often present with escalating or increasing intensity – ought to be carefully interpreted because it does not only indicate that something has gone wrong with the complementarity of distinction and relation of persons; it also indicates a protest against this *something gone wrong*. The harshness increases because breach is not sustainable; breach, in a way, is untenable. Harshness is, therefore, both 1) an indication of breach (i.e. breakdown, wound), and 2) a sign of the need for a remedy. It becomes crucial, in psychotherapy, to distinguish harshness as a cause of breach from harshness as a sign of the need to remedy breach. Clearly, the harshness presents with a *mixed meaning*. When pondering the presence and causes of breach, one may mistakenly assume (as we believe Freud and Klein did) that there is some essentially negative, destructive drive or instinct that produces breach or disorder. In our view, this conclusion is "premature" (i.e. based on initial impression) in that it fails to take into account and to recognise the *mixed meaning* in the experience of troubled feelings associated with breach.

We propose that the apparent inclination or impulse towards breach or disorder (that seems to be a feature of feelings and attitudes one may associate with superego harshness) only becomes intelligible if one gives priority to a hermeneutics of belief. It is belief that permits one to see breach or disorder against the background of complementarity. For example, with excessive guilt or shame one is attempting to solve or repair fault from within the self alone, as it were, without sufficient consideration of one's capacity to *be sorry,* and without sufficient appeal to the *other's forgiveness*: it is only a relational understanding of guilt that would allow one to make sense of the intensity or harshness of distress that is associated with such guilt, and that would set the stage for a remedy. From the perspective we are proposing, increasing harshness can be understood as a result of a continuing attempt to resolve emotional conflict *solipsistically, but it also needs to be seen as a continuing sign of frustration with, or protest against such an approach.* As a sign of such frustration or protest, harshness implies a desire to resolve the problem in a way that it can be resolved: relationally or in terms of complementarity.

To sum up the perspective we are offering here, one may conclude that superego harshness reflects 1) the failure of complementarity, 2) the *protest* against such failure, and 3) the need and striving for a remedy.[121] Similarly, with excessive suspicion or mistrust of others (i.e. where intropunitiveness becomes extrapunitiveness, as it were), one cannot find a true remedy in so far as one excludes the possibility that others can desire collaboration, or if one is utterly closed to the possibility of such collaboration. In other words, problems associated with excessive guilt or excessive mistrust only become intelligible in terms of a relational context within which one may uncover the meaning of such feelings, and within which one may ultimately bring troubled feelings to resolution.

We may conclude by saying that desperate, overwhelming, or otherwise disturbing feelings, which are directly or indirectly associated with the notion of the *harshness of the superego*, are the consequence of insularity, but they are also a complaint against insularity, and, therefore, aimed at a relational remedy.[122]

N *Priority of Belief vs. Priority of Suspicion*
  (i) *Priority of Meaning over Power and Pleasure (Viktor Frankl's Logotherapy)*
  (ii) *The Orientation of Troubled Feelings towards Meaningful Relationship vs. Pragmatic Détente in a Competition for Satisfaction*

(N-i) *Priority of Meaning over Power and Pleasure (Viktor Frankl's Logotherapy):* By approaching psychopathology and psychotherapy within a hermeneutics of belief one places the emphasis on how meaning has a healing influence on breaches of complementarity. This speaks to what we have called the *mix of reality*: one recognises in the human condition *both* breach or failure *and* a positive, meaningful core or dimension. Psychotherapeutic process requires, therefore, an appreciation of how the experience of troubled feelings expresses *both* the negation *and* the affirmation of meaning found in this *mix of reality*. Furthermore, one bases one's confidence or trust that healing has priority over damage – security over insecurity, hope over despair, reconciliation over division...– on the healing role of meaning. In other words, when interpreting troubled feelings in a psychotherapeutic context, one is not only to consider the *duality* expressed by such feelings: the meaningfulness of accord and the meaninglessness of breach. One is to consider, as well, the *unity* that arises from the presence of meaning in that *mix*: that is, troubled feelings include within them the desire to heal breach, to affirm meaning. The threat to meaning stems from that which would negate relationship, and the goal of healing involves exercising freedom and forming relationship in a manner that affirms normal accord. On the other hand, by approaching psychopathology and psychotherapy with a primary accent on the hermeneutics of suspicion, troubled feelings are essentially viewed as expressions of that which negates the self, and one places the emphasis on the need for liberation from that negation of self. Such an approach is not necessarily incompatible with one that emphasises complementarity, but neither is it necessarily compatible. Consider that as suspicion gains dominance over belief, there is the tendency to give priority to the defence of self over the defence of complementarity; and, as we have discussed in previous sections, this dominance of suspicion does lead to an approach that is incompatible with complementarity.

When belief has priority, however, one views human struggle as oriented more by the defence of complementarity than by the sole defence of ego, more by meaning than by power. One may reconsider, in this respect, Viktor Frankl's insight (discussed in previous section, "L") that to approach the human condition realistically one must "overestimate man": he says that one must become an idealist in order to remain a realist![123]   When one "underestimates man," that is, when suspicion has priority, then there is the tendency to eclipse the realm or dimension of meaning (or complementarity); in this case, the emphasis, as noted above, is primarily on the defence or protection of self from negative influence, and not primarily on the defence or protection of complementarity.

Frankl provides a succinct way of defining the importance of meaning to an understanding of human psychology where he differentiates three Viennese schools of psychotherapy. He speaks of Freud's psychoanalysis, Adler's individual psychology and his own logotherapy (*logo* referring to meaning) in terms of how these schools of thought highlight, respectively, the will to pleasure, the will to power, and the will to meaning. His own school, he notes, has been referred to as "The Third Viennese School of Psychotherapy." [124] Frankl proposes that one cannot fully grasp the human condition without considering the will to meaning. Our own emphasis is similar to his in that we speak of the *meaning* of complementarity as central to a consideration of the understanding and healing of psychopathology.

In some respects our application of the hermeneutics of belief to psychopathology and psychotherapy is an extension or development of Frankl's logotherapy. Like Frankl, we place the emphasis on meaning as a given in human experience, and as central to the understanding and treatment of many forms of psychopathology. Frankl makes reference to a statement made by Magda Arnold and John Gasson with which we are in full agreement: "'Every therapy must in some way, no matter how restricted, also be logotherapy.'"[125] Hans Urs von Balthasar expresses a similar sentiment in a comment he makes regarding the responsibility that today's *psychotherapy* inherits by taking on the role once played by "the pedagogically oriented philosophy of the Greeks":

> [Psychotherapy's] ability to play this role, however, depends on its awareness of the considerable responsibility it inherits. But there can be no talk of "inheritance" unless therapy very deliberately sets itself an analogous goal: helping man fulfill his existence through a courageous commitment to meaning. Retrospective analysis of the past, say of childhood and infancy, is not enough. Nor is the resolution of hang-ups and complexes, which in any case depends on the possibility of a new future of meaningful commitment within an equally meaningful world. In this respect what Viktor Frankl felicitously termed "logo-therapy" seems indispensable for basically every form of therapy which, if it is intent on real healing, must value the quest for meaning more than the peculiar methods and doctrines of any given school.[126]

As noted, we see our own approach as one which builds upon Frankl's logotherapy. We have sought, however, to place a greater and more explicit emphasis on abstract and universal aspects of the experience of meaning than Frankl seems to propose. In fact, Frankl defines meaning in terms of unique individual circumstances, and sees this focus on uniqueness as an essential feature of the scope of his logotherapy. He writes:

> One should not search for an abstract meaning of life. Everyone has his own specific vocation or mission in life to carry out a concrete assignment which demands fulfillment. Therein he cannot be replaced, nor can his life be repeated. Thus, everyone's task is as unique as is his specific opportunity to implement it.[127]

We agree with what Frankl intends: that is, that "realities are more important than ideas."[128]   There is, nevertheless, a universal dimension to meaning, with respect to which we believe a more general understanding and definition is possible. This is especially the case with respect to defining the accord of uniqueness and universality as a complementarity, as we have been proposing in this essay. Indeed, we see such a link to a universal dimension implied in Frankl's own emphasis on how one "should not ask what the meaning of his life is, but rather he must recognize that it is *he* who is asked," and on how the meaning of life is not to be discovered "within man or his own psyche, as though it were a closed system," but in self-transcendence. He goes on to critique how

> [w]hat is called self-actualization is not an attainable aim at all, for the simple reason that the more one would strive for it the more he would miss it. In other words self-actualization is possible only as a side-effect of self-transcendence.[129]

Frankl also says, in the context of the above, that though "the meaning of life always changes...it never ceases to be."

We believe that these points, which Frankl makes regarding the offer, call, transcendence, and enduring presence of meaning, do allow for some generalisations. Our own emphasis on complementarity and hierarchy (and their compatibility) provides a general framework within which to understand meaning, both with respect to the particular way meaning must be interpreted by each person (and in each circumstance of life), on the one hand, and with respect to the transcendent and enduring presence of meaning, on the other. It is, after all, that transcendent and enduring presence that makes a unique response possible. The universal need not negate the particular, nor the particular the universal: "The global need not stifle nor the particular prove barren."[130] Accordingly, we share and appreciate Frankl's emphasis on the unique manifestation of meaning, but also propose a more explicit understanding of the universal manifestation (and scope) of meaning, in terms of the complementarity of distinction and relation of persons, and of the compatibility of this complementarity with the experience of the higher and the lower levels of hierarchy (i.e. meaning-power, co-operation-competition, service-dominance).

Frankl speaks of the *difference* between *causes* and *reasons*,[131] and this difference has some analogy to the difference between what we have called lower and the higher levels of hierarchy. Frankl notes that a person may be subject to physically or biologically based *causes* (e.g. anxiety related to being at a high altitude and suffering a lack of oxygen), but that a person may also be affected by *reasons* based in meaning (e.g. anxiety related to concerns about emotional security). We would add that material *causes* have to be integrated into *reasons*, even if it remains important to discern the difference between *causes* and *reasons*, and even if *causes* are understood to exert their influence with relative autonomy. *Reasons*, nevertheless, are always involved because the human person *responds* to *causal* determination, and is never simply subject to *causal* determination. Indeed, our own emphasis is not only on how higher and lower – *reasons* and *causes* – differ, but, also, on how they *ought to be integrated*.

In earlier parts of this essay we propose some principles that might explain this integration (e.g. the influence of the norm of complementarity on hierarchy, the priority of co-operation over competition, the service of lower by higher, the deferral of the lower to the higher). Thus, our concern is not only to distinguish lower level factors involving striving for power, pleasure, physical safety, and biological survival, from higher level ones like striving for meaning, integrity, relationship, and transcendence. Our concern is also to consider how the lower and the higher come together in a manner that is integrative: that is, in a manner that is not reductive (reducing higher to lower) but that still allows for the relative autonomy of the lower.[132]

Human beings essentially live in a universe of meaning.[133] Such a world does not exclude the (lower) biologically-based drives or instincts (e.g. Freud's emphasis on the id – *will to pleasure*) nor does it exclude the (also lower) status- and survival-oriented needs for achievement (e.g. Adler's notions of inferiority complex and sibling rivalry – *will to power*); however, one will not fully understand the human condition and the significance of symptomatic experience without an appreciation that the human person depends on (higher) meaning. For example, human expressions of anger cannot be fully understood in terms of instinctual drive, competitive striving nor the quest for superiority, but inevitably involve questions of justice and morality. [134]

(N-ii) *The Orientation of Troubled Feelings towards Meaningful Relationship vs. Pragmatic Détente in a Competition for Satisfaction:* Both a hermeneutics of suspicion and one of belief call for an exploration of depths that take one *past the surface* of human experience. This moving *past the surface* does not imply that what is knowable is sought "*apart from* its empirical effects, only that the being ('in itself') that is known in its empirical effects is not reducible *to* those effects, either cognitionally or ontologically."[135] Moreover, "[s]ince truth is not exhausted in appearance it needs to be unpacked, not because truth lurks obscurely 'behind' appearances (where it can never logically be reached), but because it *overwhelms* appearances, as the light of the sun overwhelms the eye of the owl (Aristotle, Metaph II, 933b10)."[136] Nevertheless, there are different ways to move or see *past the surface*. And as Aristotle suggests, the cause of difficulty seeing might not lie with the things but with us (Aristotle, Metaph II, 933b10).

We have been giving particular attention to two of these ways of seeing: suspicion and belief. When suspicion has priority, one intends to *uncover* how the self may be undermined by relationship, notwithstanding some ambiguity with respect to whether a meaningful relationship is believed to be actually possible. When belief has priority, one intends to *uncover* how relationship may be undermined by the self, while also affirming trust, confidence and belief that a meaningful response (in relationship) is *always* possible. In the hermeneutical exploration based in faith one interprets the deeper meaning of troubled feelings in order to uncover how to favour healing.[137] In what follows (in this section and in the next one on *hopeful acceptance*) we will explore how a hermeneutics of belief may inform the interpretation of three troubled feelings that are commonly associated with psychopathology: anxiety, depression and anger.

We noted above that hermeneutics involves an attempt to explore more than the surface of human experience. If one applies a psychoanalytic hermeneutics of suspicion to the exploration of anxiety one may discover that unconscious factors related to instinctual drive, limits of reality, and/or superego regulation play a role in the experience of threat. One may consider that what one is *really* (i.e. more than surface) experiencing involves overwhelming instinctual drives based in the id, harsh constraints of reality associated with the ego, and/or severe pressures or demands coming from the superego. On the other hand, if one applies a *personalist* hermeneutics of belief (of the kind we are proposing in this essay – see our previous discussion of personalism) to the exploration of anxiety, one may discover that it is basically the accord of distinction and relation of persons that is in jeopardy. In some sense, therefore – from this personalist perspective – it is that accord that one is *really* seeking, whereas, from the psychoanalytic perspective, it is some form of tension reduction that one is *really* seeking. In any event, from the perspective of a personalist hermeneutics one would understand various expressions of anxiety (e.g. worried anticipation, separation fears, compulsive habits, post-traumatic reactions, etc.) as indications that the accord that defines a normal or meaningful mode of relationship is both under threat *and* being sought.

Of course, the threat to meaningful connection may arise from *within*. We are not referring, however, primarily to the threat of overwhelming instinctual forces (and conflicts associated with them) as might be proposed in psychoanalytic vein. Rather, we are referring to the kind of threat that jeopardises meaning: that is, the kind of threat that may be expressed in such *inner* attitudes as mistrust, despair, excessive withdrawal – notwithstanding that these may constitute understandable reactions to the injury that may come from *without*.

To summarise the above, one could say that, from a perspective in which one gives priority to a hermeneutics of belief, anxiety alerts one to inclinations and circumstances that threaten human freedom and human relationship, while at the same time, also alerting one to the *intrinsic*[138] accord between them. From a perspective in which one gives priority to a hermeneutics of suspicion, on the other hand, one interprets anxiety in terms of inclinations and circumstances that threaten self-interest or self-gratification.

A personalist hermeneutics focuses on the accord of self and other, an accord assumed to be ontologically given: that is, rooted in the way of being, in life itself. Therefore, even the most despairing subjective feeling, where meaning seems fully eclipsed, will contain some indication that this ontological given remains foundational and operative in the background, just as with a total eclipse of the sun, the sun's corona remains visible around the darkening disc of the moon.[139]

In giving priority to a hermeneutics of belief one comes to see that the meaning inherent to complementarity takes on a healing influence in circumstances that give rise to troubled feelings, and this, we could say, supports the trust and belief that there is *always* a good way to deal with a bad situation. A psychoanalytic hermeneutics, on the other hand, gives primacy to the tension between self and other, a tension understood to be both inevitable and accidental (i.e. dependent on both psychic structure and circumstance). The psychoanalytic hermeneutics is rooted in the understanding that there is a competition for satisfaction, which is resolved in pragmatic détente. In a personalist hermeneutics one strives for the ideal of the accord of complements, whereas in a psychoanalytic hermeneutics a pragmatic solution appears to be the best one can attain. When the accord of meaning or complementarity fails, *and* one remains under the purview of a hermeneutics of belief, we have emphasised that there is always a good way to deal with the bad situation that ensues. When, however, détente fails, *and* one remains under the purview of a hermeneutics of suspicion, there is not necessarily a good way to deal with a bad situation: indeed, one might then justify bad ways for dealing with bad situations (cf. Hatfields and McCoys).

To grasp troubled feelings in a comprehensive manner requires the application of a hermeneutics of belief through which one is alerted to the healing influence of meaning. We have noted that troubled feelings express the breach of the wound, but have emphasised that they also express or manifest the healing tendencies associated with that wound. Indeed, one could go so far as to say that without a consideration of how troubled feelings alert one to the presence of the healing influence of meaning, such feelings remain essentially unintelligible (that is, without meaning: meaning-*less*). Moreover, as we have begun to consider, it is partly through a consideration of the *telos*, final cause or aim of troubled feelings that one may become oriented to the healing influence of meaning in one's life. Troubled feelings will in some way refer to an *origin* in the experience of the breach of complementarity (while indicating that there is an even *deeper origin* in the wholeness of complementarity itself), but they will also refer to a *goal* in keeping with the experience of longing to heal that breach.

There is a desire to achieve an accord between freedom and commitment: that is, troubled feelings will in some way express the influence of a healing accord on a harmful disaccord (even if this is sometimes manifested in a form of protest).[140] One would expect to see in this process of working through anxiety both increases and decreases in the intensity of the anxiety, increases and decreases which ought to be interpreted in terms of phases of influence (and lack of influence) of *healing accord* on *harmful disaccord*. In this process there is not a simple correspondence between negative feeling and harm: that is, increases in anxiety (e.g. sensitivity to a friend's distress) may alert one to the need for healing, and decreases in anxiety (e.g. reducing one's level of distress via excessive use of pain medication) may prevent one from appreciating the level of harm to which one is subject. Indeed, the meaning of distress may not be fully decided at a given point in time: that meaning would depend, rather, on how distress alerts one to breach, and on what aim one may derive from such distress with respect to remedy or goal; the time frame for the development of such insights will naturally vary considerably.

When one approaches anxiety within the context of a hermeneutics of belief one understands the anxiety in terms of the threat posed by the *underlying* breach of accord, while the effort to intervene has, as its goal, the recovery of meaningful relationship.

When one approaches anxiety within the context of a hermeneutics of suspicion one understands the anxiety in terms of the *underlying* threat to pleasure (i.e. that which might interfere with drive reduction or instinctual satisfaction) and the threat to power (i.e. that which might jeopardise mastery, control and survival), while intervention has, as its goal, the re-establishment of satisfaction and control, respectively.

We may note similar factors with symptoms or expressions of depression or anger as we have with symptoms or expressions of anxiety. For example, in the context of a hermeneutics of belief, symptoms of depression become increasingly intelligible as one interprets them in terms of the *loss* of connection to the meaningful (i.e. referring to an origin in breach), and the longing to re-establish that connection (i.e. referring to aim or goal to heal the breach). Similarly, one could say that symptoms of anger, which often involve a reaction to the experience of an *unjust* breach of relationship, ultimately signify the quest or need for reconciliation (i.e. involving a willingness to re-engage with others – not solely or necessarily with the perpetrator of the offence, but more basically with others to whom one is close, or could become close).

One may consider that when symptoms are resistant to change, as in some conditions with post-traumatic, depressive, obsessive-compulsive, or paranoid/hostile features, part of the reason for the recurrence of symptoms may involve difficulty in working through these troubled feelings in terms of their *final* causes. For example, if the *origin* of my recurrent experience of anger lies in a breach of relationship caused by some form of injustice, then I may not be able to overcome this anger unless the *goal* of meaningful relating becomes somehow available to me. It is interesting to note, as well, how individuals who become hostile with one another following a rupture of relationship, may become, during their period of conflict, strongly *bound* to one another in their anger. Indeed, they may find themselves as bound, if not more bound, by their anger than they were by positive feelings they may have had for one another prior to their conflict. Could it be that the desire for justice and reconciliation (i.e.

the *true* aim of the feeling of anger) keeps bringing them together, and that their destructive, acting-out behaviour (a disordered expression of anger that fails to express the *true* aim of anger) keeps repeating because the anger is not being appropriately understood, and appropriately worked through? The destructive behaviour is the result of making power and control primary; however, this strategy of pursuing power does not satisfy the exigency for justice and reconciliation, which, we are suggesting concerns the deeper meaning (including goal) of the feeling of anger. The working through of anger would call for a tolerance for the distress of breach, an openness and hopefulness that the breach can be reversed, and a willingness to give priority to meaning over power.[141] In some cases, such a working through will appear to be one-sided, because one does not have the co-operation of the other party involved in the injustice (or the injustice took place in the past and contact with the other party is no longer possible). This does not diminish, however, the relational nature of the remedy, in that, in order to work through anger meaningfully, one would still need to consider relational factors. It is in view of relational factors that one could apply hopeful, patient and engaging attitudes or responses.

O *Healing via Hopeful Acceptance of All Outcomes*

We speak in the above about the need to respond with tolerance to the distress or suffering caused by a breach of accord or complementarity. Although such tolerance may appear to involve a stoic-like attitude, we are not, in fact, recommending a form of tolerance that depends primarily on one's strength to withstand and survive painful circumstances with equanimity or detachment. The tolerance we propose depends, rather, on the trust and belief that, even when complementarity fails, one may respond to the suffering associated with that failure in a meaningful manner: the wound that divides freedom from commitment to relationship provides an opportunity and opening for meaningful engagement. One has this opportunity, not in spite of the suffering or troubled feelings that the wound or breach generates, but because a way to meaningfully respond to such suffering is believed to be available. The goal (from within a personalist hermeneutics of belief) is, therefore, not to achieve – primarily and *stoically* – freedom from, or tolerance for suffering, but to achieve freedom from meaningless suffering, and tolerance that favours engaging suffering meaningfully.

All suffering points to some form of meaninglessness, but the fundamental goal within a hermeneutics of belief is not the *utilitarian* one of better managing or reducing suffering; rather, the goal is to engage with the meaning (that is rooted in the inherent dignity of persons in relationship) that might be the source of that which would inspire one – in the first place – to seek to better manage or reduce suffering.[142] In other words, the reasons that would inspire one to alleviate suffering (e.g. through compassionate care) might have a lot in common with the reasons that would inspire one to tolerate suffering. The same meaningful source inspires both alleviation and acceptance. And one tolerates or accepts the suffering one cannot alleviate or avoid because one[143] discovers that in such difficult circumstances there continues to be a *way* for freedom to support relationship, and a *way* for relationship to support freedom.[144]

Complementarity, as this *way*,[145] becomes a crucial consideration when one is seeking to find – or perhaps, more importantly, to live – the meaning of suffering. Thus, one may discover, that even, for example, with the experience of a major loss of physical or mental function as a result of an accident, there continues to be a way to meaningfully engage in life, to live a meaningful life. Moreover, in view of the twofold nature of complementarity, one may consider that this meaningful engagement of suffering depends not only (and sometimes, not even primarily) on one's own exercise of freedom – i.e. to choose to live through adverse circumstances in a manner that respects complementarity – but also on how another or others express the belief that one's life matters to them! In other words, openness to meaning often depends on a *helping hand* from others: when one faces difficult circumstances, it is *their* belief that one's life is meaningful to them that favours and permits the discovery of one's own meaning. Indeed, in view of this essential interdependence among persons, a person's failure to live meaningfully cannot be simply attributed to that person but may be related to a failure of others to be in solidarity with that person. This speaks to how we all have a responsibility for one another.

In any event, a devotion to meaning may strengthen one's capacity to *stoically* endure or withstand suffering, but this strengthening does not stem, *primarily*, from patient acceptance of discomfort, nor, *primarily*, from some form of courageous self-denial. One is to practise the tolerance required to work through troubled feelings in a meaningful manner *in order to* challenge the meaninglessness of suffering, thereby affirming the meaning that arises in the relational context of complementarity. In other words, tolerance for suffering and emancipation from expectations or desires of the self (i.e. healthy indifference or *healthy stoicism*) may signal a salutary disposition, *only* if this disposition arises in response to the call to meaningfully live complementarity, that is, to the call to meaningfully engage one's freedom and uniqueness/distinction in the context of relationship, and to the call for relationship to meaningfully favour freedom and uniqueness/distinction. One could say, therefore, that it is not enough to curb, contain or discipline the will to pleasure or power; one must take care to do so *in deference to* the will to meaning.[146] An ascetic disposition does not make sense as an end in itself, but only as an affirmation of trust and hope that a deeper connection than what is conferred by pleasure and power is essential to human life.

The experience of anxiety will often involve anticipatory thoughts about negative outcomes, and associated worries about one's inadequacy in mastering or controlling such outcomes. In addition, anxiety will reflect a sense of insecurity regarding connection (or attachment) between self and other, that is, a doubt about the reliability, solidity, or validity of such connection. Consequently, one could say that the apparent aim of anxiety is to achieve a sense of security – based on some form of control by the self – with respect to anticipation of future events, and/or with respect to the establishment of connection with others. One may realise, however, that one is unable to simply or readily exercise this type of control even if it might be appropriate for one to attempt to do so. One may further realise that even the achievement of such control – if it excludes an openness to relationship to the other beyond one's control – does not provide the mastery or fulfillment one truly desires. Indeed, attempts at *mere* control over anticipated events or relationships with others are likely to cause rather than remedy the malaise associated with anxiety and other troubled feelings.

In any case, when we limit our understanding of anxiety solely to meeting the goals of control and self-satisfaction, its exploration and treatment will involve trying to find ways to attain such goals, or, when attaining such goals does not appear possible, trying to find ways to come to terms with the lack of ability to achieve them (e.g. through detachment or tolerance). If meaning or complementarity is viewed as the focal point, however, then one realises that the *deeper* security to which anxiety aims involves something beyond the achievement of power or control and something beyond the gratification of instinct or drive. Indeed, as indicated above, one often sees how efforts that are aimed primarily at the control of events or emotion exacerbate anxious reactions or perpetuate anxious habits (like avoidant, compulsive or panic-like behaviour). It is not, therefore, control of outcome in terms of achieving power and gratification that provides the remedy to the essential breach to which anxiety alerts one. There is a deeper hope – associated with the healing orientation and influence of meaning – that provides that remedy.

Consider, as implied above, that the problem with excessive levels of anticipatory anxiety is not with having realistic expectations about the future and making reasonable plans in its regard. The problem arises, instead, with giving those expectations priority over acceptance and trust that, whatever the future may bring, there will be, inexorably, an opportunity for meaningful engagement. With anticipatory anxiety one may find oneself so highly preoccupied with the control of outcomes that one may become, for example, paralysed by panic, or trapped in the narrow focus of obsessive thoughts and compulsive habits. Applying a hermeneutics of belief to anxiety, however, opens one to the hopeful direction of which we speak, and this allows one to favour or give priority to acceptance (of all outcomes) over expectation (in the sense of a demand for a particular outcome one wants to achieve) when facing the future and engaging in anticipation.

Such priority leads to a *healthy indifference* towards one's own expectations or demands, in deferral to complementarity. Because the priority lies with complementarity, this is not an indifference about such matters as the need to take personal initiative, to exercise responsibility or to fulfill obligations in one's life, nor is it an indifference towards relationship. Consequently, it is not an indifference in which one merely tolerates whatever happens. It is a *relative indifference* to self-sufficiency (i.e. self-sufficiency implies giving priority to one's own expectations or demands over the meaning of relationship) in order to deepen one's caring about the meaning of relational ties. In this sense this indifference is to favour a deepening of caring.[147] Moreover, it is such a *caring indifference* that allows one to accept all outcomes, and that, in our view, may assist one to work through anticipatory anxiety.

With anticipatory anxiety one is alarmed by what one imagines might be, but is not yet, and one often attempts to over-extend one's control in the *now* or present on what might be in the *then* or future. In this context, excessive or escalating anxiety may indicate that one is giving priority to one's expectations or demands with respect to future outcomes and one's ability to control such outcomes, over acceptance that one is, in many respects, unable to control the future. One is not, however, simply to follow the part of the *Serenity Prayer* that says to *accept the things one cannot change*, but, to follow the prayer as a whole, and, therefore, also to deepen one's trust that one has reason to believe and hope that a meaningful way of accepting life (i.e. *serenity*) is possible in all circumstances, even in the face of those difficult things one *cannot change*. One realises that, notwithstanding the absence of the outcome one expects or wishes to have (i.e. control), there will nevertheless be a good way to deal with whatever outcome occurs. Thus, the acceptance that helps one to work through anticipatory anxiety involves neither a radical indifference, nor a passive, resigned and cynical capitulation. Within a hermeneutics of belief one appreciates that one's expectation or demand with respect to future outcome, though important, cannot be given primacy without contributing to excessive anxiety.[148]

Accordingly, the healing orientation of the hermeneutics of belief favours acceptance (hopeful, trusting and caring) over demand (of control). We ought to repeat that this is not an acceptance of only good outcomes nor is it complacency with respect to poor outcomes; it is an acceptance of all outcomes with hope, commitment and indeed, continued engagement in the quest for good outcomes. It combines acceptance of "the things I cannot change" with the "courage to change the things I can." It is a *hopeful* acceptance *for better or for worse*: one accepts, believes and trusts that there is a good, caring way to deal with whatever the future brings, the good and the bad, the favourable and the unfavourable, the rewarding and the disappointing.

Just as one applies a hopeful acceptance to the anticipation of future outcomes in working through anxiety, so too ought one to apply a hopeful acceptance to the remembering of the past in working through depressive feelings. Speaking schematically, one could say that anxiety tends to present as the fear of an imagined future (in which one might fail to have control) and depression tends to present as the sadness about a remembered past (in which one failed to keep the good), and that such feelings (anxiety and depression, fear and sadness), in the context of a hermeneutics of belief, challenge one to develop a hopeful acceptance of future and past.

We are proposing that the aim of anticipatory anxiety is, paradoxically, to attain trust and hope that there is a way to accept all future outcomes in a manner that is good and meaningful. One may further propose that the aim, final cause or *telos* for depression would similarly be that one trust and hope that there is a good, caring[149] and meaningful way to accept all past negative events (e.g. losses, failures, disappointments, regrets), as well as current experiences of diminished value. Note that with both the past and the future, the emphasis is placed on trust and belief that there *is* – in the present – a way to engage meaningfully with breaches of meaning (i.e. with wounds).

If anxiety is addressed via a hopeful acceptance of all potential future outcomes, and depression is addressed by the belief that one may similarly accept with hope all losses from the past, how might one construe the hermeneutics or working through of anger? One would interpret and work through anger with a similar spirit of *hopeful acceptance*. One would accept that there is a meaningful way of dealing with the conflict one has with the other who is angry at oneself or with whom one is angry. This hopeful acceptance would not involve an indifference to abuse and injustice, nor would it suggest a passive approach towards dealing with the injustices one may have oneself committed in one's life. It is, rather, an acceptance, in trust and hope, that a reconciliation is possible, a reconciliation that does not necessarily depend solely on one's control – indeed, one requires faith and trust in more than control by self to address the problem. Anger gives way to peace as the parties in conflict are able to give acceptance, trust and care towards one another priority over the competitive (power-based) desire to retaliate. Meaning is to have priority over power.[150]

Accordingly, one could say that the *aim* or *final cause* of anger is to favour the *meaning*-fullness of justice and mercy: justice to stop and heal the unfairness that may spark the anger, and mercy to reconcile self and other, thus healing the wound that has been inflicted by injustice. If the feeling of anger is a response to that which threatens, not only self, but more fundamentally, relationship between self and other, then the *real* aim of anger (the only aim that can provide a satisfying resolution) is that which remedies the breach of relationship. Anger has a purpose in alerting one to what one might be losing and to why one cares about it. The remedy to which anger orients one involves both justice and mercy, for *mere justice* would become revenge, and *mercy*, unconcerned for justice, might become *mere* sentimentality. True justice must be merciful, and true mercy is always concerned with justice. Echoing John Keats' poetic insight into the relation of beauty and truth in *Ode on a Grecian Urn* – "Beauty is truth, truth beauty" – one could say, "Mercy is justice, justice mercy." It is this coming together of mercy and justice that permits one to work through anger.

When I strive to believe that there is a good way to deal with bad outcomes, past losses or current injustices a problem often comes to the fore in my experience. I realise that, although I need trust and belief, and, in some ways, desire trust and belief – even see them as reasonable and supported by empirical evidence or experience –[151] I am, nevertheless, lacking in these virtues. I do not have fully in hand, as it were, the competencies and solutions that would produce the remedy I require. Indeed, I need to accept that I have difficulty accepting the troubling aspects of life. This need not lead me simply to despair, resignation or radical doubt (with respect to meaning), however, because the honest recognition that I have difficulty believing, hoping and trusting can itself be a nurturing of belief, hope and trust. There can be strength in my realisation and acceptance of my weakness, even if that weakness involves a lack of belief and hope.

We wish to emphasise that in giving priority to faith and trust we are not eschewing the value of reason, knowledge, control, prediction, outcome, power, etc. (i.e. will to power), nor are we eschewing the value of pleasure, gratification, satisfaction, drive reduction, etc. (i.e. will to pleasure). We are saying, rather, that if one is to respond meaningfully and effectively to the challenge posed by the experience of troubled feelings one cannot rely exclusively on such factors. Moreover, the priority placed on faith and trust does not lead to irrationalism. Indeed, the belief and trust in complementarity which we propose, speaks to the reasonableness of the transcendence of reason.[152]   When belief and trust (in complementarity) have priority, therefore, the excessive emphasis on control and pleasure associated with dysphoric affect is mitigated and human reason, knowledge, control, prediction, power, on the one hand, and pleasure, gratification, satisfaction, drive reduction, on the other, may regain their own relative status and meaningfulness.[153]

P   *Psychotherapy: A Hopeful Enterprise*

The purpose of this essay has been to establish a theoretical framework that identifies and explains principles of healing which underlie psychotherapeutic process. We have argued for an approach in which one recognises in symptomatic experience the real harm or danger associated with psychological wounds as well as tendencies towards healing.   In this we differ from approaches that view psychological symptoms solely or primarily as indicators of mistaken thinking, or simply as signs of illness that must be symptomatically corrected.   In our view, psychological symptoms reflect more than mistakes and illness: they are also revelatory of meaning and, therefore, may provide access to a healing or normalising tendency.

Furthermore, we propose that an in-depth view of troubled human experience cannot be limited to a paradigm which essentially reduces the scope of the meaning or explanation of human affairs to self-interest or ego-defence. For example, how prevalent is the view that some forms of psychopathology are the result of foregoing self-interest, and that the solution to such psychopathology is to somehow act in terms of self-interest ("to start doing things for me")? Naturally, we do not oppose the balancing that must take place between care of self and other; however, in contradistinction to approaches emphasising the primacy of self-interest as a solution, we have explored how such primacy – e.g. giving priority to power over right and obligation – actually contributes to or exacerbates psychopathology.

We have invoked the hermeneutics of belief as the interpretive key that would allow one to decipher and promote a more balanced understanding of human experience.[154] It is this interpretive key that allows one to extract from troubled feelings the meaning and normalising impulse that is hidden in their midst. We propose that the basis that allows for the priority of belief over suspicion in the interpretive process is the ontologically given accord of certain complements, the most fundamental and paradigmatic of which is that of the distinction and relation one witnesses in the rapport of persons. Intersecting, as it were, this horizontal dimension of persons in relation, we see a vertical dimension of hierarchy: a higher and a lower. We have proposed that this hierarchy is not simply ruled by a power dynamic; instead, we see right and obligation (to support right) as overriding power considerations. Moreover, this priority of right and obligation over power does not simply identify a static hierarchy of values. It involves an integrative movement or dynamic in which the higher serves the lower and the lower defers to the higher. We have further noted that this hierarchy of service itself depends on the normative or normalising impact of the *an-archic*, horizontal, complementary dimension, which, as implied above, provides our point of departure and our point of reference. We readily realise, however, that complements and hierarchies do not present in harmony.

The freedom associated with the distinction and uniqueness of a human person may fail to accord with the closeness and commitment associated with relations of that person; or the hierarchical order of the biological, psychological, personal and spiritual realms may be in disarray and far from *integrated*. We see here an explanation of abnormality, even as we recognise that the ultimate understanding of abnormality remains something of a mystery. We have proposed, however, that it is a *lesser mystery* (ultimately associated with an emptiness or lack regarding being and explanation), and one that is fundamentally or essentially overshadowed by a greater mystery (associated with the fullness of being and that which essentially *exceeds* human explanation), found in the features of normality or meaning: i.e. generosity, beneficence and service.[155] Nevertheless, the threat of abnormality is real. Psychological symptoms may have illusory aspects, but they are not simply illusions that are to be dispelled by forms of mental correction or detachment; they are also signs of real danger, expressing true loss, disconnection and harm. In view of the reality of such danger – in addition to the hermeneutics of belief – one requires the hermeneutics of suspicion.

Suspicion and critique are required to unmask cynicism, hostility and despair (and other negations of meaning): these latter dispositions involve the rejection of the complementarity (of distinction and relation, freedom and commitment, independence and closeness), and the rejection of the integrity (expressed in service) that constitute the core of reality. We emphasise, however, that, even when considering symptoms of extreme despair or hostility, the hermeneutics of belief retains priority. This is because, in order to make sense of the human experience of such negative symptoms and attitudes, we have to consider that they are, in some sense, protests against threats to complementarity and integrity. The critical moment of suspicion needs to always take its inspiration from the moment of belief. The breach of complementarity and integrity (of hierarchy) is *always* dependent, for its intelligibility and for its ontology, on the accord and service that express the basis and goal of life and being. It is this positive *always* (or positive *permanence*) of the complementary that is present at the heart of time that makes of time a healing time. The hermeneutics of belief that we are advocating is not centred, however, on a mere quest for the positive: that is, it is not based on an idealism that tries to ignore the painful features of the reality of human experience. Rather, a healing tendency, discovered through faith and trust (as well as supported by reason and evidence), is recognised at the heart of the hurt and harm that is a feature of the experience of human suffering.

The priority of belief allows one to approach meaninglessness with a hopeful, caring acceptance, with a belief that meaninglessness can be meaningfully engaged, even if one does not fully know, fully control how this is to happen. Indeed, one may have to recognise that one's ability, and even one's belief or trust, are weak; however, acknowledgement of weakness can be a strength, and such acknowledgement can favour the growth of this belief or trust. The closed world of primary suspicion, in which truth is rejected or reduced to what one is able to possess, control and use gives way to the open world of primary belief in which truth, like being, is acknowledged as firstly given and received, only secondarily possessed, controlled and put to use. As we have seen, with the priority of faith, one extracts meaning even from meaninglessness, truth even from falsehood; one brings trust even to suspicion. In this context one discovers and seeks to express the impulse or desire to normalise the abnormal – to heal the wound – an impulse or desire that forms the basis of psychotherapy and makes of the *talking cure*, a hopeful enterprise.

------

[1] By *hermeneutics of psychotherapy* we intend the philosophy or theory of interpretation that one applies to the approach one adopts to matters which are addressed or treated in the therapeutic encounter between therapist and patient. We believe this hermeneutics calls for a particular kind of openness in the therapist-patient dialogue. In keeping with the subtitle of the essay, we could say that this is an openness to *healing through belief*. In our theory of interpretation, we view belief as having priority over suspicion, and employ the terms "belief" and "suspicion" along the lines proposed by Paul Ricoeur. As discussed in the first essay, however, and to be elaborated in the course of this one, we offer a position that differs from Ricoeur's with respect to how one is to integrate a hermeneutics of belief with one of suspicion. Our approach leads us to consider that, in the experience of psychological symptoms, one always finds both disorder or distress, on the one hand, and a longing for *trusted connection*, on the other, that is, both *breach* and *healing*. This trusted connection speaks to what we see as an underlying ontological order to human existence: the complementarity of the distinction and relation of persons.
[2] One might object that, in the case of the *fatal wound*, healing does not occur. We would suggest, however, that in such a case, the tendency towards healing, even if not successful in saving life, is nevertheless present. Also, as we will be elaborating, we do not see the wound in isolation from the living context in which it occurs; therefore, the recovery, reconciliation and healing, to which the wound (in its connection to life) tends, is not necessarily extinguished in cases of fatality or irreparable damage, because even in such cases, a healing purpose remains a

possibility – as in when a community comes to terms with a tragic loss of one of its members in a sorrowful yet positive remembrance of that person.
[3] As noted in a previous endnote (# "1") we employ the terms of belief and suspicion with respect to hermeneutics along the lines proposed by Paul Ricoeur (Ricoeur, Paul, *Freud & Philosophy: An Essay on Interpretation*, translated by D. Savage, New Haven and London, Yale University Press, 1970, p.28, 32-36; Kaplan, David M., *Ricoeur's Critical Theory*, Albany, New York, State University of New York Press, 2003, p. 21; Itao, Alexis Deodato S., "Paul Ricoeur's Hermeneutics of Symbols: A Critical Dialectic of Suspicion and Faith," *Kritike*, vol. four, number two, 2010, p. 4, p. 7-8). Belief indicates a willingness to listen to what is presented with the expectation that it contains truth and value, and suspicion indicates that one approaches what is presented with the expectation that it expresses a false consciousness that is somehow deceptive, obscuring or disguised, hiding some ulterior, perhaps selfish, or otherwise objectionable, motive. For an extensive treatment of Ricoeur's hermeneutics of suspicion see: Scott-Baumann, Alison, *Ricoeur and the Hermeneutics of Suspicion*, London, Continuum International Publishing Group, 2009 (see: p.45, p. 69, p. 153). As we will argue over the course of this essay, by giving priority to suspicion, one adopts a primarily possessive, controlling approach (in dealing with human experience) through which one seeks to enclose the truth, as it were, in one's own mind and categories. By giving priority to faith, on the other hand, one adopts an approach in which one is less the controller and possessor of truth and more *controlled* and *possessed* by it. It is as though by giving suspicion dominance I am saying that my claim on truth comes first; whereas, by giving faith or trust dominance I am saying that truth's claim on me (perennially) comes first.
[4] See: Peterson, Christopher, and Seligman, Martin E. P., *Character Strengths and Virtues: A Handbook and Classification*, Oxford, Oxford University Press, 2004. For a philosophically oriented consideration of virtue and character along with a consideration of psychological implications, see: *The Psychology of Character and Virtue*, Craig Titus (Ed.), Arlington, Virginia, The Institute for the Psychological Sciences Press, 2009.
[5] Seligman, Martin E. P. and Csikszentmihalyi, Mihaly, "Positive Psychology – An Introduction," *American Psychologist*, Vol. 55, No. 1, 5-14, January 2000; see, also: Seligman, Martin E. P., *Flourish: A Visionary New Understanding of Happiness and Well-being*, New York, Free Press, 2011.
[6] Although positive psychology began by explicitly shifting focus from psychopathological to positive or adaptive aspects of psychological

functioning, there have been some developments in that movement in which psychopathology has become a focus, specifically in the study of what has been termed "post-traumatic growth." Yet, here too, the interest appears to be more on the adaptive and positive potential of human beings and less on understanding the meaning of the human struggle with abnormality. We agree that there can be a positive outcome to human struggle, but our own interest or concern is more with the inherent meaningfulness of psychological struggle *before* a consideration of adaptive outcome or self development. We focus on how the meaningfulness of psychological distress is rooted in the essential link or complementarity between personal and relational aspects of human experience, and see matters of outcome and self-actualisation as interpretable or intelligible only from a position that defers to the value or meaning of that complementarity. We will say more about this issue in the course of this essay. For a summary and bibliography of the post-traumatic positive psychology literature see: Tillier, William D., "Posttraumatic Growth Bibliography," June 2012, Calgary, Alberta, http://www.positivedisintegration.com/ptg.htm.

[7] Our point is that suffering cannot be equated simply with meaninglessness, but neither do we see suffering as something that is primarily functional, i.e. as a means to an end. Although suffering is naturally undesirable, we also see in it a protest against loss of meaning and a longing for meaningful forms of being and relationship. Nevertheless, suffering, generally, and psychological symptoms, in particular, appear to restrict and eclipse the capacity to be and relate in a human, meaningful way (i.e. with love and solidarity). Still, suffering does not cancel the humanity of the sufferer nor that of the one who might assist or be in solidarity with the sufferer, because suffering is intrinsically aimed at healing. In order to share in and support the healing of another who suffers one has to attend to that person with respect and compassion, and personally engage *with hope* along the hard road where one encounters the restriction and eclipse of meaning that is associated with the suffering. This kind of personal engagement is an essential feature of the work of the psychotherapist.

[8] Power, we will argue, has lower and higher expressions in human relationship (and by analogy across the spectrum of living creatures we find in the natural world). Assertive power, for example, itself depends on co-operation, from which it derives its force. If assertive power severs its ties to co-operative power, however, the quality or meaning of power is compromised. One may see this in the growth of cancer cells that *assert*

themselves in a manner that is anti-co-operative with respect to the health of the body as a whole. This example also suggests that the radicalisation of assertion is ultimately auto-destructive, in that a radicalised assertion destroys its host (i.e. the co-operative context that it requires to thrive).

[9] We intend here belief in that which is co-operative, collaborative, and *complementary*; these characteristics, we are suggesting, form the basis or core of the human experience of reality.

[10] Consider the analogous use of the expression, "sifting process" by Kenneth Schmitz: "[C]riticism is a *sifting process* based upon and subordinate to the credibility already encountered in knowledge" (italics added) (Schmitz, "A Not Uncritical Harmony," *Catholic Social Science Review, V, 2000, p. 20*). See our first essay (section "B") for further discussion of this passage.

[11] Scott-Bauman, *Ricoeur and the Hermeneutics of Suspicion*, p. 45.

[12] Moreover, we see this complementarity as analogously occurring across the spectrum and hierarchy of reality that include more than the strictly personal. Ours, however, is not a flat ontology but one in which distinction and relation of being allow for hierarchy, although as we will elaborate below, this hierarchy is not without paradox, a paradox that allows both *descent* and *ascent* of hierarchy to draw its meaning or norm from the non-hierarchical relation of persons.

[13] By "rupture, fusion or domination," we intend forms of relation that do not support the *distinct* participants. For example, instead of loyalty one might see abandonment (a form of *rupture*); instead of respect for the other one might see inordinate enmeshment or manipulation (forms of *fusion* or *domination*). Also, see the first essay in this book (section "C") for a discussion of how we understand both rupture and fusion to be forms of *disaccord*.

[14] Ricoeur, *Freud and Philosophy*, p. 8.

[15] In the wound this complementarity may be challenged or even eclipsed, but we argue that it is not eliminated. The complementarity shows itself in what we are calling the healing tendency associated with the wound.

[16] We may further conclude that (personal) *assent to* vs. *dissent from* relation, on the one hand, and (social) *support of* vs. *rejection of* distinction, on the other, are ways in which complementarity can be opposed to anti-complementarity: i.e. normality or meaningfulness vs. abnormality or meaninglessness. We ought not to conflate, however, true complementarity (such as that between self and other, freedom and commitment, diversity and unity) with *false complementarity* (such as that between normality and abnormality, meaning and meaninglessness, order and disorder, good and evil). With respect to true complementarities, both

terms of the polarity can be actually independent from each other *and* actually related to one another. However, with respect to *false complementarities*, it is complementarity itself which fails or finds itself in jeopardy. The terms cannot be reconciled and we have, therefore, an anti- or non-complementarity. We will elaborate below on how to address the unique features of the antinomy or contradiction of normality and abnormality. Also, see "Appendix B," subsection "B," for a further discussion of this issue. We explore there how the normal and the abnormal, the complementary and the anti-complementary, the meaningful and the meaningless, peace and violence, etc., are not to be viewed as a *yin and yang* harmony, but, on the contrary, as the presence vs. the absence of such harmony. Consequently, we could say that the polarity of distinction and relation represents a *paradoxical* phenomenon whereas the polarity of normality and abnormality represents a *contradictory* phenomenon.

[17] Consider Ricoeur's definition of hermeneutics: "By hermeneutics we shall always understand the theory of the rules that preside over an exegesis—that is, over the interpretation of a particular text, or of a group of signs that may be interpreted as a text" (Ricoeur, *Freud and Philosophy*, p. 8). We see giving priority to a hermeneutics of belief as a way to approach and recognise the fundamental/ontological place of the accord or complementarity of distinction and relation of persons in the human experience of both normal and abnormal events: this involves a consideration of the crucial role of accord in one's experience of the jeopardy of accord.

[18] We may note here a difference between the hermeneutics of Ricoeur and the hermeneutics we propose. The hermeneutics of Ricoeur starts with the *long detour* (see below) in approaching the symbol, thus, to some extent, endorsing the doubt and scepticism that characterise modernity. For Ricoeur, one makes one's way from suspicion and doubt to faith or belief, and beyond that one reaches a third point of integration of doubt and faith. Itao explains that Ricoeur's suspicion is initially directed towards Descartes' moment of certainty (the *cogito*), because this latter form of knowing is said to be solipsistic, empty and even narcissistic. The *cogito* has to be *doubted* in order for it to become expanded and filled, that is, in order for it to become meaningful. Ricoeur (as quoted by Itao) writes: "This positing of the *cogito* remains to be mediated by the totality of the world of signs and by the interpretation of these signs. This long detour is, precisely, suspicion" (Itao, Alexis Deodato S. "Paul Ricoeur's Hermeneutics of Symbols," p. 5, p. 11-12.)." We differ from Ricoeur to

the extent that we begin and end with faith or belief, as it were, allowing the doubt and *detour*, that Ricoeur associates with suspicion, a place in the middle part of our course, where accord and disaccord present themselves as a mixed reality (we will further explicate and develop this notion of *mixed reality* later in the essay). Note that we do not seek primarily to apply suspicion to false consciousness (as do Marx, Nietzsche and Freud) nor to the solipsistic cogito of Descartes (as does Ricoeur, noted above). We apply hermeneutics to the mixed reality of accord and disaccord of relationship, in which being (ontology) and healing, on the one hand, have priority over knowledge (epistemology – *cogito*) and breaching or wounding, on the other. The world of knowing may stray from the world of being, but our first concern is with the world of being (and its failure/disaccord), and only *secondarily* with how the world of knowledge may reflect or arise from that world of being.

[19] We recall Schmitz' notion of ontological generosity, which he applies to the intelligible connection between thought and being (and thus, knower and known), and which he says finds its basis in "a certain abundance and generosity written into being, its capacity for making a gift of itself to thought…The possibility of cognition is rooted in its ontological generosity, and in a vicariosity which permits one being to bear the presence and meaning of another" (Schmitz, Kenneth L., "Enriching the Copula," *The Review of Metaphysics: A Commemorative Issue. Thomas Aquinas, 1224-1274, 27*, 1974, p. 492-512, see: p. 511-512). See first essay in this book (section "B") for further discussion of this issue.

[20] We will elaborate this notion of *equality* in subsection "ii" below.

[21] We naturally establish a hierarchy, not only between the personal and the impersonal, but also in the impersonal realm itself, between those things that have more in common with the personal (e.g. living things) and those things that have less in common with the personal (e.g. non-living things). Note, however, that, as we will be elaborating, we see paradoxical aspects to this hierarchy, where the higher does not simply dominate the lower, but, in a significant sense, *serves* it.

[22] This integration of hierarchy arises, paradoxically, from the service of the lower by the higher and the receptivity of the lower to this service. Consider St. Paul's, 1 Corinthians 12:23: "And the parts [of the body] that we think are less honourable we treat with special honour." We will say more about this service of the lower by the higher below.

[23] We will provide some elaboration on how the question of hierarchy applies specifically to the realm of knowledge and ideas in "Appendix C."

[24] We are affirming in this an intimate relation between *is* and *ought*, as opposed to Hume's division of one from the other; we further address this issue at a later point in this essay (see: endnote "155").

---

[25] One factor that alludes to this ontological priority may be noted by considering that an entity requires the *co-operative grant of existing or being an entity, before* it can compete. We will discuss below how it is the "generosity of being" (a notion already introduced above, see: endnote # "19") that favours the compatibility between horizontal complementarity and vertical hierarchy.

[26] We will consider below how this hierarchy within hierarchy depends on a transcendence of hierarchy itself: that is, on how complementarity – with its non-hierarchical or *anarchic* features – is, somewhat paradoxically, higher than, or sets the norm for hierarchy. Note here a paradox (to be elaborated below) that hierarchy within hierarchy in a sense speaks to the influence of a certain kind of non- or an-archy on hierarchy: that is, *hierarchy within hierarchy* refers not only to *hierarchy* (within hierarchy) but also, to *anarchy* or *anarchy's* influence within hierarchy.

[27] Our point here is that, as competition is separated from co-operation, it becomes less personal in that those relational factors that establish and support the personal become eclipsed. If competition is radicalised for example, (i.e. essentially abstracted from co-operation), then personal life becomes less and less of a possibility because the relations that support the human person are being eliminated. One may generalise this principle by noting that if *distinction* is radicalised without concern, as it were, for its accord with *relation*, then distinction itself is jeopardised (because, if distinction is truly the complement of relation, then it requires the latter to continue to be itself).

[28] We are taking some liberties with the notion of personal vs. impersonal. By impersonal we are not only considering the category of things that in themselves are not persons (be they animate or inanimate objects, or even abstract principles – e.g. mathematical concepts); rather, we are also focusing here on how the human person is called to navigate between the personal, on the one hand, and the less-than-personal or non-personal features of reality, on the other, within his or her own experience. In other words, we are considering the hierarchical relation of the personal and the impersonal in the context of the human encounter with reality. One may ask, for example, about a given human situation, "Are people being treated as having greater or lesser importance than impersonal things?" In all forms of competitive striving this question becomes particularly relevant. Does competition express itself in a manner that reduces the personal to the impersonal, such that the other is reduced to an obstacle in one's path, or to a mere means to one's goal? Is the self reduced to merely seeking the *impersonal* (to *I-It* instead of *I-Thou* – to put this in Martin Buber's terms; Buber, Martin, *I and Thou*, translated by Walter Kaufmann, New York,

Touchstone, 1996, first published in German in 1923)? Or does competition, in the end, defer to co-operation, where the other is not reduced to an object of mastery, but engaged as a person, and the self is recognised in his or her orientation to interpersonal relationship?

[29] One ought to consider that one may also experience a sense of wonder – and that there is, indeed, much for which to be in wonder – in conducting a chemistry experiment. As essential as wonder is to explorations of natural science, however, such wonder cannot be captured in the strict methodology of science, but transcends (and in some ways informs) that methodology.

[30] The latter would only be valid for the complementarity in ultimate being where existence *is* essence.

[31] Consider that the transcendence of hierarchy is towards complementarity; it is this that allows the norm of complementarity to find hierarchical expression, that is, to create or contribute to what we have called *hierarchy within hierarchy*.

[32] Thus, the unity of relation transcends itself towards its complement of distinction in two ways: 1) in going beyond its unity to affirm the distinction and multiplicity of entities that share in that unity, and, 2) by being an *open* unity that encounters and affirms what appears from beyond its boundaries; because it allows and affirms what is distinct from itself, the unity of relation is not something closed in on itself (i.e. auto-referential), but presents as a unity open to diversity, an intrinsic openness to the universal scope of things.

One should also note that the transcendence of distinction towards engagement in relation, and the transcendence of relation towards affirmation of distinction are not simply sequential events: in going beyond oneself to serve the interests of relationship, one becomes more oneself, because, *coincidentally*, relationship may be going beyond itself to affirm the interests of the (distinct) one(s).

[33] With the transcendence of hierarchy towards complementarity, one does not see the extinguishing of the inequality of the former; one sees rather a transformation of hierarchy that leads to its integration. Just as distinction is not lost in its transcendent accord with relation, and relation is not lost in its transcendent accord with distinction, so too does the inequality of hierarchy not simply disappear as a result of the influence of the norm of complementarity upon it. As previously discussed, the influence of complementarity on hierarchy manifests itself in the service of the lower by the higher, and in the priority of co-operative engagement over competitive striving. Thus, the hierarchical transcends itself, not by abolishing its hierarchical structure, but, as will be further elaborated below, by adopting and adapting the *equalising/horizontal* transcendence

of complementarity within its *unequal/vertical* structure, that is, by bringing anarchy into hierarchy, as it were.
[34] Note that in speaking of *horizontal transcendence* we are not endorsing approaches that exclude vertical transcendence. Some approaches proposing "horizontal transcendence" tend towards the elimination of the vertical form of transcendence in order to replace it with a notion of transcendence limited to, or enclosed in an immanent universe, in the interest, for example, of giving priority to *life over mind*, or in attempts to address or overcome the *body-mind dichotomy*. For examples of "horizontal transcendence" that seem to us to be defined in essentially immanent (or non-transcendent) terms see: du Toit, Cornel W., "Towards a New Natural Theology Based on Horizontal Transcendence," 2009, HTS Teologiese/Theological Studies, 65(1), Art. # 186, 8 pages, DOI: 104102/hts.v65i1.186; Hine, Phil, "Some Reflections on Transcendence – II," March 20, 2012, http://enfolding.org/some-reflections-on-transcendence-ii/; Kalton, Michael C., "Green Spirituality: Horizontal Transcendence," (published as a chapter of *Creativity, Spirituality and Transcendence, Paths to Integrity and Wisdom in the Mature Self,* M. E. Miller & S. Cook-Greuter, Stamford, Connecticut, Ablex Publishing, 2000).

It is beyond our scope to address the questions raised by these approaches. We would emphasise, however, that we see no need to eliminate vertical transcendence because we see an essential compatibility between vertical hierarchy and horizontal complementarity, a compatibility in which the latter informs – provides the essential norm for – the former. Moreover, in our perspective, transcendence does not originate in the hierarchical but comes from the *horizontal*; however, horizontal transcendence, in our proposal, is not simply the environmental, biological experience of connection in the realm of an immanent, horizontal world. The latter notion of "horizontal transcendence" and our own proposal seem to us to involve something of a reversal of concepts. Indeed, in our paradigm, the immanent horizontal world, to which the proponents of "horizontal transcendence" refer, is what we consider to be the hierarchically organised world: after all, it is in this proposed *horizontally transcendent yet immanent horizontal world* that one finds, for example, the rule of the survival of the fittest as a factor of biological evolution, something eminently hierarchical. In contradistinction, we view the horizontal as inherently transcendent (distinction transcends relation and vice versa), and as that which *informs*, while transcending, the hierarchical kind of order found in the natural world; this *informing* allows the natural world and its hierarchy to, in turn, transcend itself. In addition, from our own understanding of these terms, we do not view *horizontal* transcendence as that which simply negates *hierarchy*, but as that which fulfills it. In this way the environmental, biological experience of connection in the realm of the so-called horizontally transcendent, immanent world (a world we see as inherently hierarchical) does not have a solely self-enclosed immanent explanation or scope.

[35] Thus, for example, the person may fail to go beyond immanent self-interest and, therefore, not recognise, appreciate and respond to the call to support relational commitment. Or, vice-versa, a relational association, may fail to go beyond an emphasis in maintaining its unitary status or homogeneity, and consequently not affirm the distinction and freedom of its members; or it may engage in a prejudicial exclusion of those who are outside its membership.

[36] This implies, for example, that the equality of persons is rooted in a deeper *equality* between person and relationship. We are using *equality* by analogy to its usual meaning.

[37] One may also speculate here about whether an excessive separation of individuals, as we see in the occasionalist notion of causation, sets the stage for interaction that can only be violent. One thing is said never to actually touch the other (in occasionalism), but if entities that do not normally touch should somehow come together, will they not inevitably come together in antagonism?

[38] With a mere equality of entities, their coming together in association with one another will tend towards defensive isolation from one another, on the one hand, or towards vying for competitive supremacy over one another, on the other. One may also consider that an excessively abstract notion of freedom that underlies an array of *merely* equal entities not only leads to an excessive individualism, but also sets the stage for the development of collectivist forms of control.

As discussed above and to be elaborated below, we oppose anarchic individualism but not a form of *an-archic* personalism that involves authentic regard for person and relation. The vision of the non-hierarchic or an-archic dimension which takes both person and relation into account includes more than the simple equality of entities. An equality applied solely to individuals or persons – not to person *and* relation – tends to yield a vision of competition and conflict between and among isolated interests. This implies forms of individualism that tend to be untenable (in view of the overemphasis on competition at the expense of co-operation), and which lead in turn to various forms of collectivist control (some individuals become *more equal* than others and impose on others their control). The ontological generosity of complementarity, on the other hand, does not refer simply to an equality among entities (such that one

might imagine among a multitude of solitudes each and all equal to one another); rather, the equality or *anarchy* of the horizontal dimension allows distinction and relation to co-exist. One may consider here that *mere power* (to be further discussed) is a correlate of *mere equality*, and that one requires more than *mere* power and *mere* equality to achieve genuine freedom and genuine equality among persons.
[39] This speaks to an equality of persons rooted in a transcendence that gives *equal* ontological status to the distinction of freedom/uniqueness and the relation of communion/solidarity.

By *an-archical equality* we do not mean an anarchy of the individual who does whatever he or she wishes, rejecting all authority. Such an anarchy would be one of sole power. Rather, by anarchy we are referring to a non-hierarchy that characterises relationship between or among persons, in which persons come together as equals in freedom *and* through connection, communion and mutuality. Power or hierarchy ought to ever remain secondary to this inherent equality of persons in the context of relationship. Indeed, we propose that even with respect to the inequality or power-differential found in hierarchy, the true norm is to be derived from the an-archical equality of persons (this refers to the notion of *hierarchy within hierarchy*, discussed above, which we have also designated as *an-archy within hierarchy*). A true equality of persons results from a *surprise*, that is, from a surprising ordering of power in which higher serves lower. Consider the example of how Michelangelo defers to the rough marble he is carving to find within it the statue of David. One is reminded here of the greater demand expressed in Robert Spaemann's radical restatement of the categorical imperative: "there is nothing at all that we can and may use only as a means to an end." (Holger Zaborowski's *Robert Spaemann's Philosophy of the Human Person*, Oxford, Oxford University Press, 2010, p. 255). This respect for each and every thing – and not only persons – indicates, we believe, a form of service of lower by higher that is not reductive, but *uplifting*: in the service of lower by higher, lower is raised to higher, and higher finds its fuller expression.

With modernity one comes to place great emphasis on equality and on freedom, but at the same time one faces a temptation to place power before meaningful relationship. Moreover, this happens in both totalitarian-collective social arrangements, and in what one might call the totalitarianism of the individual (e.g. relativism). With both kinds of *totalitarianism* the power of freedom is separated from the meaningfulness of relationship, such that freedom (reduced to power) dominates relation. Left and right, anarchist and libertarian, socialist and capitalist, seem often in agreement on this *separation*. With both extremes one seems to find an impoverished notion of equality: a mere equality of individuals isolated from one another, or a mere homogeneity of individuals functionally dependent on one another.

We may emphasise here that the anarchy established by the separation of individual from relational commitment is not the anarchy we are proposing. As we have said, we are not proposing a mere equality of individuals, but an *anarchy* or *non-hierarchy* in the equality of the person and relation: without relation the person cannot find meaning. With the anarchy of the individual, however, – be it the anarchy of the dictator, or of each citizen (in a relativism of values) – one grabs hold of freedom but abandons the *greater and the truer*, that is, the love that binds one person to another. Luigi Giussani speaks of anarchy as a "most fascinating temptation," but one "as deceitful as it is attractive." He goes on to say,

> The strength of its deceit lies precisely in its appeal, which makes us forget that man is made – that at one point he does not exist and then he dies. Only pure violence can make him say, 'I affirm myself against all and everything.' It is much greater and truer to love the infinite, that is, to embrace reality and being rather than to assert oneself against them. Indeed, we must recognize that man truly affirms himself only by accepting reality, so much so that, in fact, he begins to accept himself by accepting his existence, that is, a reality he has not given himself (Giussani, Luigi, *The Religious Sense*, McGill-Queen's University Press, translated by John Zucchi, Montreal, 1997, p. 10).

[40] It is beyond our scope to give an exposition of personalism. We again refer the reader to an excellent article which considers some of the basic principles and varied forms of personalism: Williams, Thomas D., and Bengtsson, Jan Olaf, "Personalism," *The Stanford Encyclopedia of Philosophy* (Spring 2014 Edition), Edward N. Zalta (Ed.), URL = http://plato.stanford.edu/archives/spr2014/entries/personalism/.

We should also consider here that human nature is such that the human person transcends the species, and is not a mere individual, but a freedom open to communion (i.e. a person). Consider the following passages: Robert Spaemann writes:

> A nature is a principle of specific reaction. With the concept of the person, however, we come to think of the particular individual as being more basic than its nature. This is not to suggest that these individuals *have* no nature, and start out by deciding for themselves what they are to be. What they do is assume a new relation to their nature; they freely endorse the laws of their being, or alternatively they rebel against them and 'deviate'. Because they are thinking beings, they cannot be categorized exhaustively

as members of their species, only as individuals, who 'exist in
their nature'. That is to say, they exist as persons (Spaemann,
Robert, *Persons, The Difference between 'Someone' and
'Something,'* New York, Oxford University Press, Oliver
O'Donovan, Trans., 2006, p. 33).
Kenneth Schmitz presents a similar elucidation of the meaning of person:
After tracing the dynamic inclinations of our human nature our
story does not come to an end, for we are not only human beings;
precisely as individual human beings we are persons. Now a
person is not simply the contraction from the specific and general
character of our humanity to the particular instantiation of that
specific character, as though our story ends with our membership
in the species.... Rather, our personhood marks in each of us the
inner transcendence that characterizes our individuated human
nature and gathers that nature into a surpassing of our destiny
(Schmitz, Kenneth L., *Person and Psyche*, Arlington, Virginia,
The Institute for the Psychological Sciences Press, 2009, p. 33).
Roger Scruton, as well, makes a similar point:
What do we mean when we refer to 'creatures like us'? Do we
mean to include only humans? Homer tells us of the 'laughter of
the gods,' and Milton of laughter among the angels. Here is the
beginning of a profound metaphysical problem. We belong to a
natural kind: *Homo sapiens sapiens,* which is a biological species.
But, when we talk of creatures like us, it seems that we do not
necessarily refer to our species-membership. Our 'glassy
essence,' as Shakespeare calls it, refuses to be contained in our
species-life (Scruton, Roger, "Confronting Biology," in
Philosophical Psychology, Craig Steven Titus, Ed., *The John
Henry Cardinal Newman Lectures*, Volume 5, Arlington, Virginia,
The Institute for the Psychological Sciences Press, 2009, p. 68-
107; see: p. 87).
[41] Where individualism and collectivism respectively favour the support of
one term at the expense of its complement, personalism is able to support
the richness of both diversity and unity.
[42] We refer above to the compatibility between the horizontal and vertical.
Note, however, the subtlety of how the compatibility between the accord of
the horizontal and the integrity of the vertical arises with reference to the
priority of the anarchical over the hierarchical. The anarchical or non-
hierarchical, precisely because it is non-vertical, supports the vertical: it is
compatible with the hierarchical as that which is *less*-than-fully-personal
(the personal is that which more fully expresses distinction and relation,

freedom and communion in terms of having a nature receptive to and
oriented towards personal qualities such as responsibility, conscience and
love). This is in contradistinction to a conception and expression of the
vertical in which priority is given to itself, to its *mere* hierarchy. Giving
priority to *mere* hierarchy makes hierarchy incompatible with anarchic
equality. In other words, horizontality (of persons), in itself, does not
exclude verticality; however, verticality, without openness to the norm (of
complementarity) transcendent to itself, *does* exclude horizontality. Note
our paradoxical use of the term *horizontal*: by horizontal we intend that
which is *higher* than the vertical. This *higher*, however, is a matter of
service, that is, of responsibility to care for the *lower*.
[43] The co-existence inherent to complementarity is offered to hierarchy by
infusing the latter with the principles of service and co-operation,
principles that support hierarchy and define its limits, even as they express
origins transcendent to it, origins in an accord that is itself, as outlined
above, an expression of mutual transcendence of complements. It is via
the service of the lower by the higher, and the openness and reciprocal
response of the lower to this service, that hierarchy achieves compatibility
with complementarity, while retaining a hierarchical order.
[44] By *complements that are in accord* we mean expressions of distinction
and relation between such *equal* terms as freedom and commitment,
singular and communal, multiplicity and unity, *male and female* – the
prototype of which is the relation of persons: self and other.

It is of interest to note that with the complementarity of *male and female*
one is dealing with something archetypal and cosmic, that is present in all
of nature (as Peter Kreeft proposes: see reference at the end of this
endnote). With human beings the complementarity of male and female
found in nature, takes on personal meaning: that is, the relation of male and
female – despite stereotyping or reduction to political or power
considerations that may misrepresent this distinction/relation – essentially
demonstrates the characteristics which we identify with complementarity:
accord, transcendence and equality are essential features of the
relation/distinction of male and female persons. We do see, however, not
only throughout the course of human history, but as well in the current
zeitgeist, tendencies to reduce complementarity to a power differential, that
is, to *mere* hierarchy. When power is permitted to dominate
complementarity, however, meaning collapses. See the following video
produced by Humanum (2014) that considers the question of the
complementarity of male and female from a variety of perspectives;
speakers include Peter Kreeft, Maria Fedoryka, Chady Rahme, Fernando
Pliego Carrasko, Robert Barron, Thérèse Hargot-Jacob, and Philippe
Ariño; URL=

http://www.aleteia.org/en/society/article/moving-beyond-gender-stereotypes-video-5771034837909504.

[45] By *hierarchy that is integrated* we mean ways in which descent and ascent function to integrate such *unequal* aspects of reality as spirit and flesh, Eros and Agape, biological needs and companionship needs, competitive inclinations and co-operative inclinations, interactions based on instrumental requirements and interactions based on friendship.

By way of summary of this section – on the normality of the compatibility of the complementary and the hierarchical – we could say that the normal involves, in terms of complementarity, the following: freedom that unites (assents to unity), unity (solidarity) that liberates (defends and supports freedom); and, in terms of hierarchy, descent of the higher that supports ascent of the lower, and ascent of the lower that is open to the integration offered by such descent. Conversely, we could add, that the abnormal involves: freedom that divides (dissents from unity or relationship), inauthentic or superficial unity that offends freedom, and non-integrative descent that does not allow ascent, and non-integrative ascent that rejects or remains closed to integrative descent.

[46] One may speak of *power* and *degree* of being, and their association. There is the *existence* of an entity, on the one hand, and its *essence* (or limit/*degree* of that existence), on the other: its *power* to be (i.e. existence or that it is) and its *degree* of existence (i.e. a feature of its essence or what it is) (for a development of this notion see: Carlo, William E., *The Ultimate Reducibility of Essence to Existence in Existential Metaphysics*, The Hague, Martinus Nijhoff, 1966). As we discuss above, the relational principle is embedded in the hierarchical features of reality, in that hierarchy fundamentally unfolds from relation, and relation continually informs hierarchy through service. Metaphysically, therefore, each thing carries the imprint of relation in itself, in the service of *what it is* by *that it is*. We may also consider, as previously noted, that existence and essence achieve equality of ontological status only in the Absolute; this means, interestingly, that existence and essence are true and *equal* complements only in terms of their ultimate realisation; otherwise they are hierarchically arranged with existence being higher than (and in the framework we present above, *serving*) essence.

[47] As we have considered, this equality is not a mere equality of entities but occurs through a mutual transcendence of distinction and relation. We are proposing that any equality that entities (such as persons) may have with respect to one another depends on that more primary distinction-relation transcendent accord: this speaks to an equality through transcendence. One may consider here, that if one approaches an entity solely in terms of

hierarchy, the distinct being of an entity will be given greater ontological weight than its relations, because there will be the tendency to regard the latter as accidental properties (cf. Harman in the first essay); and substantial features are of greater ontological importance than accidental ones in defining an entity. When one leaves the purview of sole hierarchy, however, and considers the priority of complementarity over hierarchy in defining personal existence, one may then realise that relation contributes to distinction in as fundamental a way as distinction contributes to relation. Thus, there is an *equality* of ontological status between distinction and relation; but it is an equality in which distinction ever transcends itself to enter relation, and relation ever transcends itself to affirm distinction.

[48] We intend here a scale that is not simply one of power or brute force, but one of the meaning of power: thus, for example, one party may gain the advantage over another in terms of sheer force (i.e. power), but, nevertheless, remain *defeated* in terms of truth and justice (i.e. meaning).

[49] One may consider that hierarchy, as a whole, is itself subject to the norm of non-hierarchic or an-archic equality. One may appreciate, therefore, that the purpose of hierarchy (as we are outlining it) is not simply to define and assert the order of higher and lower levels of being, the dominance of one over the other (which we saw in the examples of individualism and collectivism). The purpose of hierarchy, when viewed in this comprehensive manner, is to orient that order (of higher and lower) to the *normative* dimension of equality. There is in this a transcendence of the hierarchy of dominance to affirm a hierarchy of service, (i.e. hierarchy transcends itself by allowing complementarity to transform it from within).

One may also consider that, by remaining basically oriented by power and hierarchy, an individualism or collectivism, although it may include a reference to egalitarianism, will tend to lose touch with the basis of that egalitarianism (i.e. we are proposing that the basis of a viable egalitarianism lies in the distinction and relation of persons).

We may further speculate about how complementarities may themselves be arranged hierarchically and by analogy. For example, consider that the polar complementarity of *chance and necessity* applies at the *lower* levels of reality, while it has an analogous counterpart in *freedom and commitment* at the *higher* personal levels.

[50] Note the change in meaning of the *higher* in this context: the higher refers to a reductive understanding of power, more akin to a notion of brute force, and not the higher in the sense of the fullness of being and the expression of conviction, meaning or truth.

To summarise this section, distinction and relation are to be *equally* balanced with respect to complementarity, whereas, in order for *an-archy* (non-hierarchic equality of complementarity) to inform hierarchy, co-operative service is to have *priority* over competitive dominance. In other words, the influence of the order of an-archic equality does not abolish the inequality of hierarchy, but it only supports a particular kind of *inequality*: the form of inequality characterised by the priority of co-operative service over competitive dominance. Also, and as previously noted, when complementarity rules hierarchy the latter achieves integration, whereas when (mere) hierarchy rules complementarity the latter is breached. [51] It is this dependence of vertical hierarchy (as distribution of power) on horizontal complementarity of persons in relation (as expression of love) that allows us, we believe, to provide an approach that meets the exigency of secular interest and autonomy. Consider a comment made by Hanna Arendt to the American Society for Christian Ethics in 1973, in which she emphasises the difference (if not incompatibility) between a secular and religious vision of social and political reality: "there is no doubt that the notion of covenant is itself somehow Biblical in origin...[but a] covenant of mutuality—this covenant which relies on *mutuality*—cannot possibly be compared to covenants in which one party is God, to whom we owe existence, creation and so on, also law, and [in which] we only pledge our *obedience*" (as cited by Moyn, Samuel, "Hanna Arendt on the Secular," *New German Critique*, No. 105, Political Theology, Fall 2008, p. 76-96, see p. 87). Yet an ontological order in which the hierarchical distribution of power is informed by and defers to a complementarity of personal relationship, and in which complementarity in turn *serves* hierarchy would, in our view, support compatibility between the secular and the religious, and would precisely allow one to favourably compare the two kinds of covenants Arendt describes. Indeed, it would seem that the priority of *mutuality* over *mere* hierarchical power could be compatible with *both* a religious *and* a secular vision in which power defers to relationship. The compatibility of complementarity and hierarchy, which we propose, could find expression in what Margaret Somerville has defined as a *post-secular society*. She starts by defining an *exclusively* secular society as one in which there has been some confusion between freedom *of* and *for* religion (i.e. no state religion and no restriction on religious practice by the state), on the one hand, and freedom *from* religion (exclusion of religion from the public square), on the other. Freedom *of* and *for* belong in a "properly secular society," but according to Somerville, freedom *from* "is not a valid requirement for a secular society." She outlines a post-secular society – i.e. one in which *freedom from religion* is not required – in terms of four points: 1) a post-secular society "would not simply be a return to the past" secular or pre-secular world; 2) all beliefs, religious and non-religious would be allowed in the public square; 3) one ought to avoid *ad hominem* attacks based on others having beliefs; 4) exclusion of those who do not agree with one's beliefs constitutes a "serious mistake." See: Somerville, Margaret, "Building Ethical Bridges in a Secular Age" *Comment, Public Theology for the Common Good*, September 1, 2014, published by Cardus, http://www.cardus.ca/comment/article/4373/building-ethical-bridges-in-a-secular-age/.

[52] We have previously spoken of *hierarchy within hierarchy* as actually involving the introduction of *non-* or *an-archy* into hierarchy. Consider, for example, how the sculptor may chip away at the rough stone in the creation of a statue with a deep respect and deference to that material, which, from a *merely* hierarchical perspective, is but something to be shaped as the sculptor wishes to shape it. The sculptor does not simply rule the material being sculpted; rather, the influence of the norm of complementarity has the sculptor *serve* the material, discover it, work with it collaboratively and not only in terms of power/control.

[53] This approach is opposed to a pragmatist or utilitarian notion of functional relation in which the lower explains the higher: i.e. where the extrinsic "cash value" (c.f. William James) dominates and explains away, as it were, the intrinsic (ideal) higher value. The principle of service of the lower by the higher does not, however, exclude the practical, since it does not abstract the ideal from the real – or even the ideal from the empirical. We will elaborate further on this integral vision where we critically explore below some of the ideas of Isaiah Berlin on negative and positive liberty (see: endnote "115").

[54] It is beyond the scope here to consider many of the implications of the priority, in principle, of collaboration over competition. One may think, for example, about how one's view of biological evolution, whose prevalent explanation remains largely linked to the competitive notion of natural selection, might appear differently if one were to give priority to the co-operative principles that contribute to life's development. Similarly, shifting to social theory, one might ask, questions like the following: Is all competitive striving ultimately rooted in a more fundamentally co-operative striving? Is all negative liberty (involving some form of individual assertion) rooted in positive liberty (involving some form of collective support for personal freedom)? See our further discussion on this issue in endnote "115," where we explore Isaiah Berlin's "Two Concepts of Liberty."

[55] Complementarity – as the accord of distinction and relation, freedom and communion – provides the credible and trustworthy *substratum* to the hermeneutics of belief.

[56] Note how, in the contemporary zeitgeist, one will come across confusion with respect to distinguishing the notions of acceptance and permission,

and one finds, as well, forms of intolerance that express neither acceptance nor permission. One ought to appreciate, however, that it is often challenging to maintain an authentic self-acceptance in which one seeks to be accompanied in one's troubles, or to maintain a genuine acceptance of the other, such that one genuinely accompanies the other who is troubled. One may be tempted to follow one of two extremes, and sometimes even to subtly combine them. At one extreme one turns acceptance into permission, and at the other one adopts neither acceptance nor permission, but intolerance or rejection. Permission is inappropriate when it involves an attempt to fix the problem and alleviate the suffering that accompanies it through denial of either problem or suffering or both. In this way one eclipses the promise of healing. Moreover, this form of permission turns out to be a pseudo rather genuine acceptance that only has the semblance of support or accompaniment. This would be like an acknowledgement/acceptance of alcoholism without the offer of any hope of sobriety, or it would be like the simple endorsement of a patient's desire to commit suicide without any offer of hope in living. One must also avoid the other extreme, also prevalent in the contemporary zeitgeist, in which one offers the other neither acceptance nor permission. One fails to accompany the other by excluding the person as a result of equating the person with his or her error or difficulty (e.g. one equates the person with alcoholism without distinguishing person and error, that is, again, without offering hope of sobriety). It is of interest that these two extremes both involve the exclusion of the person: in one I cancel the problem by refusing to take seriously the suffering of the person (e.g. I deny the problem of alcoholism); in the other I affirm the problem but refuse to take seriously that there is a person who is suffering (e.g. I affirm alcoholism but deny the hope that defines a human person: that is, I conclude, "He's just a drunk"). A true acceptance allows one to care for and accompany the person *with* the problem. Mere permission and mere intolerance fail to express this accompaniment.

[57] Meaninglessness is not identical to nothingness, but the two terms have something in common. Meaninglessness refers to a failure of meaning, whereas nothingness has a more neutral connotation, which refers to the absence of being/existence. However, both terms imply lack. In any case, the association between meaninglessness and nothingness may help to explain why, when one confronts meaninglessness (i.e. the failure of freedom to support relationship and the failure of relationship to support a meaningful expression of freedom), one faces the absence of sense or meaning, thus something akin to nothingness. One may also note the close

ties between fundamental terms like sense and meaning, on the one hand, and being and existence, on the other.

[58] Lorenzo Albacete speaks of the origin of suffering – which one may consider to be closely linked to the experience of meaninglessness – as "something 'irrational,' where rational indicates the human capacity to make sense of it. It is not only something merely unknown, but *unknowable*, a break in the fabric of understanding itself. No 'cause' can explain it adequately." (*God at the Ritz, Attraction to Infinity*, New York, The Crossroad Publishing Company, 2002, p.110)

[59] We speak of this positive mystery as exceeding our sensing, reasoning and explaining because the grant of being is always presupposed to one's human sensing, reasoning and explaining, a grant that exceeds one's grasp but that paradoxically allows one to grasp.

Consider, as well, Pascal's, *the heart has its reasons that the reason does not know*. We see here that the heart is not unreasonable but exceeds reason, and has access to a generosity and fullness of being that reason alone does not reach.

Yet another reference to consider with respect to how meaning exceeds human capacity comes from Viktor Frankl. He writes: "What is demanded of man is not, as some existential philosophers teach, to endure the meaninglessness of life, but rather to bear his incapacity to grasp its unconditional meaningfulness in rational terms. Logos is deeper than logic" (Frankl, Viktor, *Man's Search for Meaning*, translated by Ilse Lasch, Boston, Beacon Press, 2006, first published in English 1959, first published in German in 1946, 118).

[60] By *descent* and *ascent* of hierarchy we mean the descent or service of the higher for the lower, and the ascent of lower in its deferral to, and participation with the higher.

[61] See section "M" below, for discussion on the harshness of the superego.

[62] As long as we are within time – which is where psychotherapy takes place – we have hope. Consider Hans Urs von Balthasar's theological perspective on this issue as analogous to that which we are approaching from a philosophical and psychological/psychotherapeutic perspective: *Dare We Hope that All Men Be Saved*, San Francisco, Ignatius Press, 1988.

[63] In other words, where we find time we also *always* find hope: this *always* is the sense of *eternity* (akin to what we earlier called *positive permanence*) that enters time; an entry that is the *origin* of hierarchy (by this we mean that the patterns of hierarchy ultimately come from or depend upon the differentiation of eternity and time, the heavens and the earth, etc.). In a sense the wound is itself this openness of time to the trans-temporal, an openness that makes of time a healing time.

[64] Let us reconsider, at this point, what role (secondary) suspicion ought to have with respect to the wound. Suspicion is to be directed against all forms of despair, subtle or obvious, covert or overt, which attack the truth that the wound is enclosed by a living body (co-extensive with a living community), and that it is intrinsically open to the opportunity to renew and strengthen life in relationship – which means life in the complementarity of freedom and communion. On this do we found the hermeneutics of belief, and in view of stopping or negating an ultimate despair that would reject such complementarity, do we allow a (secondary) hermeneutics of suspicion.

When we compare what we are proposing to the views of Ricoeur's three Masters of Suspicion one might suggest that we are simply replacing the explanatory substratum in each of their systems with our own. Instead of the economic and social class factors of Marx, the will to power of Nietzsche, or the id of Freud we speak of the complementarity of being and relation (and the integration of hierarchy associated with this). It is the case that this complementarity has analogous explanatory significance for us. It could also be argued that we too are suspicious of what does not agree with our emphasis. Indeed, we are suspicious of that which radically negates complementarity, just as Marx is suspicious of ideologies that obscure the *actual* nature of class struggle, Nietzsche of the alleged slave morality that presumably would inhibit the super man, and Freud of the pretense in the conscious mind that disguises the rule of unconscious instinctual drives. We do not believe, however, that our proposal follows the essential pattern or structure proposed by the Masters of Suspicion. The main difference is that we do not give priority to that to which (primary) suspicion orients one. Dialectical materialism, will to power and instinctual drive all refer to an origin in conflict, and the positing of such an origin has one start the process of interpretation with primary suspicion. We recognise conflict, but not in the origin. There is not, in our view, an original conflict or some form of irreconcilability between distinction (of being) and relation (of one to another). There is original accord, compatibility, complementarity and harmony. Any conflict comes, not *in the beginning*, but *afterwards* (an *afterwards* or *wound* that is itself oriented to an ultimate healing). The priority thus remains with the accord and, consequently, favours an interpretive process that begins with belief – we are proposing here that belief, in a sense, arises from, or is rooted in ontological accord.

---

[65] Consider the notion of "hitting bottom" in AA. This notion makes sense retrospectively but would become foolish and cynical if applied prospectively. The wisdom of a retrospective application rests on a confidence that a meaningful way is offered to one even and sometimes especially in moments of extreme powerlessness. The foolishness and cynicism of a prospective application lies in reducing value to a pragmatic principle that ultimately undermines meaning (i.e. within an outlook that is primarily pragmatic, mere hierarchy or power is given priority over meaning: truth is reduced to "cash value," as it were).

[66] Lorenzo Albacete writes in *God at the Ritz* (p. 88): "suffering is the cry of meaning in the human heart refusing to be defined by any power. Suffering then is a sign of hope."

[67] We employ this term in some ways similar to Kenneth Schmitz' use of "mixture of reality." With that term he refers to "those clouds and shadows that are part of the reality of the make-up of each of us," that involve negations and privations through which the "texture of being [nevertheless] shines with its positive values." By "negations" he means the limits that naturally define any entity, whereas by "privations" he means that which ought not to be (Schmitz, Kenneth L, *Person and Psyche*, p. 31).

[68] We should emphasise that, in this essay, when we refer to *wound*, we intend something whose ultimate intelligibility occurs in a personal and interpersonal/relational context. In other words, the ultimate meaning of the wound is as a wound of a person (or persons) that is, moreover, always, at least implicitly, shared (since being a person involves, intrinsically, in addition to distinction, sharing in relation).

[69] Love is a feature associated with the wound because the wound, even in its weakness, tends towards healing. This love involves both receiving love (being loved) and giving love (loving). If I am wounded, then it follows that I share in, or am touched by the loving that is the healing tendency in my wounded state. Moreover, if I discover that I love, then I ought to recognise that, firstly, I *am loved* (as a human being, before I love, I am ontologically or in principle loved, and it is this being-loved that grants me existence and freedom – if *I am* it is because I am being given being or being loved into being). One has to see beyond Sartre's "existence precedes essence" to the given or gifted nature of both existence and essence (Sartre writes about this in his famous paper, "Existentialism is a Humanism," originally given by him as a lecture in 1946; see: Kaufmann, Walter, *Existentialism from Dostoevsky to Sartre,* New York, New American Library, 1975, p. 345-369). And if I am loved (and receive this love in freedom), then the love I in turn (freely) express is actually a

response to being loved (and love then *increases* through mutuality). Consider that the terrible *waste* of the past (associated with regret, victimisation, and essentially due to the failure or lack of love in that past) must be overcome by challenging the even *greater* waste (or lack of love) of the present. The greater threat is not that I do not receive what is due to me, but that I respond to such injustice with a despair about what I am currently given and fail to consider what I may in turn currently give. And my concern with giving (including, ultimately, my regret about my failures or my anger about injustice) is *proof* (if priority goes to faith) that I have received what I need in order to be and continue to be who I am, a *receiver* who is, therefore, also a *giver* of love.

[70] *Weakness* here refers to my experience of limited or diminished strength to express my freedom as a power to make things be as I choose: my weakness to be an *agent of being*, as it were. Yet, by engaging my freedom in relationship in the context of experiencing a weakness I cannot avoid, my freedom is strengthened by the meaningfulness of relationship. Relationship confers its strength onto my weakness. One may also consider that there could be a reciprocal expression of this *healing through weakness*, where the weakness is not present in terms of diminished freedom of action (i.e. as an agent of being) but in terms of failed or damaged relationship. In that case, there is a sense in which failed or damaged relationship can be *equalised* and strengthened via acts of freedom – examples of which would be acts of freedom involving generosity such as altruistic giving or forgiveness. In some ways all acts of healing involve reciprocal influences of complementarity, with the emphasis being sometimes on one, sometimes the other side of the *equation* (i.e. sometimes on freedom, sometimes on relation).

[71] As we will go on to discuss, this engagement in the deepening of love will depend on attitudes and actions rooted in belief or trust in relationship; belief and trust speak to transcendence and surrender, not mere immanent control; with love there is a willingness to grow beyond the apparent safety of knowledge and mastery.

[72] Although writing in a different context, Jacques Philippe expresses an idea similar to the one we propose, where he says, "The exercise of human freedom is arbitrary and trivial unless it is a response to an invitation from something that transcends it" (Philippe, Jacques, *Called to Life*, translated by Neal Carter, New York, Scepter, 2008, fourth printing 2012, p. 5).

[73] In corollary fashion a "love" relationship that imposes unity in a manner that crushes freedom also demonstrates breach rather than accord, immanence rather than transcendence, inequality rather than equality.

Thus, when love does not *accord, transcend and equalise* with freedom, and vice-versa, when freedom does not *accord, transcend and equalise* with love, one notes a respective failure of love and freedom. Freedom and love fail to be freedom and love when their accord, mutual transcendence and equality fail. But in the above we are considering how love may grant or confer its equality to freedom when the latter finds itself diminished or even powerless. One may also consider that freedom could grant or confer its equality to a weakened love. Consider in this respect the words of St. John of the Cross: "Where there is no love *put* love, and you will harvest love" (italics added; quoted by Jacques Philippe in *Interior Freedom*, translated by Helena Scott, New York, Scepter, 2007, p. 74). Then, in viewing complementarity as a whole, one may say that, in the healing of the wound, the complements *equalise* one another.

[74] See Jacques Philippe discussion of freedom in *Interior Freedom* (p. 56-57 in particular).

[75] We made an earlier reference to the Star Trek movies in which Kirk and Spock have an exchange on the sacrifice of the few for the many and the many for the one. It is of interest to note that in *The Wrath Khan* Admiral Kirk receives, as a gift from Spock, a copy of the book *A Tale of Two Cities*, and repeats some of the words of Sydney Carton in the final scene of the movie when the casket containing Spock's body is sent into space and lands on a planet on which new life is beginning.

[76] We could elaborate "one is powerless to change" by adding that this refers to situations, issues or problems which the mere exercise of power cannot change; such situations, issues or problems call for trust in the accord or complementarity of freedom and love.

[77] It is beyond our scope to address questions pertaining to universal human rights, but we would offer that the distinction we are proposing speaks to different ways in which one might approach universality: there is a generic and abstract kind of universality, in which the highest expression of freedom is the indefinite, and there is a universal and concrete kind of universality in which freedom flows from the call to engagement, solidarity, sharing. The highest expression of the latter kind of freedom involves commitment that combines right with obligation, freedom with love. The highest expression of the former (indefinite) kind of freedom involves, possibly, some kind of neutrality or indifference with respect to the concrete expression of freedom. In this essay we emphasise the hierarchy of power and right in which the priority is to be given to right. This implies that any neutrality or indifference involved in the notion of freedom is similarly to give way to, and take its norm from commitment to relationship. We will further consider below how freedom cannot be

ultimately or radically separated from the truth of love without a loss or failure of freedom.

[78] See section, "C-ii" above for discussion of how complementarity constitutes the norm of hierarchy.

[79] In *The Need for Roots: Prelude to a Declaration of Duties towards Mankind,* which Simone Weil wrote shortly before her death in 1943 at the age of 34, she says: "The notion of obligations comes before that of rights, which is subordinate and relative to the former. A right is not effectual by itself, but only in relation to the obligation to which it corresponds, the effective exercise of a right springing not from the individual who possesses it, but from other men who consider themselves as being under a certain obligation towards him. Recognition of an obligation makes it effectual. An obligation which goes unrecognized by anybody loses none of the full force of its existence. A right which goes unrecognized by anybody is not worth very much" (Weil, Simone, *The Need for Roots: Prelude to a Declaration of Duties towards Mankind,* preface by T.S. Eliot, translated by Arthur Wils, Routledge Classics, London, 2002; first published in English by Routledge & Kegan Paul, 1952. p. 3).

[80] See previous discussion of collective and individual aspects of complementarity above in the section, "C-ii-b & -c."

[81] See above: "C-ii."

[82] Our distinction between power and right resonates well, we believe, with the framework proposed by Viktor Frankl, in which he differentiates the three Viennese schools of psychotherapy: the school of psychoanalysis, founded by Freud, the school of individual psychology, founded by Adler, and the school of logotherapy, founded by Frankl, himself. He speaks of three basic modes of human motivation and relationship, respectively associated with these schools: *will to pleasure, will to power,* and *will to meaning.* The consideration that the human being is oriented by will to meaning is central to Frankl's psychotherapeutic approach, which he calls *logotherapy* or meaning-therapy (Frankl, Viktor, *The Doctor and the Soul,* translated by Richard and Clara Winston, Toronto, Bantam Books, 1955, p. x). We could say that limiting human freedom to pleasure and power fails to do justice to authentic freedom, which is not solely oriented towards pleasure or power but to meaning. We note a tendency in the modern zeitgeist to reduce freedom to the mere power of choice, without consideration of that to which the choice is linked (including consideration of the reality of the human person, which is the basis of the reason one ought to respect freedom of choice to start with). Thus, this not only eclipses the will to meaning, but it fails to recognise that that which grants

value to the will to power (and pleasure), and to the freedom to choose without coercion, that is such a central value in modernity.

[83] This question of power and right is also the question of the meaning of freedom. One notes the extremes that have arisen in addressing this question: from those views that would abolish freedom by proposing various forms of determinism to those views that would (effectively and more subtly) abolish freedom as a result of proposing restricting human freedom to an individualistically conceived private sphere.

[84] This individualist emphasis finds expression in the politically and ethically unchecked influence of economic forces, whose power is defended on the basis of the *rights* of individuals to wield economic influence as they choose: competition is given priority over co-operation. Another example is the eugenic practices on a seeming *individual* basis (as opposed to the explicitly collective proposals and measures of the early to mid-twentieth century), not only to control undesirable defects in human offspring (by elimination of those humans), but also to control normal characteristics – sometimes viewed as undesirable – such as female gender.

[85] Hart, David Bentley, *Atheist Delusions: The Christian Revolution and Its Fashionable Enemies*, London, Yale University Press, 2009, p. 6.

There are many examples of this inversion in which it is said that meaning has to be invented or created either individually or collectively. On the other hand, Viktor Frankl provides a perspective that emphasises meaning as a given, as something to discover. He noted, for example, that we are not to find the courage to learn to face the ultimate meaninglessness of our lives, but the courage to learn to endure our inability to fully comprehend ultimate meaningfulness (Frankl, *Man's Search for Meaning,* p. 141).

[86] See: Weil, *The Need for Roots*, p. 3.

[87] It is interesting to note how constructivists and constructionists equate declaration (of truth) with truth and therefore create a perspective basically rooted in the triumph of the power to declare. This is an idolatry of power that rejects any other principles above itself: other principles such as truth and love (e.g. the obligation to respect and care about the dignity of human persons).

[88] How often are we mesmerised by the dominance, in human affairs, of power that disregards human rights, and then mistakenly declare this dominant power as the norm, thereby failing to distinguish the prevalent from the true?

[89] See essay by George Grant on Nietzsche, "Nietzsche and the Ancients." Grant writes: "There is no escape from reading Nietzsche if one would understand modernity. Some part of his whole meets us whenever we listen to what our contemporaries are saying when they speak as moderns"

(Grant, George, "Nietzsche and the Ancients: Philosophy and Scholarship," in *Technology and Justice*, Toronto, Anansi Press,1986, p. 79-95, see: p. 89).

There is some resonance between our manner of explicating power and right, and Max Scheler's discussion of what he called the *classical and the negative theories of man.* He views the negative theory as proposing that the spirit arises from the negation of nature, that is, in the negation of the more primitive anterior stages of development. He associates this *negative theory* with such thinkers as Buddha, Schopenhauer, and Freud. For Schopenhauer, for example, the source of all "superior forms" of knowledge and consciousness is the negation of the will-to-live of which humans are capable, a "liberating" negation animals are unable to accomplish. Scheler argues that, similarly for Freud, the repression and sublimation of instinct *is* the explanation of the formation of human culture. Scheler sees the *classical theory* (which he assigns not only to Aristotle, Plato and to Judeo-Christian belief, but also to Fichte and Hegel), on the other hand, as proposing that the spirit possesses an original activity and capacity to act. Scheler challenges the negative theory by arguing that that which it claims to explain via negation, it presupposes. Thus, he proposes that the reason libidinal energy is repressed and sublimated has to do with the spiritual values that such negation is supposed to generate. He is also critical, however, of the classical theory, in that he does not accept its claim that the spirit possesses an original activity and capacity to act. His resolution of the conflict or quandary he sees between the classical and negative theory involves asserting that in principle or at the origin there is a *powerful*, demoniacal, blind force of nature, as well as a *powerless*, yet somehow *informative* spirit (one is reminded here of Rabbi Kushner's' proposal of a non-omnipotent God, which Kushner is offering as a solution to the problem of the suffering of innocent human beings – this issue is further discussed in endnote # "103" below). In Scheler's perspective the interpenetration of a powerful, if blind, life force, and an *informative*, if powerless, spirit, contributes to development.

We see value in Scheler's attempt to consider how human life is based on the complementarity – or indeed, *hierarchy* – of the natural world and the spirit; however, we do not see him as really going beyond the negative theory he critiques. His nature is "demoniacal" and blind and his spirit is fundamentally or inherently powerless. The higher spirit takes its power from the lower life-force. The lower life-force takes its meaning from the spirit. In our own approach we see a relation of service in hierarchy that does not exclude power. The spirit can indeed be powerless or helpless because it is within the power of the spirit to be gentle: e.g. the father of the Prodigal Son. Moreover, the power of nature is itself a gift, a given; therefore, when we recognise power in nature we cannot conceive of it as lacking a link to the spirit which has it be. We could also say that the power of nature is only blind and demoniacal in its separation from the accord of freedom and relation, and in the disintegration associated with the failure of service. We disagree, consequently with Scheler's notion of an original combination of a powerless spirit and a demoniacal nature or life force. The disintegration of hierarchy may render spirit powerless and power demoniacal, but such is the result of disintegration. In our view, to approach such disintegration meaningfully calls for an appreciation of an original and ultimate complementarity, and an original and ultimate integration in which spirit *serves* power and power *defers* to spirit (Scheler, Max, *La situation de l'homme dans le monde*, translated by M. Dupuy, Paris, Editions Montaigne, 1951, p. 77-90).

[90] Williams, Bernard, *Truth and Truthfulness: An Essay in Genealogy*, Princeton, Princeton University Press, 2002, p. 12-19.

[91] Nietzsche, Friedrich, *The Antichrist*, 1888, section 52; quoted by Kaufmann, Walter, *Existentialism from Dostoevsky to Sartre,* New York, New American Library, 1975, p. 19.

[92] We have mentioned this notion previously, and will elaborate on it below in the section "O" titled, "Healing via Hopeful Acceptance of All Outcomes."

[93] See: Hanby, Michael, "Absolute Pluralism: How the Dictatorship of Relativism Dictates," *Communio*, Summer-Fall 2013, Volume XI, Number 2-3, p. 542-576; in particular, see: p. 571.

[94] This speaks to the complementarity of love and truth. The relation of love depends on truth in order for such relation to be loving, and the relation of truth depends on love in order to be true. Thus one may speak of a dialogue of love and a dialogue of truth, or indeed a dialogue in love and truth. See the report on an interview with Ecumenical Patriarch Bartholomew regarding relations between Roman Catholicism and Orthodoxy on the occasion of the visit of Pope Francis to the Holy Land. The Patriarch emphasises the need for a "dialogue of truth" *and* a "dialogue of love." See article in Osservatore Romano May 24-25, 2014: http://www.news.va/en/news/on-the-eve-of-the-popes-trip-to-the-holy-land-inte.

[95] We should add that we are not suggesting that the principle of complementarity is easy or straightforward in its application, only that it is a principle which both person and society, individual and community, should strive to apply.

[96] See Jacques Philippe, *Interior Freedom* (p. 58). On p. 76 he quotes Christiane Singer.

[97] Frankl, *Man's Search for Meaning*, p. 130.

[98] See: *Minnick's Klein Academy: Melanie Klein's Models for Understanding the Baby Core of the Personality,* "The Manic Defense," by Chris L. Minnick M.D., 2014;

http://minnickskleinacademy.com/module-2-2-kleins-baby-core-coping-defensive-maneuvers/manic-defense/

[99] The interpretative process in psychoanalytic therapy aims at unmasking the role of defences, and thus freeing the person from excessive ego defensiveness. We will discuss in a later section ("L") of this essay our own proposal of a more comprehensive vision of defence, as fundamentally involving more than ego defence; we also discuss this issue in the first essay in this book.

[100] Antonio Lopez, "Christian Culture and the Form of Human Existence," *Communio*, 40, Summer-Fall 2013, p. 473-509; see: p. 491.

[101] As noted earlier, an authentic power is one in which freedom and good come together in truth; a freedom divorced from good – i.e. reduced to mere power of choice – is a failure of freedom.

[102] One may interpret Nietzsche's vision of power with reference to Klein's explication of manic defences. In a sense, Klein's manic/*omnipotent* defences of control, contempt and triumph all involve a denial of relationship. One may see such defensiveness in a variety of forms, from substance abuse to sexual abuse, from extreme insularity or withdrawal from others to manipulative or even tyrannical approaches to others. In all cases where there is some form of denial of relationship one may see indications of inauthentic or false omnipotence. But we propose above a distinction between inauthentic or false omnipotence, on the one hand, and authentic or true omnipotence, on the other. If true omnipotence is reflected in the "gift of oneself to the end for the sake of another" (Lopez), then one may interpret the false mastery that denies the other in order to affirm the self as a misguided quest for true mastery; in *true mastery* one *denies* the self in order to affirm the other, a *denial* that is also *affirmation*. In other words, an authentic denial of self is also an authentic affirmation of self. Consequently, mastery or affirmation of self is not necessarily cancelled in powerlessness; this is an option that Nietzsche seems to view with disbelief or suspicion, if not with contempt. He speaks of those who are noble, self-glorifying, with power over self and others vs. those who are contemptible, cowardly, "intent on narrow utility." He thus distinguishes the master and slave morality (see: Kaufmann, Walter, *From Shakespeare to Existentialism*, Garden City, New York, Doubleday and Company, 1960, p.208-214). As we noted previously, Nietzsche may have been seeking meaningful expressions of power, but in our view, this cannot

be done via a glorification of power, nor a rejection of the notion that meaning (including the deeper meaning of power itself: as expressed in the notion of *hierarchy/anarchy within hierarchy*) is also to be found in weakness and powerlessness.

[103] Here we would have to disagree with Rabbi Kushner's hypothesis of a non-omnipotent God as the way to explain *When Bad Things Happen to Good People.* (New York: Anchor Books, 2004; originally published in 1981). Admittedly, one confronts a mystery in the omnipotent God's granting of any sort of fundamental freedom or autonomy to his creature. In our view, however, one cannot claim that omnipotence is radically absent from the experience of powerlessness and abandonment, even if the mix we thereby confront of omnipotence and powerlessness is a paradox and mystery. Indeed, when it comes to love, the reach and meaning of a genuine power – one that expresses love and is in conformity with right – cannot be restricted to powerful displays alone. In other words, if authentic power is rooted in love, then love, not power constitutes the ultimate meaning and norm of power itself. Kushner himself recognises the transcendence of faith, and how it puts one in touch with dimensions of life that reason or science alone (i.e. factors that allow us to exercise power or control over things) does not grasp. In fact, it seems to us that at times Kushner is more attempting to make room for a religious attitude in which one may relate to a God whom one cannot master (in contradistinction to a God whom one might master like one masters a product of technology), than limiting the omnipotence of God. In that respect, he is less seeing or proposing a limit to God's omnipotence than a limit to human power. See another of his books, *Who Needs God?* New York: Summit Books, 1989, for an insightful examination of these themes.

Moreover, one may also find greater signs of omnipotence in powerlessness and poverty than in human power and riches. Consider: "Not to be limited by the greatest but to be contained in the tiniest – this is the divine" (Ignatius of Loyola: reference in "A Big Heart Open to God: A Conversation with Pope Francis." Interviewer: Antonio Spadero, S.J., *America: The National Catholic Review*, September 30, 2013, http://www.americamagazine.org/pope-interview).

[104] This identification of power emptied of meaning (power that is therefore blind), on the one hand, with empty powerlessness, on the other, may remind one of the Hegelian dialectic in which being and nothingness are identified. Schmitz comments regarding understandings that employ a Hegelian dialectic, "In these understandings, being has been confined within the polarities of rational thought, between the universal and the particular, so that an all-important factor has been assumed but not

articulated, and so overlooked." Schmitz goes on to articulate a more comprehensive understanding of *being* such that one may recognise in it the "actuality of presence." It is this "wonder of presence," we would suggest, that can manifest itself not only in moments during which one may exercise power but also in concrete experiences of powerlessness (Schmitz, *Psyche and Person*, p. 2-3).

[105] We place *consent* in italics here, because a consent to hopelessness is ontologically a failure of consent, a failure of freedom.

[106] For freedom to be freedom requires a living, dynamic link between freedom and the responsibility to respect and promote relation. In asserting this link one is not diminishing the value of freedom or self-determination, nor restricting its scope. On the contrary, both in principle and practice, the value of freedom or self-determination must constantly be rooted (both in terms of origin and goal) on a love, solidarity and care that supports, nurtures, and promotes it. In other words, there is no authentic human freedom that is not, in some fundamental way, supported by, and oriented to relationship.

[107] Consider how psychoanalysis is a *talking cure*, that is, a form of healing that requires relationship, not just self-analysis. See the first essay in this book (section "A") for a consideration of how, in the early history of psychoanalysis there was some debate and ambiguity surrounding the question of whether an analyst needed to be analysed.

[108] Consider the following comment by J. Jacob Tawney on the themes of dialogue, power and truth:

> "There is a certain tendency in recent political circles to conceive 'dialog' as the process by which each party states his or her opinion, listens to the other without offering criticism or critique all in the service of a vague conception of 'tolerance,' and then a 'compromise' of sorts is arrived at, often in an arbitrary manner. Nowhere in this process is there room for objective truth guiding the discussion, and thus the term 'dialog' is inappropriate. 'Dialog,' after all, has as its root the concept of *logos*, meaning rational objective truth. The danger in conceiving of dialog in this errant manner is that it places the resolution in the hands of the more powerful, not the more truthful." See: Tawney, J. Jacob, "Content and Form: From Linguistics to Abstract Art," *Communio*, Winter, 2013, p. 818 (footnote 40).

[109] In our first essay, "Applying a Hermeneutics of Belief to the Understanding of Psychopathology," we discuss the ambiguity of the internal object in psychoanalytic theory: that is, the internal object is presented as both a sign of linkage to the other and a sign of defence or

withdrawal from relationship. One may note here a similar ambiguity with respect to the role of defence. Just as the internal object can express a link to the other so too can defence exceed self- or ego-defence.

[110] Frankl, Viktor, Video on "Realism and Idealism," http://www.youtube.com/watch?v=R_bjOeECpjl.

[111] Freud said of the ego: "The poor ego…serves three severe masters…the external world, the super-ego and the id" (*New Introductory Lectures on Psychoanalysis*, translated by James Starkey, 1965 (original published in 1933), New York, W.W. Norton and Company, p. 96-97).

[112] Collective self-interest of the bourgeoisie for Marx, self-interest of the slave class for Nietzsche, and autoerotism or narcissism for Freud are all presented as both expected and problematic by these Masters of Suspicion.

[113] Erikson, Erik, *Childhood and Society*, New York, W. W. Norton & Co., 1963 (original published in 1950), p. 264-265.

[114] The psychoanalyst interprets the ways in which defensive reactions express themselves in the person's life, and particularly in the ways these might find expression through the transference.

[115] Isaiah Berlin gives priority to this form of liberty, ostensibly to protect against totalitarianism or other forms of imposition that might flow from *positive* liberty. But to give priority to this *negative* aspect of liberty may lead to relativism, a position which Berlin seems to propose, in fact, in the concluding paragraph of his essay ("Two Concepts of Liberty"). It is difficult to see, however, how relativism can effectively protect any liberty, including negative liberty. For even negative liberty is rooted in a positive liberty in which one agrees not to force the other to act contrary to self-interest, in view of the *positive* acceptance of the other's human dignity. Berlin, it seems to us, confuses or does not sufficiently distinguish subjective and objective aspects of the "deep and incurable metaphysical need" which he dismisses as a quest "for the certainties of childhood or the absolute values of our primitive past." He thinks that to allow the "incurable metaphysical need" to influence one's practice "is a symptom of… [a] deep, and…dangerous, moral and political immaturity." He thereby, in our view, reduces or restricts this "metaphysical need" to the subjective sphere, thereby turning all positive liberty (including – without realising it – the expression of positive liberty required to promote negative liberty) into a matter of imposition of power (subject over object). Berlin is critical of the modern quest for subjective certainty, but he seems to implicitly accept the modernist fallacy that if one can demonstrate that a single metaphysical error has or might occur, then one is to retreat into the security of some kind of anti- or non-metaphysical framework: perhaps, the cogito of Descartes, the mind-minus-noumena of Kant, the positivism

of Comte, the dialectical materialism of Marx, the pragmatism of William James, the radical subjectivism of the constructivist, etc., or, indeed, the relativism of Berlin. Yet, it is only a metaphysics which validly (subjectively *and* objectively) identifies human dignity that can provide the basis for support of any political freedom, including the negative freedom which Berlin seeks to defend (Berlin, Isaiah, "Two Concepts of Liberty" 1958; in *Four Essays on Liberty*, Oxford, Oxford University Press, 1968; quoted passages are taken from the last paragraph).

[116] Here we may consider once again the conclusion reached by Jacques Philippe in *Called to Life*: "The exercise of human freedom is arbitrary and trivial unless it is a response to an invitation from something that transcends it" (p. 5). Philippe refers to a transcendence that involves relationship. He is speaking in a religious context, but we too have emphasised that transcendence is a feature of the complementarity in which freedom finds meaning (i.e. distinction transcends itself towards relation and relation towards distinction: see section "C-ii-b" above).

[117] By "requirement of complementarity" we mean a positon in which one respects freedom, because freedom is the complement of relationship. In other words, we consider a position in which one does not respect freedom, or in which freedom separates itself from the support of relationship to be a position that fails to meet the "requirement of complementarity."

[118] Freud, Sigmund, *Civilization and Its Discontents*, translated by J Riviere, Mansfield Centre, CT, Martino Publishing, 2010 (originally published New York, Jonathan Cape & Harrison Smith, 1930), p. 116; see also Perlow, Meir, *Understanding Mental Objects*, New York, Routledge, 1995, p. 16-23, & Hughes, Judith, *Reshaping the Psychoanalytic Domain*, Berkeley, University of California Press, 1989, p.58, for discussion of this topic.

[119] This is, perhaps, less a drive to die than a drive to return to *before life* (i.e. from dust to dust); it is an *anti-Eros* drive, as it were. The idea that death might be – in addition to a negation of life – a culminating and novel point in life (i.e. more than a return to nothingness: a potential passage or way to deeper fulfillment) is lacking in this conception.

[120] This breach of complementarity may also involve a corresponding breakdown of hierarchy in which power, competition and dominance eclipse meaning, co-operation and service.

[121] We may think of these as three steps of *working through*.

[122] In proposing an alternative explanation for the harshness of the superego we are emphasising how the presence (and, at times, escalation) of this harshness has two meanings: it indicates the negative effects of an

excessive insularity or auto-orientation, and it alerts one to the need and desire to remedy the negativity arising as a result of such insularity or auto-orientation. Note the difference between this explanation of superego harshness, and the explanation offered by invoking the death instinct. The death instinct is posited as a primal negative force, whereas the negativity arising from insularity is posited as the consequence of the failure of persons in relation, the failure of complementarity, the failure, that is, of something positive. Where the death instinct has an essentially negative origin and meaning, the negativity arising from insularity remains essentially linked to the positive meaning of complementarity, even if this link involves some degree of opposition. In addition, the death instinct presents as having an essentially negative aim, whereas the excessive insularity that leads to superego harshness ought to be interpreted in the context of a mix of positive and negative factors. That is to say, there is a mix of negative effect and positive aim: as noted above, harsh feelings express the negative effects of insularity, on the one hand, and the positive aim of seeking a remedy, on the other. In other words, the intensity of distress not only shows what is wrong; it also contains indications of what is and could be (further made) right.

[123] Frankl, Viktor, Video on "Realism and Idealism": http://www.youtube.com/watch?v=R_bjOeECpjI.

[124] Frankl, *Man's Search for Meaning*, p. 98-99.

[125] Ibid., p. 108. The quote is taken from Magda B. Arnold and John A. Gasson, *The Human Person*, Ronald Press, New York, 1954, p. 618.

[126] von Balthasar, Hans Urs, "Health between Science and Wisdom," *Communio*, Volume XLI, Number 3, Fall 2014, p. 666; taken from *Explorations in Theology*, Volume 5: *Man is Created*, translated by Adrian J. Walker, San Francisco: Ignatius Press, 2014.

[127] Frankl, Man's Search for Meaning, p. 108-109.

[128] Pope Francis, *Evangelii Gaudium*, November, 2013, # 231-233, http://w2.vatican.va/content/francesco/en/apost_exhortations/documents/papa-francesco_esortazione-ap_20131124_evangelii-gaudium.html.

[129] Frankl, *Man's Search for Meaning*, p 110-111.

[130] Pope Francis, *Evangelii Gaudium*, # 235.

[131] Frankl, Viktor, *The Unheard of Cry for Meaning,* New York, Simon and Schuster, 1978, p. 44-63.

[132] For a further discussion of this issue, see section "D" above, and see also, "Appendix C."

[133] The notion that the human universe is one of meaning is reminiscent of Teilhard de Chardin's concept of *noosphere*: the sphere of thought encircling the earth with the advent of human life (de Chardin, Teilhard,

The Phenomenon of Man, New York, Harper & Row, 1965, originally published in French in 1955, p. 180-184).

Also, consider this from Margaret Somerville: "Our human spirit is that which makes us human and enables us to experience amazement, wonder and awe at the mystery of life, and through it we reach for meaning. This search for meaning is of the essence of being human; we are meaning-seeking beings and, as far as we know, uniquely so. I believe everyone searches for meaning, even if they won't admit or perhaps, in some cases, don't recognize that is what they are doing" ("Building Ethical Bridges in a Secular Age" *Comment, Public Theology for the Common Good*, September 1, 2014, published by Cardus, http://www.cardus.ca/comment/article/4373/building-ethical-bridges-in-a-secular-age/).

[134] It is not the instinctual forces in themselves that pose the threat to the meaning or normality of complementarity, but the response one develops, in freedom, to their influence. Thus, interpretation, judgement, discernment and even psychological working through of the experience of instinctual drive will play a greater role than the mere force of the instinctual drive itself. In other words, the basic threat to my meaningful engagement will not stem, for example, from an angry feeling or reaction, but from the way in which I respond to and work through such a feeling, including, in particular, how I deal with the intrinsically human aim of this experience.

[135] Hanby, Michael, "Reconceiving the Organism: Why American Catholic Bioethics Needs a Better Theory of Human Life," *Communio*, 41, Fall 2014, p. 615-653; see: p. 651; Hanby is quoting David L. Schindler's *"Agere sequitur esse*: What Does It Mean? A Reply to Father Austriaco," *Communio: International Catholic Review* 32, Winter 2005, p. 805.

[136] Hanby, Michael, *No God, No Science?: Theology, Cosmology, Biology*, Chichester, West Sussex, Blackwell Publishing Ltd., 2013, p. 16.

[137] We are referring here to our previous exposition of normality or meaning in terms of the accord of complements and the integration of hierarchy. As previously discussed, it is interesting to consider that Frankl's threefold distinction of schools in terms of will to pleasure, power and meaning, could be framed hierarchically. Pleasure (e.g. instinctual release) and power (e.g. need for survival and status) would be lower on the hierarchy than meaning. Thus, incorporating these terms into the framework we propose, pleasure and power ought to *defer* to meaning, and meaning ought to *inform* and *serve* pleasure and power.

[138] As discussed previously, this accord refers to an original wholeness and to a striving for ultimate healing. The accord is a feature of *what ought to*

be that – in contradistinction to Hume's position on this matter – cannot be separated from *what is*. We will say more about Hume's distinction between *is* and *ought* in the last section of this essay (see: endnote # "155").

[139] To continue the analogy one may consider that the ontological given of which we speak not only shows signs of its presence in the background or context of one's troubled feelings – in the way that the corona of the eclipsed sun shows that the sun is present in the background behind the darkening disc of the moon. In addition, this ontological given speaks to the aim or direction of troubled feelings towards a desired or hoped for remedy – in the way that the coronal light presages the full splendor of the sun that is to appear when the eclipse has passed. We will further explore this question of *aim* below.

[140] Circumstances associated with feelings of insecurity, loss and injustice often call for an attitude of protest (i.e. a negation or suspicion of breach), which is *ipso facto* oriented to the restoration of healing. In other words, the troubled feelings associated with psychological symptoms involve, in some sense, a protest against that which might jeopardise complementarity, and, consequently, orient one to the healing influence of accord over the damaging influence of disaccord. As emphasised above, this accord is one of freedom and relationship (and analogous complements), whereas disaccord refers to the breach of such complementarity.

With respect to the role of human freedom in response to relationship, one may realise that, in the *mix of reality*, breach is, on the one hand, entirely possible, but, on the other, never necessary or inevitable. A hermeneutics of belief highlights the dramatic struggle of freedom in the experience of breach: the suffering of troubled feelings associated with breach always offers an opportunity to respond *freely* with either a further rejection of meaning or a deeper engagement with meaning.

[141] This is consistent with what we argued in the previous section regarding the harshness of the superego. This harshness (including its projected form expressed in hostility/harshness towards others) increases the more one tries to resolve it *solipsistically*; that is to say, it increases the more one stays insulated from reality beyond oneself. Only with openness beyond self or with a relational emphasis does it become possible to respond to the experience of harshness in a manner that may meaningfully modulate it.

[142] The meaning of complementarity is that which allows one to consider that the *useful* might be valuable, but it also allows one to see that the *useless* can be valuable (including the *uselessness* of meaning itself: meaning is *useless* because it is ever greater than *useful*, and thus not merely subject to the *useful*). And there are two senses to the *useless* here: 1) the *useless* includes that which exceeds human expectation, explanation,

practicality, that which demonstrates the sheer generosity and superabundance of being (consider how the world of art and beauty may be seen as *useless*); 2) the *useless* also includes that which fails to reach explanation because it contributes to the rupture of complementarity or meaning (i.e. failures of freedom or relationship). Moreover, the rupture of complementarity (lesser mystery) remains subject to the remedy of complementarity (greater mystery), but only to the extent that, as we have seen, the person in freedom, distinction and uniqueness, transcends himself or herself towards relational existence, and only to the extent that relational existence transcends itself in supporting the person in freedom, distinction and uniqueness (i.e. we have referred to this as an equality in transcendent accord). Thus, *empty uselessness* is to be essentially overshadowed and remedied by *full uselessness* (as, for example, seen in beauty).

[143] By *one* we intend, not just the solitary individual, but the one, unique person *in the context of relation with others*, and this relation with others occurs in turn *with reference to the one, unique person*. As well, we are not implying that, in each and every human experience of suffering one will have a clear vision of meaning. Indeed, lack of clarity with respect to meaning is often a feature of human suffering. We are implying, however, that there is a solidarity in human experience that allows one person to complete the experience of another, and that full intelligibility would, in some sense, require a grasp of all who have suffered and will suffer. Consequently, such intelligibility remains beyond the grasp that is immanent to the single individual, and beyond the grasp that is immanent to a given collectivity of individuals. This does not preclude, however, a participation with universal meaning through the hope and faith that depends on that *always* which allows the individual to transcend self towards the collective, and the collective to transcend itself towards the individual. It is this participation that draws together uniqueness and relationship.

[144] Recall our reference to *Star Trek* and the conversation between Kirk and Spock in which they speak of the needs of the many outweighing the needs of the few, and the needs of the one outweighing the needs of the many. The suffering or sacrifice of the one for the many, and of the many for the one speak to the transcendence (within *complementarity*) of self towards relation, and of relation towards self.

[145] To speak of complementarity as the *way* to address the suffering that results from the breach of complementarity may seem redundant, but, as we have been proposing, we see in suffering (of the wound) not only the sign of rupture but also the indication of a healing influence. As we have previously discussed, that influence speaks not only to an original

wholeness, but, as well, to the potential for a reconciliation greater than original wholeness.

[146] One may consider an analogous emphasis in the AA approach to the relation between sobriety and abstention from drinking. As crucial as abstaining from drinking alcohol might be for the alcoholic, it does not, in itself, confer sobriety. One may still, in AA terms, behave as a *dry drunk*: one's behaviour may still be ruled by addiction, by the lack of sobriety one sees, for example, in a failure of maturity, wisdom or respect for others. (With respect to the use of the term, "deference," in the above, one may consider that meaning *reigns* but also *serves*. Indeed, we saw, with respect to the notion of *hierarchy within hierarchy*, discussed previously, that to reign means to serve.)

[147] This caring about the other, because it is a caring for relationship, is also a caring for the self. Indeed, keeping in mind what we have said about complementarity, it follows that to care for relationship is the only way to care for self in a manner that respects one's own uniqueness and freedom.

[148] Let us consider, yet again, what Viktor Frankl says regarding what life asks of me rather that what I ask of life: "Ultimately, man should not ask what the meaning of his life is, but rather he must recognize that it is *he* who is asked." Frankl, *Man's Search for Meaning*, p. 109.

[149] Consider how with depression one often finds a lack of confidence, trust and hope that caring is possible, yet one also finds the longing for a time or circumstance (before loss occurred) in which caring was possible, and by implication, a longing for a time in which caring will become possible again.

[150] We noted earlier in this section that it may not always be possible, for a variety of reasons, to reach agreement with an opposing party, but also noted that this does not alter the fundamentally relational character of the remedy towards which anger is ultimately oriented – if anger is interpreted in the context of a hermeneutics of belief. In addition, by placing an emphasis on an ultimate remedy to anger one is not to diminish – indeed, one ought to amplify – one's attention to, or concern about the destructive potential of anger.

[151] I may recognise that there is a reasonableness to believing in a trusted connection or a meaningful world, even in the face of rupture and meaninglessness. Moreover, in my own past experience, or in the example of the experiences of others, I may recognise a witness to how troubling events and failures of meaning did not cancel the opportunity to respond meaningfully. Yet, each new circumstance calls for more than a recall of the past and of others' good example; it calls for trust and belief that one has *now* an opportunity to participate in changing, accepting and living in a

way that accords with the world of meaning, a world of meaning that
envelops and penetrates one's life in the present.
[152] We may again consider here the oft-quoted statement by Pascal: "The
heart has its reasons which the reason does not know," or another reference
regarding the limits of reason, expressed with humour by Chesterton: "The
madman is not someone who has lost his reason. The madman is someone
who has lost everything but his reason" (the passage is found in G. K.
Chesterton's book, *Orthodoxy*, Chapter II; see *The Collected Works of
Chesterton, Volume I*, David Dooley, Editor, San Francisco, Ignatius Press,
1986, p. 222; Josef Pieper refers to this passage in his book, *Leisure, The
Basis of Culture*, translated by Alexander Dru, New York, New American
Library, 1952, p. 102). Consider as well a statement that also, in its own
paradoxical way, speaks to the transcendence of reason as reasonable; it is
a statement by Lessing, quoted by Viktor Frankl: "There are things which
must cause you to lose your reason or you have none to lose" (Frankl,
Man's Search for Meaning, p. 20).

These passages speak to the transcendence of reason, but we must also
consider how reason is to be meaningfully integrated with that which
transcends it. Reason or thought cut off from reality or being is madness,
but if being is generous to thought (recall, Schmitz' *ontological generosity*;
"Enriching the Copula," p. 511-512; Chesterton also said, "Thanks are the
highest form of thought": Chesterton, G. K., *A Short History of England*,
London, Chatto & Windus, 1917, p. 59), then the epistemological moment
can find its value and integration by deferring to being or truth (to the
ontological/metaphysical moment). Moreover, if our notion of hierarchy
applies to the relation between thought and reality, between epistemology
and ontology, then the lower (epistemology/ideas) ought to defer to the
higher (ontology/realities), but the higher ought also to *serve* (ought to be
generous to) the lower (see "Appendix C").
[153] One might raise objections or concerns about giving priority to faith
over reason or knowledge. One may believe that this will lead to various
kinds of fundamentalism or forms of fideism. Moreover, the latter
inclinations involve, not only a tendency towards irrationalism, but may
also, at times, demonstrate a tendency towards violence. There is some
complexity to this question and it is beyond our scope here to provide a
comprehensive discussion. We wish to emphasise, however, that
movements based in fundamentalism and fideism are often more similar
than dissimilar to scientistic or exclusively rationalist approaches. Indeed,
fundamentalism or fideism is more akin to narrow rationalist and narrow
scientific perspectives than different from them. There are, for example,
more similarities than differences between the approaches of literal biblical

creationists and the evolutionists with whom they tend to engage in debate. What is striking is the literalness and *fact*-bound approach each side takes. One reads the scripture only literally, and the other reads nature only literally. The exclusively *literal* approach seems to limit access to the depths of value and meaning that both scriptures and nature have to offer. [154] An understanding that is *balanced* is an understanding that is open to the inherent complementarity of human experience.

[155] To put it in ontological terms, we could say that the greater mystery stems from Leibniz and Heidegger's *why there is something rather than nothing,* why – we could elaborate – there is sheer generosity in being, a generosity whose eminent expression is not only the presence of *something rather than nothing*, but also the presence of *someone rather than no-one*. Moreover, we have proposed that this generosity is the norm of relationship. We have noted that the lesser mystery is that such being (-in-relationship) fails to be, and as human beings we share in that failure, both actively and passively. To speak of *failure to be*, however, implies an *ought to be*, an *ought to be* that arises from the complementarity inherent in being.

Some (traditionally Hume) dismiss the notion that an *ought* arises from an *is*. Yet, as human beings, we inevitably recognise the *ought to be* of things: even the most convinced cynics and sceptics, the most suspicious and doubtful, who (like Hume) claim that things, as they are, *ought* not to be viewed as having any *ought to be* in them, have, of course, already ventured into the world of *ought* in defining how the world of *is* ought to be *evaluated*. Sometimes proponents of this form of scepticism will suggest that the type of argument that we are making in response to them – that an *ought* arises from an *is* because one has to appeal to an *ought* in distinguishing *ought* from *is* – could be used to claim the existence of anything we might think up. They might argue that making a reference to the concept of *ought* does not make the *ought* ontological or real (i.e. part of what is), and they might suggest, by analogy for example, that mentioning leprechauns does not prove that they exist as real creatures. That analogy does not, however, capture the true irony found with extreme scepticism and with the radical separation of *ought* from *is*. In our view, an appropriate analogy would be one where one would have to somehow make use of an actual leprechaun in one's attempt to prove that such a creature did not exist. In other words, we are suggesting that one cannot escape asserting the reality of *ought* when contemplating the *is*. Even in declaring that something is a mere, brute fact, without any question of value as a feature of its existence, one *evaluates*. One is saying, "This thing occupies the place of the merely empirical, it is a mere fact; that is, its value is in its *non-value*." The irony in such a declaration (in which one adopts the position of denying the ontological basis of value) is akin to the sceptic's insistence that there is no truth, and that such is *truly* so! If I have to rely on truth to deny the truth, then my denial would appear to be an error; if I have to imply there is *value in being* to deny that value is a feature of *being*, then my denial would appear to be an error. Nevertheless, one might still argue at this point – with some validity perhaps – that the *is* proposed by Hume, as merely empirical or factual, has no inherent value (indeed, by definition), and that we are somehow trying to introduce value (an *ought*) where there is none (i.e. where we have only an *is minus ought*, as it were). One could agree that this is so, but note that it is so by definition or design. It is akin to agreeing that the parts of a frog that have been subject to dissection in biology lab no longer have the life of the frog in them: such is true, but only because the frog has been killed and dissected. In other words, an empirical datum or fact becomes *merely* fact or *merely* empirical as a result of a defining action or conceptual operation; it is not a *mere fact* as a feature of actual (one could say, *original*) experience (just as the parts of the frog were not lacking life when they were still in the living frog). When *ought* is withdrawn from *is*, *is* is reduced to a mere fact or to the merely empirical; *ought* is thereby banished, as it were, usually to the subjective/emotional/mental sphere or to the sphere of pragmatic function (i.e. for Hume, to *sentiment*). There is further irony in this because the banishment to subjectivity or pragmatics is itself the product of a subjective or pragmatic operation: value is thus said to be subjective or pragmatic because one has declared it to be so for subjective or pragmatic reasons (or, indeed, for logical reasons in which logic and reason are circumscribed or separated from logos and being, epistemology from ontology). Envisioning the empirical realm in this way, however, is neither a way to remain true to objective reality nor is it a way to remain true to human experience. It is a subjective operation which reduces the empirical to a conceptual derivation arising, precisely, from analytically separating fact from value (see Appendix B, endnote "1," for further discussion of this issue). However useful such a dissection might be, the whole remains greater than the sum of its parts. A reductive separation may have its place or purpose (e.g. in some investigations of natural science such as the study of physiology or anatomy), but one need not essentially nor generally reduce the realities of human experience to the merely empirical, the merely functional, the merely controllable, the merely logical, or the merely subjective in this way. In fact, in the current zeitgeist one may need to guard against this kind of reduction of reality in order to protect the whole, and so that the merely empirical, the merely practical, and the merely rational do not become a runaway train.

We would further propose that there is no *is* except in relation. *Ought* is derived from the complementary nature of self-other, in contradistinction to self or other, *per se*....the truth of self is distinction-relation....the truth of other is distinction-relation...the *ought* is not solely obligation to other...rather it includes consent to the gift of relation...consent to accept this gift. To dissent, to deny the gift, is to deny truth, to deny freedom. The *is* is truth...the *ought* is its acceptance. The *ought* is truth...the *is* is its foundation. If to be is to be free ("[t]he very rhythm of being itself pulses with...ontological freedom," Schmitz, *The Recovery of Wonder*, p. 104), then the complementarity (of *is* and *ought*) of being-free and being-in-relation demonstrates that truth involves the intimate connection of freedom and the good of relationship, freedom and the good of the other. In other words, "[t]he ties of love call freedom into existence and freedom exists in view of the ties of love" (Carelli, Roberto, *L'uomo e la donna nella teologia di H. U. von Balthasar*, EUPRESS FTL, Lugano – Reggiani SpA, Varese, 2007, p. 11, translation by authors). Consider that "[i]t is much greater and truer...to embrace reality and being rather than assert oneself against them" (this passage is from, Giussani, Luigi, *The Religious Sense*, translated by John Zucchi, McGill-Queen's University Press, Montreal, 1998, p. 10).

We should note that the argument we are making above against separating *is* from *ought* in a radical manner – and in favour of an essential complementarity between them – leads to partial agreement (but also partial disagreement) with both those who critique the *naturalistic fallacy* and with the proponents of *naturalistic ethics*. To speak in terms of the frog analogy discussed above, the naturalistic fallacy would be like saying that one can put the dissected parts of the frog together and return to the living frog. On the other hand, the proponents of naturalistic ethics tend to say that the *ought* somehow does originate in the reality of nature. The problem with naturalistic ethics, however, is that one is mistakenly looking for that reality, not in the living frog, but primarily in the dissected parts, that is, through a reductive vision of the human experience of (and connection with) nature and, consequently, a reductive vision of the nature of the human (e.g. evolutionary psychology, social Darwinism, utilitarianism...).

APPENDIX A

A SYNOPSIS OF
"APPLYING A HERMENEUTICS OF BELIEF TO
THE UNDERSTANDING OF PSYCHOPATHOLOGY"

A *Introduction*

The intent of this synopsis or digest is to provide a more straightforward rendition of the key issues that we address in our first essay in this book, "Applying a Hermeneutics of Belief to the Understanding of Psychopathology." We have also limited endnotes in this synopsis and refer the reader to the original essay and to the "Bibliography" at the back of this book for more complete information on sources.

In the original essay we seek to establish a philosophical basis for understanding psychological normality and abnormality, in which we emphasise basic ontological/relational aspects of human experience. This does not exclude definitions of "normality" that refer to personal opinion, social convention, statistical average, or even historical context. Rather we attempt a more fundamental formulation on the basis of which one might evaluate such other definitions.

We propose that there is a basic accord between what it means *to be* and *to relate*, and that this accord, agreement or complementarity constitutes normality. We also propose that disaccord, disagreement and disharmony (i.e. *anti-complementarity*) between *being* and *relation* constitute core aspects of abnormality, and that these aspects underlie more conventional definitions of abnormality in the field of psychopathology, such as mood or anxiety disorders. This appeal to being and relation (and their accord or complementarity) may seem somewhat abstract, but we believe these terms capture important and universal aspects pertaining to questions of psychological normality and abnormality. We will outline and summarise in what follows how we explain and develop our proposal regarding the normal and the abnormal in the original essay.

B   *Object and Defence*

We begin the essay with an examination of two central concepts found in Freud's theory of psychoanalysis: object and defence. By object, psychoanalysts mean *the other*: in relationship, there is self and *other*, or subject and *object*. This other or object, however, takes two forms: 1) the other as the person with whom one actually interacts (i.e. the external or real object); 2) the other as an inner representation of those who have had a psychological influence on one's life (i.e. the internal or mental object). In psychoanalytic theory the internal object is not only developed on the basis of one's actual encounter with the *real other*; the internal object is also shaped by one's own feelings, inclinations and imagination, and it becomes a feature of the very structure of one's mind or psyche. One sees an example this kind of internal structuring in Freud's understanding of the development of the superego. The superego acts as an inner representation of one's parents and, more broadly, as the reflection of social requirements, expectations and ideals one derives from one's experience of relationships with others. One could say that the superego structure is like an internal place or part of the psyche where the influence of significant others *resides*. In order to better understand, however, how Freud views the development and origin of the superego (and the internal objects that are part of its formation) one ought to consider – in addition to *object* – another central concept in psychoanalysis, that of *defence*.

In psychoanalysis defence refers to a protective manoeuvre by the ego (or *I*) to reduce the threat posed to it by anxiety. Threats to the ego come from various sources. Biologically based drives may at times overwhelm the ego – such drives originate in what Freud called the id. Punitive reactions from the superego may also pose a threat. Thirdly, harsh experiences in the encounter with reality could jeopardise the ego's stability (as occurs, for example, with traumatic experiences). Defences are many and varied and include: denial, repression, reaction formation, projection, sublimation.... We will elaborate below on how, in psychoanalysis, ego defence is understood to play an essential role in the development of the internal object.

C *Relational Ambiguity of the Internal Object*

There are two seemingly contradictory explanations for the development of the internal object in psychoanalytic theory. One is that the internal object develops essentially on the basis of contact with the real other with whom the infant or child identifies. For example, and as noted above, the object-based structure of the superego is said to develop out of the relationship the child has with parents and other significant social influences. From the psychoanalytic perspective, it is not simply, however, the positive connection with others that gives rise to the formation of the internal superego structure. Rather, there is a sense in which this internal development results more from frustration and threat than positive alliance to actual others: the child defensively withdraws from others (external objects) as a consequence of conflict and threat (e.g. oedipal issues), and internalises prohibitive social influences in order not to lose support it needs from others. It is this defensive withdrawal that gives rise to internal object development. The explanation offered is that when the child cannot satisfy instinctual or id-based attractions he or she withdraws energy and interest (libido) from the real others and redirects this energy towards a split-off part of the self or ego, creating an internal object: a sort of internal relating that substitutes for the threatening and unsustainable external relating, all the while protecting one's connection to the threatening external reality. Moreover, this threat – that is associated with internal object formation – does not simply originate in external relations but also involves internal conflict generated by desires arising from id and ego. Thus, since I cannot have or possess what I want in relation to the external world I withdraw into my internal world, and develop internal *structures* in lieu of that external world. It is thus, according to Freud, that a split off portion of the ego develops to represent the parents and becomes the superego. This withdrawal gives me separation and independence from external, real relationships, and from the threat that my own inclinations or drives produce in my experience of those relationships. This separating movement occurs as a result of a defensive manoeuvre that protects against and lowers anxiety associated – in this case – with not being able to have what I desire or with being threatened because of what I desire (Freud sees the superego development as significantly shaped through the child's efforts to resolve the oedipal conflict).

In the above we note two factors influencing the development of the internal object. One factor seems to involve positive attachment to others (and the desire to protect that attachment), while the other seems to involve the opposite: ego-defensive detachment and withdrawal from actual relationships to others. In our view these contrasting factors suggest an ambiguity in the psychoanalytic concept of the internal object: Is the internal object a positive development and sign of attachment or connection, or is it an indication of detachment or disconnection resulting from disappointment and frustration regarding external or real relationship? In response to this question one could say that it might be possible for a psychic structure such as the internal object to have two contrasting foundations or functions: a linking and a separating one. Although we see both perspectives expressed in the theory of psychoanalysis, the stronger or dominant tendency, in our view, is for psychoanalysts to resolve this ambiguity by emphasising that the origins of internal object development stem more from the separation or alienation of self from other, than from positive attachment of self to other. We develop a position that involves the latter emphasis: we argue that the primary origin to the internal object world is to be found in the linking of self to other.

D   *The Hermeneutics of Belief and the Hermeneutics of Suspicion*

We see some analogy between the psychoanalytic emphasis on the defensive origin and development of the internal object, and the emphasis, in some philosophical currents, on how the structure, content and function of the human mind involves an essential disconnect with, rather than link to, reality. We go on to consider broader aspects of this matter of connection vs. disconnection between mind and reality in the light of the hermeneutics of belief vs. the hermeneutics of suspicion. We propose that the hermeneutics of belief allows one not only to consider the epistemological question of mind and reality, but, more fundamentally, the ontological question of the relation of self and other, and more comprehensively, the relation between one thing and another. In addition, we consider how this ontological dimension of *being and relation* is associated with the epistemological level of knowledge and the analogous psychological realm of the internal or mental object.

Hermeneutics refers to the theory or understanding of rules of interpretation. Originally the term was used with respect to the interpretation of biblical or legal texts, but its meaning has been broadened to include a focus on the rules of interpretation that apply to a wide range of content one may seek to understand and interpret. The French philosopher, Paul Ricoeur, invokes the distinction between the hermeneutics of belief and the hermeneutics of suspicion. David M. Kaplan provides an explanation of this distinction:

> Hermeneutics is a contested term. There is not general hermeneutics but multiple hermeneutics, with different rules of interpretations, often competing and even conflicting with one another. At one pole of the hermeneutic field is the 'hermeneutics of belief,' aimed at recovering a lost message, animated by faith and a willingness to listen; at the other pole is the 'hermeneutics of suspicion' aimed at demystification, animated by mistrust and skepticism. The counterpole to a hermeneutics that recovers meaning is a hermeneutics that removes illusions."[1]

Ricoeur speaks of three Masters of Suspicion, Marx, Nietzsche and Freud. Each of these looked upon what people claim and think, with basic suspicion. Broadly speaking, Marx applies suspicion and critique to ideology, Nietzsche to the morals and conventions of society, and Freud to the conscious mind and consciously stated motives. For Marx it is economic factors, and the class structure to which these give rise, that determine social ideas, beliefs and attitudes. For Nietzsche conventional beliefs and ideals regarding service to others are inauthentic, and he interprets them as signs of weakness that eclipse the self-affirming and creative will to power. For Freud consciousness hides more than it reveals about the *actual* motives of the human person. These hidden motives are rooted in the unconscious discharge or pleasure oriented drives or instincts found in the id, and may also involve unconscious aspects of the ego and superego (often in conflict with the id). In any case, the Masters of Suspicion view the conscious or explicit expression of human inclinations as disguised, and such expression is to be interpreted via what Ricoeur characterises as a hermeneutics of suspicion.

In other words, with the three Masters the realm of thinking, especially with respect to what is manifest (ideology, socially promoted values, and conscious process) comes under suspicion. Ricoeur does not fully accept, however, the critical, suspicious approaches of the three Masters of Suspicion, for he goes on to indicate that, although they unmask what is false, they also themselves fall victim to some forms of false consciousness. Ricoeur does, nevertheless, appear to accept the priority of suspicion in the hermeneutical process. He proposes that one ought to achieve an eventual balance between suspicion and belief, but he affirms the value and apparent priority of an initial suspicion. We share some of Ricoeur's views, but also differ in fundamental ways.

First of all, we see a problem in defining hermeneutics with an initial emphasis on factors closely associated with knowledge (ideology, moral prescription, consciousness).   Our focus is ontological before it is logical, epistemological or even ethical: that is, we do not approach belief and suspicion solely in terms of their influence on thinking, because we see thinking (about reality, conduct and experience) as rooted in being. We do not, therefore, see the interpretive process or hermeneutics as *primarily* oriented to unmasking false ideologies or consciousness. In other words, we do not believe that thoughts are primarily about other thoughts, but we consider that they are primarily about being (or realities). We see hermeneutics as rooted in how "to be" and "to relate" are given as an accord – yet may be threatened by disaccord – and how the "relating" implied by human knowing and consciousness must depend on this prior, ontological accord or "relating."[2]   In our view, belief and suspicion ought to apply, respectively, to the accord and disaccord that may exist between being and relation. Moreover, we argue that it is because thought cannot be radically separated from being that belief always has priority over suspicion in the hermeneutical process – even in the case of disaccord, we argue that accord retains its ontological priority. Unlike the Masters of Suspicion, we do not begin by attending to the matter of true or false thinking, but to the matter of how thinking has to be rooted in the accord or complementarity of being and relation. In other words, one may consider thinking as having two aspects: the more fundamental aspect speaks to its origin in, and basic compatibility with the accord or complementarity of being and relation; the secondary aspect speaks to its distinction from such an origin: it is distinct from this origin as *reflection*. Thus, for example, thinking about eating food may have its origin in the actual experience of eating food, but thinking about eating food is not the same as, and can be relatively independent of actually eating food.

Moreover, we consider that the ontological accord of "to be" and "to relate" is the foundation of the internal object, and is prior to it, as it were. We may speak of the internal object, broadly speaking, as an analogue of thought or knowledge, and as a feature of the ordering of the psychological realm. Moreover, although the internal object, as a feature of the internal world, is relatively independent from the actual world (e.g. as analogous to what is noted above: thinking about food need not be the same as actually eating food), it is at the same time fundamentally connected to the actual world, since it is the actual world (of being and relation) that allows such a world of ideation to be.

Furthermore, we propose that, if the internal object arises fundamentally from actual human relationship, then it cannot, *in a primary or fundamental sense*, be the result of ego-defensive withdrawal. Any ambiguity it may display cannot be resolved by giving primacy to ego-defence, and to the negation or suspicion of relation implied in the notion of ego-defence. In our view the origin of the internal object has to based on the accord of being and relation, that is, on some degree of trusted (relational) connection.

Recall that the ego-defensive origin of the internal object proposed in psychoanalytic theory implies a recoil from the failure of actual relationship: that is, psychoanalysts are inclined to view the object as arising primarily out of withdrawal from relationship (see original essay for arguments in support of this conclusion). In contradistinction, we see the internal object as arising primarily out of engagement. Our focus shifts from the psychoanalytic one on suspicion of consciousness to one that begins with trust and belief that consciousness (along with unconsciousness: that is, taking into account the whole of the psychic realm) fundamentally reflects and rests upon the accord of being and relation. We are not thereby bypassing or ignoring the possibility that consciousness might, at times, be false, but we are considering consciousness in its deeper, ontological context, in its fundamental accord with being, and we are consequently giving that deeper context priority. In our view, trust and belief are not simply optional ways of thinking that one might choose to adopt or not. Trust and belief arise from being; they cannot be eliminated, only misapplied: like the sceptic who denies truth but to do so must make use of a connection to truth that is prior to doubt.

E   *Graham Harman, Kenneth Gergen and Kenneth Schmitz*

The attitude of doubt and suspicion, combined with the quest to exercise mental and technical power and control over reality characterise modern thought. Descartes sought certainty and clarity of thought by starting with radical doubt. Kant, in a sense, *institutionalised* the division implicit in doubt by positing a radical separation of mind from things-in-themselves (what he called "noumena"), and making access to such things impossible in principle. We also see in the modern era the natural sciences making dramatic strides by their exclusive focus on those aspects of reality that can be measured, predicted and controlled, with an associated tendency to relegate anything that cannot be mastered in such a manner to the *unscientific*. What cannot be mastered tends to fall under "suspicion," even if natural science itself depends on insights, assumptions, and a sense of wonder that originate from beyond its *mastery* or *control*. This mix of doubt and control (that characterise our modern era) has borne dramatic results (both constructive and destructive, one could say) in terms of social change and revolution, technological innovation and development, and it has resulted in shifting beliefs about how we are to understand human experience.

We should note that we are placing Ricoeur's distinction between the hermeneutics of belief and suspicion in a broader context than he intended. His was a specific look at the interpretive practice of applying suspicion to unmask forms of false consciousness in which actual motives or factors might be hidden (he also saw the need to then balance that initial suspicion by resuming an attitude of belief or faith as a result of the further unfolding of the hermeneutical process). Instead, we are seeing in the hermeneutics of suspicion (especially of the kind practised by the *Masters of Suspicion*) an instance of a broader movement of thought in which one gives primacy to the elements of doubt, critique and control in a way that could limit access to certain important dimensions of reality.

We see giving primacy to suspicion, in this broad sense, as an eclipsing of the influence of the complementarity or accord of being and relation on thought in general and on the internal object in particular. We argue that this complementarity or accord, and its influence on the development of the internal object (and associated psychic structures) are central to understanding normality and the healing of abnormality. In order to further articulate a hermeneutics that would be open to the reality of such accord, and its influence or implications for psychological development, we consider the work of three contemporary thinkers: two philosophers, Graham Harman and Kenneth Schmitz, and a psychologist, Kenneth Gergen.

We chose Graham Harman because, in his philosophical approach, he, in a sense, emphasises the being of things-in-themselves, analogous to what we refer to as "distinction" (by *distinction* we mean the uniqueness, independence and freedom associated with "to be," a distinction we view as the complement of *relation*). In his philosophy Harman affirms the reality of things-in-themselves and is strongly opposed to reducing them to mental constructs. In this sense he is critical of the Kantian-like reduction of all reality to human experience or mind. Yet, in our view, he remains critical (akin to suspicious) of relation: from his perspective, in order for things to be, they withdraw from relation. Harman critiques Kant for privileging human knowing but, by proposing a fundamental *suspicion* of relation, he actually retains the Kantian notion of an unbridgeable gap between thought and reality (or, in Harman's framework, between one thing and another). He universalises Kant's understanding of that relation (or should we say non-relation) between the mind and things-in-themselves, in that he applies this Kantian chasm or gap (between mind and noumena) to the *space* separating each thing from every other. For Harman no thing can *know* any other in itself. Just as the mind does not touch the noumena for Kant, so does each thing not touch any other for Harman. Harman's purpose seems to be opposite to Kant's, however. Kant was trying to salvage the mind from Hume's scepticism, whereas Harman is trying to salvage the reality and being of each thing as it is in itself from a mind or relational component that would reduce that reality to mere mental relation.[3] Thus Kant is an *idealist* whereas Harman is part of a movement called "speculative *realism*."

We chose to consider Kenneth Gergen's views next because in some ways he presents a contemporary position that is opposite to Harman's. Gergen is a constructionist, and therefore rejects any sense that something is in itself. Things are said to be the products of social construction and Gergen therefore speaks of all things as *relational*. This is a Kantian-like position, but it is not the forms of the mind which construct reality in Gergen's system; rather, it is the interactive social process that constructs reality. Gergen refers to this process in terms of "relational being." Despite his use of the word "being" he explicitly rejects ontology, which he says would have things be before the relational process that gives rise to or constructs them (a relational process that may deconstruct as readily as it constructs, and that therefore makes all things arbitrary or "optional"). Where Harman protects the reality of things-in-themselves and sees them as having, as it were, to flee from relation in order to affirm themselves, Gergen sees things-in-themselves as a *threat* to their supposed origins in "relational being": they have to be perennially reduced to the knowing process that is a feature of social interaction. Gergen will not even allow that this social interaction occurs among given persons or selves, because such persons or selves are themselves products of "relational being," or simply optional constructs. Thus for Gergen the unique being of each human self or person is not a basis for relationship, and he goes on to propose that "relational being" allows one to overcome what he calls the "prison" of the self.

We see, in both Harman and Gergen, positions which do not allow one to recognise that being and relation are in a fundamental accord with one another; in addition they do not allow one to consider that thought both arises from, and is compatible with this accord – even if, in our view, the *virtual* quality of thought may show a relative independence from the *actual* quality of being. At the risk of oversimplification, we suggest the following. With Harman, for being to endure as being, then being must flee from relation. With Gergen it is the opposite: for relation (-al being) to endure as the formative influence on reality, then relation must flee from being. After considering the views of Harman and Gergen we go on to interpret the work of Kenneth Schmitz because we believe that Schmitz' philosophy allows for an accord between being and relation: in his approach relation does not negate being nor is being *obliged* to radically withdraw from relation; moreover, thought or knowledge is viewed as fundamentally compatible with being.

In our view, both Harman and Gergen present an understanding of relation that is too limited, that empties relation of its fuller meaning. Albeit, this occurs in different ways: Harman sees the relation of knowing as failing to engage the depths of things-in-themselves (failing to grasp or touch their identities) while Gergen sees the process of knowing (the social construction of knowledge) as all that the thing is. Like Harman, Schmitz distinguishes the thing as known and the thing as it is in itself, but Schmitz does not see being as intrinsically alien to knowing. He emphasises that things are not simply known objects or "objects of consciousness"; they are also "subjects of being." However, instead of seeing the realm of knowledge or "objects of consciousness" as intrinsically separate from that of "subjects of being," he speaks of "the credibility already encountered in knowledge."[4] We interpret this reference to "credibility" as implying the priority of a hermeneutics of belief. The relation that occurs in knowledge is not intrinsically severed from its ontological roots. The intelligible connection between thought and being (and thus of knower and known) is based in "a certain abundance and generosity written into being, its capacity for making a gift of itself to thought…The possibility of cognition is rooted in its ontological generosity, and in a vicariosity which permits one being to bear the presence and meaning of another."[5] It is this generosity that allows us to give priority to trust and belief in the process of interpretation (or hermeneutics), and that allows us to speak of normality as the complementarity, accord or harmony of being and relation.

F   *Extracting the Normal from the Abnormal: The Opaque vs. the Transparent Object & the Defence of Self vs. the Defence of Complementarity*

The above exploration of philosophical questions regarding whether *to be* and *to relate* can be in accord, and whether thinking or knowing can be compatible with this ontological foundation has application to our earlier discussion on the ambiguous status of the internal object in psychoanalytic theory.   We note that the tendency in psychoanalysis is to resolve this ambiguity by seeing the internal object as the product of an alienating encounter with an other, and a consequent withdrawal into the self or ego, where a split off part of the latter comes to *take the place* of the external object. The internal object is therefore more the result of separation than linkage between self and other. In this conception the internal world develops as a consequence of a negation of an actual connection in the real world, an alienation imported, as it were, into the internal reflective world of psychic life and structure. We also note that there is a philosophical analogy between the psychoanalytical separation of the internal object world from real connection with others, and the philosophical separation – in some currents of modern thought – between knowing and being, or between thought (or mind) and reality. Moreover, we see such separation as broadly in keeping with the *hermeneutics of suspicion* and with scepticism or doubt about whether human beings (both as individuals and/or collectively) ever really know anything beyond themselves.

At this point our goal becomes to resolve the ambiguity of the internal object in terms of a hermeneutics that starts with trust rather than mistrust, belief rather than suspicion. We propose that *to relate* does not intrinsically negate *to be*, and *to be* does not intrinsically negate *to relate*, even if there can be a failure of accord between *to be* and *to relate*, and even if this failure will have an impact on the internal representations (i.e. internal objects) that *reflect this accord* (and disaccord). Indeed, in our view, it is this failure that defines a key feature of abnormality; however, we see the normality of accord as foundational (i.e. such accord is a necessary point of comparison that permits us to recognise and interpret abnormality).

This conception of normality will have an impact on the psychoanalytic notions of defence and object. We accept the possibility that an ego-defensive response to troubled relationship may result in a withdrawal that influences the development of an internal object: there is an attempt to create some form of self-sufficiency when relationship seems to fail. We see this, however, as an example of abnormality, and propose that there is a prior and underlying normality in which relational connection (between self and other) and the internal representation of connection (internal object) arise in basic harmony with one another. Furthermore, this *normative foundation* has implications for how one ought to understand psychological defence. Defence cannot be limited to being solely the defence of ego or self against threat. We argue that the need to defend does not apply solely to self but applies, more comprehensively, to the accord of self and other in relationship. This means that the internal object is not simply a sign of withdrawal and alienation, but more fundamentally a sign of relationship. It is fundamentally *transparent* (or relational) even if in the experience of abnormality it may take on *opaque* (i.e. a- or anti-relational) properties. In the experience of abnormality, normality is not definitively lost or eliminated, even if it may become eclipsed.

It is this expansion of the notion of defence (i.e. to include not only defence of ego but also defence of relational accord or complementarity) that permits one to extract normality from the experience of abnormality. In our view, the ontological accord of being and relation calls for an expansion of the (ego-) defensive horizon that is generally proposed or implied in psychoanalysis. We propose, on the other hand, that it would not be actually satisfactory or fulfilling for the ego to defend *only* itself from anxiety. We believe that a careful and attentive consideration of the threat that confronts the human person in the experience of anxiety will reveal that it is not simply the self or ego that is under threat but it is the *accord* that has *being* complement *relation* that is under threat. It is not enough simply to dispel anxiety as a feeling; one has to address the greater threat to which anxiety ultimately alerts one: the threat that would undermine (by breach or fusion) the accord of freedom and commitment, independence and communion, self and other, being and relation. When anxiety is simply treated as a problem of feeling or a problem of self-affirmation, it tends to recur. For a defence to be authentic, therefore, it has to extend beyond the sole defence of ego. This expansion of the very meaning of defence – from defence of ego to defence of accord or complementarity – allows one to recognise that there is a need to extract from the experience of the breach or fusion of abnormality the accord or complementarity of normality. This *extraction* is an essential feature of healing.

---

[1] Kaplan, David M., *Ricoeur's Critical Theory*, Albany, New York, State University of New York Press, 2003, p. 21.

[2] The "relating" that characterises human thought, knowing and consciousness rests on an ontological foundation. We discuss below how there is, in the words of Kenneth Schmitz "a certain abundance and generosity written into being, its capacity for making a gift of itself to thought" (Schmitz, Kenneth L., "Enriching the Copula," *The Review of Metaphysics: A Commemorative Issue. Thomas Aquinas, 1224-1274, 27,* 1974, p. 492-512; see: p. 511-512). The generosity and relational quality written into being is the starting point, therefore, for interpretation or hermeneutics. We go on to discuss how this priority of being and relation sets the norm for thought or knowledge, supporting the priority of belief over suspicion in hermeneutics (see, in particular, Appendix C, for further discussion of this point).

[3] In order to be authentic or true, the relation of knowing need not be exhaustive with respect to either the object known or the relation itself. In our conception, distinction and relation are ontological *before* they are epistemological, with the ontological providing, as it were, an ever greater basis and horizon for the epistemological: we could say that the ontological is the *whole* and the epistemological the *part.*

[4] Schmitz, Kenneth L., "A Not Uncritical Harmony," *Catholic Social Science Review*, V, 2000, p. 17-22; see: p. 20.

[5] Schmitz, "Enriching the Copula, p. 511-512.

APPENDIX B

A SYNOPSIS OF
"A HERMENEUTICS OF PSYCHOTHERAPY: HEALING THROUGH BELIEF"
(WITH ADDITIONAL ELABORATIONS)

A   *Introduction*

The main intent of this synopsis or digest is to provide a more straightforward rendition of the key issues addressed in our second essay in this book, "A Hermeneutics of Psychotherapy: Healing through Belief." We have also limited endnotes in this synopsis and refer the reader to the original essay, and to the "Bibliography" (at the back of this book) for more complete information on sources. In addition, we have provided some further reflections and elaborations on the hermeneutics of psychotherapy.

In our first essay, "Applying a Hermeneutics of Belief to the Understanding of Psychopathology," we propose an understanding of psychological normality in terms of the basic accord we experience between being (a person) and relating (to other persons), and abnormality in terms of the disaccord or rupture that may occur between these complements. In developing this understanding we apply a *hermeneutics of belief* to the subject matter of psychopathology: that is, we see an attitude of openness and receptivity to the trusted connection between self and other as essential to the process of trying to make sense of troubled feelings associated with psychological symptoms. We explore the notions of internal object and ego-defence as developed in psychoanalysis, and propose that the linking, relational role of the internal object has priority over its separating role, and that the defence of the *person in relationship* has priority over defence of the *ego from relationship*.

Although we give priority to a hermeneutics of belief we also see a place for suspicion or doubt; however, it is trust or belief in the accord of complements that provides the basis for interpretation and investigation; it is this basis in trust and belief that allows us to extract the normal from the experience of the abnormal.

In our second essay we go on to apply this hermeneutics of belief to the healing process that takes place in psychotherapy. We are basically considering how to approach, with (a hermeneutics of) belief, the rupture, breach or wound within self and/or between self and other. We argue for the appropriateness of a hermeneutics of *belief* in approaching the wound, because, as we will further discuss below, although the experience of the wound indicates rupture, a comprehensive look at it reveals in its midst a normalising or healing tendency.

In view of the focus on the negative or abnormal aspects of human experience, our hermeneutics of psychotherapy does not present as a work of positive psychology, although we do focus on the positive meaning that is available to the person facing abnormality in so far as we emphasise normalisation or healing. The perspective we adopt also differs from a cognitive behavioural approach, in which one views symptomatic experience primarily as a product of cognitive distortion or negative thinking. Although we see a disordered aspect to symptomatic experience, we also emphasise that the quest for meaning is invariably a key feature of that symptomatic experience, such that symptoms reflect both order and disorder. Whereas the tendency in cognitive approaches (including the *third wave* emphasis on mindfulness-type interventions) is to see symptoms as the product of distortion/disorder that must be somehow overcome (e.g. through correction of distorted thinking or through setting such distortion aside via detached observation) we emphasise that symptomatic experience reveals both meaning and meaninglessness, a *mixed reality*.

With respect to psychoanalysis, we share some aspects of the interpretative stance it adopts in that we believe that one ought to explore the depths that lie beyond the surface of symptoms. However, in contradistinction to psychoanalysis, we give priority to belief rather than suspicion in exploring what lies beyond that surface. This has corollary implications with respect to how we understand 1) that which motivates human behaviour, 2) the meaning of dysphoric affect, and 3) the ultimate significance of defensive reaction. In each of these areas, our emphasis is on the fundamentally relational meaning of human existence, and, consequently, on the disordered quality of radically self-oriented attitudes. Our point of departure, in defining the psychotherapeutic treatment of psychopathology, is openness to, and trust in the healing tendency that one may observe in all living things. When hurt or wounded in their passage through the vicissitudes of life, living things have a natural tendency towards healing: that is, the living organism seeks or tends to heal the wound from which it suffers. We broadly apply this notion of healing to the harm, hurt and discomfort which is the material or content for psychotherapy. We emphasise that healing is a given before it becomes something that one deliberately attempts to execute: the psychotherapist and patient are participants in a healing process that, in a sense, has begun already, before they set to work on promoting and seeking repair.

B   *Complementarity*

Paul Ricoeur proposes that hermeneutics is the theory or philosophy of the rules of interpretation. In our proposal of applying the hermeneutics of belief to psychotherapy, our hermeneutical theory rests upon the complementarity of distinction and relation of persons and analogous complements such as freedom and commitment, independence and solidarity, uniqueness and commonality…. This complementarity refers to an *original* and *ultimate* accord of these complements: *original* in the sense of basic or fundamentally given, and *ultimate* in the sense of the further accord that may result after the repair or healing of the rupture or disaccord of complements. Consequently, the experience of the wound is neither radically circumscribed from *original* wholeness nor from an *ultimate* opportunity for repair. In a sense, the actual healing process manifests an intermediate phase *after* the original accord has been jeopardised and *before* the healing of the breach has been completed.

It is as if one could simultaneously experience the despair of suffering and the hope of recovery: *a mixed reality*.

In this context, we speak of healing time, because, in addition to experiencing the reality of breach, and the *negative permanence* associated with that reality (e.g. the despair of suffering: *no light at the end of the tunnel* associated with depression; *never-ending feud* associated with the holding of a grudge), one may also experience a *positive permanence* associated with hope and trust that an accord is continually possible over the course of time (e.g. the hope of recovery; *light at the end of the tunnel*; justice and mercy that reconcile warring factions). In view of original and ultimate accord (noted above) one may also consider that the influence of this positive permanence on mixed reality has greater import or significance than negative permanence.

To recapitulate, complementarity reveals itself, not only in terms of an essential origin and an ultimate goal to human existence, but, as well, in the human experience of mixed reality, where accord and disaccord co-exist. The disaccord or breach of complementarity indicates real harm or danger for the human enterprise, but we argue that, even in times when one faces the meaninglessness of breach, the influence of meaning remains present in some way. This healing influence stems from both sides of the *equation* of complementarity: from the side of the distinct and unique personal act of freedom, and from the side of relational support. Indeed, both are essential to effect healing or recovery.

Moreover, we propose that there is an equality and transcendence between the two sides of complementarity. The person transcends self to engage meaningfully in relationship, and the relationship transcends itself to meaningfully support the person, and both of these (e.g. the one and the many) have equal importance (see reference to Star Trek, in section "C-ii-c" of the original essay, regarding the meaningfulness of the sacrifice of the *few for the many*, and of the *many for the one*).

Consequently, when we speak of disaccord or breach of complementarity, we intend any form of dis-association between complements in which there is 1) negation of one complement or term by the other, 2) sole immanence of either term, and 3) inequity between the terms.   These three factors essentially define abnormality. In contradistinction, normality calls for an opposite definition of these three factors: 1) affirmation of one complement or term by/with the other 2) immanent *and* transcendent relation of complementary terms, and 3) equality between terms.

As noted, in the mix of reality, the factors that define the normal and the abnormal co-exist. Moreover, we see a connection between these factors and the hermeneutics according to which one is to apprehend them. Granting priority to the hermeneutics of belief assumes an accord of complements (transcendent/immanent and equal), while granting priority to the hermeneutics of suspicion assumes the disaccord of complements (solely immanent and unequal).

Furthermore, the complementary terms or pairs of which we speak are to be distinguished from other *contradictory* (anti-complementary) pairs, such as accord and disaccord, meaning and meaninglessness. In the case of the *complementary* pair (e.g. the distinction and relation of persons), the fulfilment of the one term is associated and only possible with the fulfillment of the other term; there is a form of equality or symmetry (in distinction) between one term and the other. In contrast, with *contradictory* pairs, the fulfillment (or logical conclusion) of the one term does not depend on the fulfilment of the other. In fact the fulfillment, or logical conclusion of the one depends on the diminution of the other. These latter *contradictory* pairs – accord and disaccord, meaning and meaninglessness – in contradistinction to *complementary* pairs, are more appropriately described as unequal or asymmetrical. One could say that they are false or pseudo-complements.

The wounding or breaching of complementarity as a feature of the mix of reality exemplifies this inequality or asymmetry: the wounding expresses purposelessness or meaninglessness, while the healing tendency associated with the wound expresses purpose and meaning. This twofold aspect of the wound is not a matter, as it were, of a *yin and yang* balance or connection. It is, rather, a matter where the complementarity of yin and yang is itself jeopardised. Indeed, it is in and through the influence of complementarity that the inequality and asymmetry associated with the wound may be healed. This is because intelligibility and healing depend on, and result from accord, not disaccord.

Consequently, we emphasise the *secondary* role of the hermeneutics of suspicion with respect to the hermeneutic process as a whole. The hermeneutics of suspicion, as a response to disaccord, finds intelligibility and purpose if it remains nestled within or dependent upon a hermeneutics of belief: belief is a response to the *accord-seeking* or healing tendency one discovers in the mix of reality. In other words, the priority of belief over suspicion – in the hermeneutics of psychopathology and psychotherapy – depends on the priority of accord over disaccord in the mix of reality. It is for this reason that the association between belief and suspicion ought to remain an *unbalanced, asymmetrical* one, in favour of belief. Indeed, if the purpose one discovers in the wound involves a healing or normalising tendency (i.e. where accord seeks to heal disaccord), then the purpose of bringing belief and suspicion to bear on the mix of reality is to favour belief: it is for this reason that one is to apply suspicion only *secondarily*.

C   *The Nature of Hierarchy*

In the above we have defined the basis of psychopathology as a breach or disaccord between the complements of *distinction* and *relation* of persons, and have viewed psychotherapy as a process that seeks to heal this breach through the recovery and development of a meaningful accord of these complements. We have also indicated that, although distinction and relation of persons define a prototypical form of complementarity (or normality), there are various other analogous forms of this complementarity: freedom and commitment, uniqueness and solidarity, one and many.... In elaborating the characteristics of the connections between the terms of each pair of complements, we have highlighted three essential features as normative to this complementarity: accord, mutual transcendence and equality.

One may note that these features speak to a *horizontal* emphasis: that is, one has normality when each term accords with, *mutually* transcends itself towards, and remains *equal* to its complement. This all takes place on the same *non-hierarchic* or *an-archic* plane, as it were. For example, to engage my unique capacity for freedom meaningfully I must not betray but uphold loyalty or commitment to relationship. And, in order for relationship to be meaningful it ought to support and not undermine the authentic freedom and uniqueness of the person (i.e. the uniqueness of both self and other in relationship). Thus, normality or complementarity calls for a balance (accord), transcendence, and equality of terms; and this speaks to a mutual, *horizontal* arrangement.

One ought also to consider, however, that, in the human experience of reality, one readily encounters distributions of power and value that speak to a higher and a lower, that is, to an inequality. For example, with respect to distribution of power, consider such notions as *survival of the fittest*, or *pragmatic interest*, notions that one sees applied not only to biological evolution, but, also, to economic exchanges, political interaction, competitive sports, educational achievement, and other forms of social interaction. One notes, in these various examples, a distribution of power favouring those who are stronger – with a dominance based on skill, advantage, circumstance, privilege, striving, chance....

This power distribution speaks to a *vertical* or *hierarchical* dimension within the reality encountered in human experience. With respect to this hierarchy of power, relative positions on this hierarchy are said to depend on the exercise of power or advantage that plays out in some sort of competitive way. At the same time, however, one notes that the hierarchy one observes in nature and in human society is not only predicated on competitive advantage and striving, but, also, depends on what one may call a distribution of meaning or value. For example, one may look to instances from human experience where co-operative practices and principles prove to be higher than competitive ones (such priority of co-operation over competition may be noted, for example, with acts of generosity). Furthermore, one may look to how service, as a value (or virtue), *ought* to have priority over dominance, as a form of *mere power*. Some will readily reduce value or meaning to power as if competition and pragmatic achievement somehow rule the day, and they may then define co-operation or service as simply the *handmaid* of competition. Thus, it is said, for example, that the self-sacrificing behaviour of some animals is simply a way to promote survival of their genetic code, or it may be said that greed and power are the central motives that explain the movements of human history. We see significant limitations in a perspective that emphasises pragmatic self-interest as explanatory, but also recognise two points of validity in it. We will elaborate on both the two points of validity and on the limitations of this perspective below.

One reason that power may take priority over value or meaning, and even eclipse the latter, is that one may indeed have situations where competitive power rather than co-operative disposition rule the day. Yet, as human beings, we cannot, nor do we in ususal practice, approach reality solely in terms of a circumscribed empirical realm, that is, in terms of the *mere facts of the matter*. We invariably consider what happens in terms of what *ought to be* (value) *and* not only in terms of a circumscribed notion of what *is* (i.e. by "a circumscribed notion of what *is* we mean an *is* separated conceptually from value). Such is the case, perhaps, despite, or indeed, because of Hume's distinction between *is* and *ought*. Even when one wants to assert that an *is* (e.g. competitive power has dominated a period of conflict in history) has nothing to do with an *ought* (e.g. the parties in the conflict failed to act co-operatively, even if it is recognised that they *ought* to have done so), one is, at least implicitly, asserting that this separation of *ought* from *is* is how the situation *ought to be viewed*, thus confirming how much *ought* is part of one's vision of *how something is*. In other words, we are arguing that one inevitably considers *ought* as a feature of *is*. This is the case even when one is attempting to deny that such is the case, because, such a denial speaks, after all, to how things *ought to be* viewed. Consequently, discovering that an historical event or a biological process has been ruled by competitive power more than co-operative value does not discount the priority of co-operation over power, because the *mere facts* of empirical data or of functional relations cannot be radically circumscribed from the meaning of what *ought* to be (because such a radical circumscribing, in terms of a perspective such as Hume's – i.e. the claim that an *ought* cannot be derived from an *is* – is itself an engagement in the world of value, thus suggesting that the claim of a radical separation between *is* from *ought* is a questionable one).[1]

The other point of validity, in the notion that co-operation is the *handmaid* of competition, has to do with the subtlety of the way in which the hierarchy of power and the hierarchy of meaning/value influence one another. A consideration of the *ought* (meaning/value) in the human experience of reality reveals that the hierarchy of value or meaning (i.e. the realm of *ought*) does not simply call for *dominance* of the higher towards the lower, but for *service* of the higher towards the lower. It is co-operation and service, therefore, that provide the deeper order or rule to hierarchy (when hierarchy is viewed as a whole or comprehensively, as we will elaborate below), not competition and dominance.

Indeed, co-operation has ontological priority over competition. This (hierarchical) ontological priority arises from the (horizontally) given quality of one's existence as a person: that is, as a human person one always starts with *having being as given* to oneself in the context of relationship.[2] This *having being as given* calls for a reciprocal response: that is, in the experience of one's being or existence as given, one discovers one's own uniqueness and freedom, and it is natural to orient that freedom towards *giving back* to relationship in terms of the uniqueness one has to offer the other. This reciprocity basically defines what we have called complementarity.

In addition to the ontological priority of co-operation over competition, one may also speak of a moral priority of the former over the latter: that is, the appropriate or moral exercise of power depends on the deferral of competition to co-operation, or the deferral of the striving to dominate to the striving to serve. These (hierarchical) *moral* deferrals in turn depend on (horizontal) *ontologically given* complementarity, that is, on distinction (of persons) supporting relation (of persons), and on relation supporting distinction. It is this *horizontal*, complementary dimension that provides the inner norm for the *vertical*, hierarchical dimension (pertaining to ordering power). Furthermore, the priority of co-operation does not eliminate competition, because it is, in the end, a priority of service, not one of mere dominance or power. Co-operation provides the norm for competition, allowing the latter to find fulfillment it could not otherwise attain. In other words, it is in its deferral to co-operation that competition attains meaningfulness.

This not only indicates the relative autonomy of competitive striving, but it also indicates that competitive striving, and lower levels of being generally, enjoy *only* a relative autonomy: relative to the normative influence of complementarity on hierarchy, an influence which finds expression in the hierarchical priority of collaboration over competition, service over dominance.

It is in view of the priority of service (and co-operation) that we may speak, comprehensively, of a *hierarchy within a hierarchy*: the hierarchy of power or dominance does not ultimately exist in a circumscribed manner; there is a hierarchy of service *within* it that supports it and has it *be*. As previously discussed, however, we face a mixed reality, not one of perfect harmony of complements nor of perfect order of hierarchy. Consequently one may witness various ways in which the hierarchy of power may fail – both ontologically and morally – to remain true to the *inner hierarchy*, and to the complementarity on which that inner hierarchy is itself based. These failures (encountered in the mixed reality) do not cancel ontology and morality; if anything, the experience of these failures only becomes intelligible when it is recognised that the failures point to and affirm the ontological and the moral. In the experience of the mixed reality one may always find, therefore, indications of the *hierarchy within a hierarchy*. This *inner* hierarchy is a reflection of the fullness of being-in-relationship, and is that which invites one to consider the priority of service over dominance, co-operation over competition.

D   *Right and Power*

The ontological and moral disorder noted above has implications for our understanding of psychological disorder. Symptomatic experience expresses in some way the breach of meaningful connection,[3] and at the same time, indicates a longing for repair. This repair is fundamentally *horizontal*: that is, it is fundamentally a repair of complementarity. Yet, as we have seen, human experience also involves a hierarchical (non-horizontal/vertical) dimension, having to do with the distribution of power, and internal to that hierarchy there is another more fundamental hierarchy, having to do with the distribution of meaning or value (e.g. service and co-operation). We emphasise that this service-oriented, co-operative inner dimension of hierarchy is a reflection and expression of the influence of horizontal complementarity. Thus one may say that horizontal complementarity confers its non-hierarchic *norm* (i.e. referring to an equal, mutually transcendent, *an-archic* accord of persons in relationship) onto the hierarchic structure of service and dominance, co-operation and competition.

It is in view of this hierarchical distribution of service and dominance, co-operation and competition, that we may speak of the importance of the hierarchical relationship of *right* and *power*. If we only had *powers* (e.g. survival of the fittest, the rule of the powerful, utilitarian goals, collective or individual supremacy) we would have no *rights* (e.g. respect for the person regardless of his or her power status).

Consequently, right, along with its complement, obligation, ought to have priority over mere power. Indeed, it is the language of rights *and* obligation that provides a context within which to understand many essential aspects of the human experience of meaning or value. It is interesting that Viktor Frankl, who, as the founder of logotherapy, is, we could say, a champion of (will to) meaning over (will to) power and (will to) pleasure, said that there ought to be on the west coast of the United States a *Statue of Responsibility* to complement the *Statue of Liberty* on the east coast.[4] In the framework we are presenting, one could say that the complementarity of right and obligation/responsibility (respectively represented by the two statues) ought to have priority over and inform the hierarchies of power and pleasure – we have not spoken specifically of a hierarchy of pleasure, but may consider that, like power, pleasure does not make a good ultimate *master* in human affairs: that is, pleasure, like power, should not be circumscribed from meaning and granted some kind of absolute status in human affairs. In any case, right speaks to the exercise of freedom and the affirmation of being, while obligation or responsibility speaks to the relational commitment within which that freedom finds meaningful support and expression. There is analogy to complementarity: right is to obligation (or responsibility) as distinction is to relation (of persons).

Freedom or right cannot be essentially separated from the exercise of power; consequently considerations of hierarchy come into play when we consider rights and obligations. The breach of complementarity that underlies psychopathology does not only involve the breakdown of complementarity but, as well, a breakdown in the order of hierarchy in which the priority of co-operation over competition is compromised, as is that of service over domination (or that of right/obligation or meaning over power). When one seeks to understand and treat abnormality or psychopathology, one has, therefore, both a breach of complementarity *and* a dis-integration of hierarchy with which to contend. Conversely, healing calls for a recovery of horizontal complementarity (of freedom/right in accord with obligation/responsibility) and a recovery of vertical or hierarchical order (granting priority to co-operative service over the mere exercise of competitive power). Indeed, healing calls for an overarching harmony or *compatibility* between these two dimensions, between the *horizontal* and the *vertical*.

E   *Powerlessness and Hopeful Acceptance*

Psychotherapy involves an effort to normalise the abnormal, and the therapist and patient apply this effort to symptoms arising from both breaches of complementarity and dis-integrations of hierarchy. If co-operation is the authentic interior (i.e. the norm or principle) of competition, and if complementarity is, in turn, the authentic interior of co-operation, then one may see how this nesting of complementarity within co-operation, and co-operation within competition gives rise to the *compatibility* and harmony (noted above) between the accord of complements *and* the integration of hierarchy.

Psychological symptoms often involve feelings of alienation, meaninglessness, powerlessness, hopelessness.... In dealing with these issues through psychotherapy one has, on the one hand, to come to terms with (i.e. accept) the mixed reality in which they present, and on the other hand, to attend to the healing dynamic or influence that renders that mixed reality intelligible and workable. Human experience is human because it occurs in a world of meaning, and to understand and work through troubled experience involves addressing issues in terms of this world of meaning. Although power and pleasure also rule the human world, these factors never exist independently of meaning: one could say that meaning lies both within and beyond power and pleasure. For example, in circumstances where there is interpersonal conflict, those involved do not concern themselves solely with issues of power and control, but more typically raise questions of whether such power and control are exercised in a manner that is just. Accusations are not only levied against others because of their superior strength, but also because of the perceived or presumed unjust or dishonest exercise of that strength. It may be true that sometimes questions of meaning or value will simply be used as excuses to disguise actions that are primarily oriented to seeking power or advantage; however, the negation of meaning does not cancel meaning, no more than claiming that the law of gravity has no relevance will prevent one from falling as one steps off a precipice. Moreover, even in circumstances where human behaviour shows a callous disregard for respect of others, there will often still be some pretense or lip service paid to questions of meaning. There is a remnant of meaning that cannot be excised from human affairs, even when the realm of meaning is in fact being transgressed (recall the previous discussion in which we emphasised that one cannot – contrary to Hume's claim – fundamentally or ultimately excise or separate *ought* from *is*: such an excision may be made, but it remains essentially conceptual, not actual).

If the meaning of complementarity, co-operation and service is at the heart of the human experience of mixed reality, then the radical absence of power (i.e. powerlessness) and of pleasure (i.e. extreme pain) – although such absence might be an indication of meaninglessness – cannot be equated with meaninglessness. Power and pleasure cannot be separated from meaning, but, as we have seen, this is because the world of meaning includes, yet exceeds, the worlds of power and pleasure. Indeed, the obligation or responsibility we have as a society of persons to reduce the powerlessness and pain of others does not stem from norms derived from the worlds of power and pleasure, but from norms derived from the world of meaning.

In working through troubled feelings one is to consider, therefore, not only how power and pleasure are compromised, but also how meaning is compromised. It is the world of meaning that will allow one to ultimately make sense of one's troubled feelings; that world of meaning will permit one to find the sense even in the challenging circumstances of powerlessness and extreme displeasure. One naturally strives to affirm power, tries to avoid pain, and seeks to find pleasure and happiness, but in confronting the mix of reality one will encounter limits to this search. One will not only experience limits on one's power and pleasure, however. One will also experience limits in the very quest for power and pleasure: one experiences an insufficiency not only in terms of what power and pleasure have to offer, but, more fundamentally, in terms of what power and pleasure, if cut off from meaning, cannot offer.

If the human being lives fundamentally in a world of meaning, then adaptation and adjustment oriented by power (e.g. survival, dominance, success, achievement...) or pleasure (e.g. comfort, instinctual release, drive reduction...) will not suffice to provide fulfillment. Indeed, where human beings are limited to power and pleasure, one should see signs of frustration and displeasure that do not arise from limitations of power and pleasure as such, but come from a more fundamental malaise: a loss of meaningful, trusted connection. There is a more basic or fundamental adjustment or adaptation that the human being seeks than one involving power or pleasure, and that is an adjustment to meaning, an adjustment to the accord of distinction and relation, an adjustment that involves the deferral of competitive striving to co-operative service.

Consequently, there will be two inclinations associated with experiences of powerlessness and discomfort: one of these is to overcome the powerlessness and discomfort, but the other is to accept the *better* and the *worse* of whatever happens with hope and trust that a meaningful response is continually available or possible. This does not involve an abandonment of, and detachment from the worlds of power and pleasure, but their (hierarchical) reintegration and rehabilitation, such that power and pleasure defer to meaning, and meaning *serves* and *informs* power and pleasure. This deferral to meaning remains possible even in conditions that one might perceive or believe to involve extreme powerlessness or displeasure. In other words, powerlessness and displeasure, like power and pleasure, are also to defer to meaning; or, conversely, meaning is also to inform powerlessness and displeasure, as it is to inform power and pleasure. Consequently, when it becomes necessary to do so, even conditions of powerlessness and displeasure may be accepted, because the potential to meaningfully exercise freedom *and* meaningfully benefit from relationship will not be absent from such conditions. It is this opportunity to engage freedom and experience relationship meaningfully – even in circumstances where one suffers unavoidable powerlessness and displeasure – that makes of psychotherapy a hopeful enterprise.

---

[1] The mistake that is made with overstating empirical claims is to consider the *merely empirical* to be somehow the original, fundamental or even ultimate datum of the experience of reality. We are proposing that in the context discussed above – i.e. regarding distinctions of *is* and *ought* akin to Hume's – the empirical is, rather, a conceptual derivation, arising from analytically separating fact from value. Such analysis does not yield negative consequences as long as one does not succumb to the illusion that this product of analysis (i.e. the mere fact) stands on its own, outside of the unity from which it comes, a unity that includes value or meaning. Further confusion arises if this conceptually derived empirical realm is granted powers and qualities it does not possess, and, after having been explicitly stripped of value, viewed, with some irony, as *the* source or basis for making determinations of value and meaning (one may see here expressions of the problems with both the naturalistic fallacy and naturalistic ethics: see last endnote, # "155," in second essay for elaboration of these points). We see this kind of mistaken attribution in pragmatist and utilitarian visions of reality, and in forms of secularism that exclude non-secular views from public discourse.

[2] Consider this from Luigi Giussani: "being loved is the substance, the nature of your 'I.'" The statement emphasises that the distinction of 'I' depends on the relation of love, and this, in our view, describes the horizontal complementarity of distinction and relation; we have noted that it is this complementarity that provides the inner norm of hierarchy, a norm that establishes the priority of co-operation over competition. The statement by Giussani is quoted in Zucchi, John, "Something Always

Eludes Us," *Convivium*, Volume 3, No. 16, October/November, 2014, p. 33-37; see: p. 37.

[3] By meaningful connection we intend one's connection to that which really matters in life in ways that are particular, fundamental and comprehensive.

[4] Frankl, Vikor E., *Man's Search for Meaning*, Boston, Beacon Press (first published in English in 1959; originally published in German in 1946), 2006, p. 132.

APPENDIX C

SOME REFLECTIONS ON THE COMPATABILITY OF THOUGHT AND BEING, IDEA AND REALITY, INTERNAL REPRESENTATION AND ACTUAL RELATIONSHIP

In our first essay in this book, we regard the psychoanalytic understanding of the internal object as ambiguous.[1] We propose that the internal or mental object, as viewed in psychoanalysis, has both a linking and separating function (with respect to human relationship), and suggest that the tendency in psychoanalytic theory is to resolve this ambiguity by emphasising the internal object's separating, ego-defensive function over its linking, *relationship-defensive* function. We also draw an analogy between psychological issues associated with this ambiguity (re: how the internal object is linked to actual relationship), on the one hand, and philosophical issues (re: how epistemology is linked to ontology), on the other.

We consider the philosophical perspective of Graham Harman who places the emphasis on the ontological status (reality) of objects, but who views the relation between objects as a form of Kantian-like *knowledge* in which one thing or person never actually connects with another thing or person (each thing-in-itself remains essentially inaccessible to every other). Harman proposes that things meet only at their surfaces, as it were. We also consider the contrasting perspective of Kenneth Gergen who places the emphasis on the non-reality of (*independent*) objects, on their continual resolution back to a *constructive relational* process, which is said to create them (i.e. from Gergen's contructionist perspective people's agreement about what something is, is, indeed, an agreement that is forever optional and subject to modification or cancellation). One could say that there are no depths, only surfaces in Gergen's constructionist vision. Lastly, we consider the personalist/metaphysical approach of Kenneth Schmitz whose perspective, in our interpretation of his work, allows for both the relation and the reality (being) of objects to co-exist, giving both an ontological status, as it were. One also sees, in his approach, a way to distinguish thought or knowledge from being (echoing Harman's emphasis), and yet a way for thought or knowledge to arise from being through an act of the latter's *generosity*, and not through a process in which there is some form of intrinsic opposition or alienation between one term and the other (i.e. between ideas and reality or between thought and being).

In some ways, Schmitz, in our view, speaks to the critical moment in Harman's perspective in that he does not reduce *subjects of being* to *objects of consciousness*: that is, the relation of knowing need not be exhaustive (this would be consistent with Harman's emphasis, and contrasts with Gergen's in which knowledge – agreeing something is – is *all* it is). For Schmitz, however, subjects of being are related to one another in a manner (i.e. *community of beings*) that exceeds relations restricted to mere subject-object consciousness: relationship has ontological and not only epistemological underpinnings.

Schmitz' approach also speaks to the critical moment in the perspective of Gergen, in so far as Gergen is seeking a relational basis to the world of reality. However, whereas Gergen limits that basis to the knowing, constructive, *relational* activity (that is somehow associated with human beings),[2] thereby excluding ontology (i.e. excluding all things that are in themselves) and reducing being to optionality, Schmitz sees being as something that is *generous* and allows the diversity of beings to have a true existence: i.e. to be in themselves. Moreover, this generosity supports not only relations that have an epistemological basis (i.e. involving thinking, knowing or ideational activity), but, in addition, relations that have an ontological basis: that is, there is a community or solidarity of diverse beings *before* there are relations of *mere* knowledge or consciousness.

For Schmitz thought rests or depends on being, arises from it. He writes about "a certain abundance and generosity written into being, its capacity for making a gift of itself to thought…The possibility of cognition is rooted in its ontological generosity, and in a vicariosity which permits one being to bear the presence and meaning of another."[3]   We may also consider here a comment by G. K. Chesterton that similarly suggests that the origin or basis of thought lies in a generosity to which thought responds with gratitude: "Thanks are the highest form of thought."[4]   Thus, the generosity of being is reflected and acknowledged, as it were, in thought.

We went on, in our first essay, to consider how the internal object in psychology may be viewed as the analogue of the epistemological moment in philosophy.   If thinking, ideation and knowledge arise from being, then – by analogy – the internal object in the human psyche arises from human relationship.   Moreover, if "realities are more important than ideas"[5] (i.e. if ontology has priority over epistemology), then actual relationship has and retains priority over the internal representations (i.e. psychic structures and internal objects) that arise from, or in the context of relationship.   One may consider that this is consistent with our emphasis on how complementarity (the ontologically given accord of distinction and relation of persons) provides the norm to hierarchy.   The compatibility of the complementary (horizontal dimension) and the hierarchical (vertical dimension) finds expression in the compatibility of ontologically-based relationship (e.g. community of beings) with epistemological expressions of relationship (e.g. philosophically: the world of thought, knowledge, ideas; psychologically: the world of internal objects and psychic structure).   This compatibility does not exclude the possibility of incompatibility, however.   We have referred to disorders of complementarity and hierarchy, and these are possible, as well, with respect to how the world of ideas (the epistemological realm) could separate itself from the world of distinction and relation of persons (the ontological realm of complementarity).

We may draw further analogies. If, as discussed in our second essay, the exercise of mere power[6] leads to incompatibility between complementarity and hierarchy (and to breach of complementarity and dis-integration of hierarchy), then the same applies to the epistemological moment (which we are saying ought to defer to the ontological one): that is to say, if we restrict our scope to the *merely ideational*, then the ideational itself loses its meaning, its connection with truth; its truth depends on its remaining compatible with the ontological moment (i.e. that ontological moment involves the accord of distinction and relation of persons, and by analogy, as we will discuss below, the accord of freedom and truth, freedom and the good of relationship).[7]

One notes in Gergen's perspective an emphasis on constructive activity, which he implies underlies the realities we experience. His intention seems to be to celebrate the freedom and creativity that becomes possible, if we but abandon ontology (and related notions such as the independence of things and the principle of truth), and consider realities to be, simply, products of agreement (i.e. cognitive constructions). It is as though he sees remaining in the *merely ideational* as a form of liberation. Is there some sense in which one can retain the value of creative freedom to which Gergen seems to allude without the chaos and contradiction of absolute relativism, to which, in our view, Gergen's position seems to lead?[8] We will consider below how to understand creativity and freedom in a manner that allows things to retain their being, depth, and independence, and, in addition, allows the principle of truth to remain central to human dialogue as opposed to being excluded from it (and replaced by pragmatics, as Gergen proposes).[9]

We have referred in the second essay to a complementarity of freedom and truth where "truth is integral to freedom," but "freedom is also integral to truth."[10] We have argued that truth refers, not only to the adequation of mind to reality, but, in view of (person-based) freedom's reciprocal relation with truth, to the relation between freedom and the good of relationship (i.e. the mind's grasp of reality finds its ever higher expression in the accord between the distinction/freedom of self and the good of relationship with the other). In other words, truth is not simply the adequation of mind to reality (in the abstract) but refers to, and includes (more concretely) the union, relation or *adequation* of freedom to the good of relationship, freedom to the good of the other (and vice-versa: the adequation of the good of relationship to the freedom of those in relationship). Within this framework, things in general and persons in particular (and prototypically) are free and creative,[11] both in their distinction from one another (i.e. "freedom is integral to truth") but also in their ontological/epistemological relation to one another (i.e. "truth is integral to freedom"). In this way there is not an essential nor a necessary disaccord between freedom and truth, and it follows that there need not be an essential separation between creativity (i.e. construction) and truth or being. Indeed, such a separation would nullify the truth or being in creativity, a proposal of nullification which Gergen, perhaps in some ways echoing Nietzsche, seems to commend.[12]

In view of these considerations, the epistemological moment (as a feature of hierarchy) need not be incompatible with the ontological moment from which it derives its norm. Just as the ontological normative influence of complementarity does not negate hierarchy, but informs it with the order of priority of co-operation over competition, service over dominance, meaning over power, so too does truth[13] provide a norm for ideational activity.[14] If truth involves the adequation of freedom to the good of relationship, and if freedom is an essential component of creativity, then there cannot be an authentic (creative) construction of reality without truth. Gergen emphasises construction, but fails to appreciate that freedom *and* truth ought to be its essential components.

Is power freer when separated from meaning? Is competition more successful when separated from co-operation? Does dominance become stronger when separated from service? Do ideas become more creative when separated from truth? We have argued that complementarity provides the norm (the authentic order of priority) to hierarchy. It is because of this *in-formation* that meaning has priority over power, co-operation over competition, service over dominance, and truth over knowledge. This order arises from the fundamental ontological accord of the distinction and relation of persons, from the fundamental accord of freedom and the good of relationship: a freedom in truth, and a truth in freedom.

Our work in this book has been on the subject of psychopathology and its treatment. Consequently, we have not only considered the realm of normality: ontological accord, hierarchical order, and their compatibility. Our focus has also necessarily included a consideration of how complementarity may be breached, hierarchy may be disordered, and the compatibility between the one and the other – between horizontal complementarity and vertical hierarchy – may become an incompatibility. This does not vitiate, however, ontological accord, nor hierarchical order, nor the compatibility of accord and order; nor does it justify giving priority to a hermeneutics of suspicion, a priority which, in our view, obscures rather than enhances the possibilities of understanding and healing, because it tends to eclipse the influence of the truth of ontological accord. Such truth is not cancelled when one confronts disaccord because reality is a *mixed reality*, and the paradigmatic expression of mixed reality is the *wound*. In the mixed reality of the wound, truth becomes a healing influence. We propose that giving priority to a hermeneutics of belief opens one to the opportunity and challenge of participating in that healing influence. Belief allows one to seek accord, order and compatibility in the *mixed reality* that includes disaccord, disorder and incompatibility.

The application of the hermeneutics of belief depends continually on the accord and truth that provide the healing influence whenever there is a breakdown of complementarity and a corresponding breakdown of the hierarchical order.[15] Furthermore, we have implied that ideational activity itself has higher and lower expressions that are features of hierarchy. Accordingly, we could say that the norm of truth[16] that informs ideation arises from the same ontological accord that informs the distribution of power generally. One may conclude, therefore, that just as co-operation and service provide power with meaningful form so do *thanks*[17]– and we may add that belief, wonder, and expectation also provide thought with meaningful form.[18]

We are indicating that thought, as an expression of power, presents one with a hierarchical order. Accordingly, one may appreciate that the higher forms of thought are characterised by thankfulness, wonder, contemplation, receptivity, expectation, surprise..., whereas the lower forms of thought are characterised by possession, mastery, control, production, demand, prediction.... By giving primacy to belief one may ascend and descend the order of hierarchy while staying true to the norm that forms that (interior/intrinsic) order, the norm that comes to hierarchy from the reality of complementarity. By keeping to this inner hierarchical order, human thought and knowledge (containing objects of consciousness or internal objects) remain *transparent*. As wonder and expectation give way to control and demand, however, the world of human thought becomes *opaque*, and the distribution of power becomes disordered with domination eclipsing service, competition eclipsing co-operation, ideas eclipsing realities, control eclipsing wonder, suspicion eclipsing belief.... When power or hierarchy becomes separated from complementarity, both complementarity and hierarchy are compromised. This wound, however, does not occur without a cry for healing from the midst of the human experience of mixed reality. On the one hand, there is the cry for the uniqueness of the person in freedom to newly find accord with the trusted connection of relationship. On the other hand, there is the cry for co-operation to newly inform competition, service to newly inform authority, wonder to newly inform reason, belief to newly inform suspicion....

---

[1] Please refer to the first essay for a more complete explanation and discussion of the psychological and philosophical concepts described in this section. We only present a schematic summary of these concepts here.
[2] We say "somehow associated with human beings" because, although Gergen asserts that things are as a result of our agreeing that they are, he rejects the idea that there are actual entities in relation that construct reality. For Gergen the entities themselves are somehow the product of a

relation that constructs them, even if one may consider that relation seems to require the entities to be in order for them to be in actual relation. Gergen is, evidently, wary of this requirement (i.e. *to be*) because he believes it will undermine relation and construction. We propose, in contradistinction, that there is no contradiction but a profound complementarity between *to be* and *to relate*, a complementarity essential to human creativity.

[3] Schmitz, Kenneth L., "Enriching the Copula," *The Review of Metaphysics: A Commemorative Issue. Thomas Aquinas, 1224-1274, 27,* 1974, p. 492-512; see: p. 511-512.

[4] Chesterton, G. K., *A Short History of England, London,* Chatto & Windus, 1917, p. 59.

[5] Bergoglio, Jorge (Pope Francis), *Evangelii Gaudium,* November 2013, #231-233.
http://w2.vatican.va/content/francesco/en/apost_exhortations/documents/papa-francesco_esortazione-ap_20131124_evangelii-gaudium.html.

[6] *Mere power* refers to hierarchy not informed by the norm of complementarity, such that one does not give priority to co-operation over competition, and to service over dominance.

[7] Consider how Gergen, who explicitly separates the ideational from any independent reality beyond it, also concludes that the principle of truth poses some kind of threat. This is because, for Gergen, truth cannot be the common ground on the basis of which one may enter dialogue with another; it can only be the restrictive imposition of one merely ideational perspective on another: dialogue is essentially reduced to competition or to parallel solitudes that never really encounter one another (cf. Harman's occasionalism).

[8] If ideational or cognitive construction is said to be the source of reality, then reality is indeed reduced to the product of the *power of agreement,* and truth itself will be a mere product of subjective choice, either individual or collective. The declaration that truth is to be limited to subjective imposition claims for itself an objective status, however; it thus gives rise to the contradiction of an *absolute relativism.* To assert the relativity of truth requires that one employ a notion of truth that is absolute, thus turning one's negation (relativizing) of truth into a contradiction.

[9] See our discussion of Gergen in the first essay for further considerations of the connection between truth and dialogue.

[10] See Hanby, Michael, "Absolute Pluralism: How the Dictatorship of Relativism Dictates," *Communio,* Summer-Fall 2013, Volume XI, Number 2-3, p 542-576; see: p. 571.

[11] Schmitz writes: "The very rhythm of being pulses…with ontological freedom" Schmitz, Kenneth, *The Recovery of Wonder: The New Freedom*

and the Asceticism of Power, Montreal, McGill-Queens University Press, 2005, p. 104.

[12] Nietzsche seems to reject relativism with respect to the question of truth, whereas we interpret Gergen as implying that only a relativism is possible. Nietzsche, like Gergen, however, seems to give the *final say* in matters of truth to power, thus raising doubts as to whether Nietzsche really avoids relativism: for Nietzsche the will to power seems to be the final arbiter of truth and, perhaps of goodness; whereas for Gergen it is the power of declaration of agreement that establishes reality.

[13] We have proposed above that truth is more than an adequation of mind to reality; it is also deeply personal and involves an *adequation* of freedom to the good of relationship, and relationship to freedom – this *adequation* is a feature of complementarity.

[14] In this way there will be no conflation between ontology and epistemology, a conflation which Hans Urs von Balthasar warns against in his *Theo-Logic* (see reference below). The *generosity* of being (cf. Schmitz) informs thought, and thought defers to being in *thanks* (cf. Chesterton). The norm of persons in relation (i.e. complementarity) effects an integration on the hierarchy of being and thought, *reality* and *ideas* (cf. Pope Francis, *Evangelii Gaudium*), such that the object enjoys its autonomy (cf. Harman) and the idea or thought involves intrinsic relation (cf. Gergen). In this way, as von Balthasar proposes, the "object's whole essence would [not] consist in being an object for a subject" and there could be "a free self-revelation" on the part of the object to the subject. The autonomy of the object rests upon ontologically based relation and encounter, a relation and encounter from which thought may become alienated; however, in human experience such an alienation would be a wound (a dis-integration) in search of healing. Thus we could say, as it were, that ontology serves epistemology and epistemology defers to ontology, both in an original sense and in an ultimate sense of a quest for renewal, recovery, healing. See: Hanby, Michael, "Reconceiving the Organism: Why American Catholic Bioethics Needs a Better Theory of Human Life," *Communio*, 41, Fall 2014, p. 615-653; see p. 650 for reference to von Balthasar. Passage from von Balthasar taken from the following: von Balthasar, Hans Urs, *Theo-Logic I: The Truth of the World*, trans. Adrian J. Walker, San Francisco, Ignatius Press, 2000, p, 81.

[15] By breakdown of complementarity and hierarchy we are referring to a *wound*. The capacity to be wounded (i.e. vulnerability) is a feature of living in a *mixed reality*. This reality is mixed because, on the one hand, one is subject to breach and disintegration, while, on the other hand, one is subject to a healing influence. The mixed reality need not be split in

ambivalent, borderline fashion, nor does is it have to be regarded as solely indicative of a destructive force in *paranoid* fashion, nor approached by primarily identifying with the destructive force that inflicts the wound in *anti-social* or *psychopathic fashion*. One is to orient one's experience of wound by recalling the original wholeness that was there before the wound was inflicted, and, as well, by trusting in the healing influence that constitutes the heart of the wound. Without the original wholeness and healing influence the wound is unintelligible.

[16] The norm of truth is expressed in "truth is integral to freedom" and "freedom is integral to truth" (Hanby, "Absolute Pluralism," p. 571), and in our elaboration of truth as freedom adequating the good of relationship and, vice-versa, the good of relationship adequating freedom. In addition, we could say that we are viewing the hierarchical realm of the world of thought as a feature of the hierarchical realm of the world of power/meaning.

[17] Referring to Chesterton above, we noted that "[t]hanks are the highest form of thought." Chesterton, *A Short History of England*, p. 59.

[18] We could restate this with greater elaboration: just as the priority of co-operation or service over competition or dominance permit a meaningful expression of the latter, so does the priority of thanks or gratitude permit a meaningful expression of more *possessive* or *controlling* forms of thought. By "more *possessive* and *controlling*" we are referring to forms or aspects of thought in which one emphasises mastery of the object as one of consciousness or knowledge, as opposed to forms or aspects of thought in which one emphasises encounter with the object as a *subject of being*. We are not suggesting, moreover, that such *controlling* aspects of knowledge are necessarily inappropriate, no more than competition is necessarily inappropriate. Rather, our point is that *mere* control in thought or knowledge just like *mere* competition suggests a disintegration of the order of hierarchy.

BIBLIOGRAPHY

Albacete, Lorenzo, *God at the Ritz, Attraction to Infinity*, New York, The Crossroad Publishing Company, 2002.

Allport, Gordon W., "The Functional Autonomy of Motives." *American Journal of Psychology,* 1937, *50*, 141-156.

Arnold, Magda B., and Gasson, John A., *The Human Person*, Ronald Press, New York, 1954.

Betz, John R., *After Enlightenment: The Post-Secular Vision of J. G. Hamann*, Chichester, West Sussex, Wiley-Blackwell, 2009.

Bergoglio, Jorge Mario (Pope Francis), *Evangelii Gaudium*, November 2013, http://w2.vatican.va/content/francesco/en/apost_exhortations/docum ents/papa-francesco_esortazione-ap_20131124_evangelii-gaudium.html.

Berlin, Isaiah, "Two Concepts of Liberty" 1958; in *Four Essays on Liberty*, Oxford, Oxford University Press, 1968.

Borch-Jacobsen, Mikkel, and Shamdasani, Sonu, *The Freud Files: An Inquiry into the History of Psychoanalysis*, Cambridge, Cambridge University Press, 2012.

Buber, Martin, *I and Thou*, translated by Walter Kaufmann, New York, Touchstone, 1996 (first published in German in 1923).

Burnham, John (Ed.), *After Freud left: A Century of Psychoanalysis in America*, Chicago, The University of Chicago Press, 2012.

Caldecott, Stratford, *Not as the World Gives: The Way of Creative Justice*, Kettering, Angelico Press, 2014.

Carelli, Roberto, *L'uomo e la donna nella teologia di H. U. von Balthasar*, EUPRESS FTL, Lugano – Reggiani SpA, Varese, 2007

Carlo, William E., *The Ultimate Reducibility of Essence to Existence in Existential Metaphysics*, The Hague, Martinus Nijhoff, 1966.

Chesterton, G. K., *A Short History of England*, London, Chatto & Windus, 1917.

Chesterton, G. K., *Orthodoxy*; in *The Collected Works of Chesterton, Volume I*, David Dooley, Editor, San Francisco, Ignatius Press, 1986.

de Chardin, Teilhard, *The Phenomenon of Man*, New York, Harper & Row, 1965 (originally published in French in 1955).

du Toit, Cornel W., "Towards a New Natural Theology Based on Horizontal Transcendence," 2009, *HTS Teologiese/Theological Studies*, 65(1), Art. # 186, 8 pages, DOI: 104102/hts.v65i1.186.

Erikson, Erik H., *Childhood and Society*, New York, W. W. Norton & Co, 1963 (original published, 1950).

Fairbairn, William Ronald Dodds, *Psychoanalytic Studies of the Personality*, London, Routledge, 1952.

Falzeder, Ernst, "A Fat Wad of Dirty Pieces of Paper: Freud on America, Freud in America, Freud and America." In Burnham, John (Ed.), *After Freud left: A Century of Psychoanalysis in America*, Chicago, The University of Chicago Press, 2012, p. 85-109.

Fower, Blaine J., "Placing Virtue and the Human Good in Psychology," *Journal of Theoretical and Philosophical Psychology*, *32*, 2012, p. 1-9.

Frankl, Viktor E., *The Doctor and the Soul: From Psychotherapy to Logotherapy*, translated from the German by Richard and Clara Winston, Toronto, Bantam Books, 1965, first published in 1946.

Frankl, Viktor E., *Man's Search for Meaning*, translated by Ilse Lasch, Boston, Beacon Press, 2006 (first published in English, 1959; originally published in German in 1946).

Frankl, Viktor, *The Unheard of Cry for Meaning,* New York, Simon and Schuster, 1978.

Frankl, Viktor, Video on "Realism and Idealism," 1972: http://www.youtube.com/watch?v=R_bjOeECpjI.

Freud, Anna, *The Ego and the Mechanisms of Defence*, London, Hogarth Press.1968 (original published in English, 1937; in German, 1936).

Freud, Sigmund, *Civilization and Its Discontents*, translated by J. Riviere, Mansfield Centre, CT, Martino Publishing, 2010 (this translation, originally published: New York, Jonathan Cape & Harrison Smith, 1930).

Freud, Sigmund, *New Introductory Lectures on Psychoanalysis*, translated by James Strachey, New York, W. W. Norton & Company, 1965, original published in 1933.

Freud, Sigmund, *Group Psychology and the Analysis of the Ego*, translated by James Strachey, London, The Hogarth Press, 1949 (original published in 1922).

Freud, Sigmund, *An Outline of Psycho-analysis*, translated by James Strachey, New York, W. W. Norton & Company, 1949 (original published in 1940).

Gergen, Kenneth J., *An Invitation to Social Construction*, London, Sage Publications Ltd., 2009 (First Edition, 1999).

Gergen, Kenneth J., *Relational Being: Beyond Self and Community*, Oxford, Oxford University Press, 2009.

Gergen, Kenneth J., "Response to Book Reviews: Relating to My Reviewers," *Journal of Theoretical and Philosophical Psychology, 31*, 2011, p. 69-70.

Giussani, Luigi, *The Religious Sense*, translated by John Zucchi, Montreal, McGill-Queen's University Press, 1997.

Grant, George, "Nietzsche and the Ancients: Philosophy and Scholarship," in *Technology and Justice*, Toronto, Anansi Press, 1986, p. 79-95.

Hanby, Michael, *No God, No Science? – Theology, Cosmology, Biology*, Chichester, West Sussex, Blackwell Publishing Ltd., 2013.

Hanby, Michael, "Absolute Pluralism: How the Dictatorship of Relativism Dictates," *Communio*, Summer-Fall 2013, Volume XI, Number 2-3, p. 542-576.

Hanby, Michael, "Reconceiving the Organism: Why American Catholic Bioethics Needs a Better Theory of Human Life," *Communio*, 41, Fall 2014, p. 615-653.

Harman, Graham, "On Vicarious Causation," in Robin Mackay (Ed.), *Collapse Vol. II: Speculative Realism*, Falmouth, Urbanomic, 2007, p. 187-221.

Harman, Graham, *Circus Philosophicus*, Winchester, U.K., Zero Books, 2010.

Harman, Graham, *The Quadruple Object*, Alresford, Hants U.K., Zero Books, 2011 (original Published in 2010 in French: *L' objet quadruple: Une metaphysique des choses d'après Heidegger*, Paris: PUF).

Harman, Graham, "The Road to Objects," *Continent, 3.1*, 2011, p. 171-179 (originally given as a lecture at the CREA club, Amsterdam, on March 10, 2011).

Harman, Graham, "Everything is Not Connected," Lecture given in Berlin February 2, 2012, http://www.transmediale.de/content/keynote-graham-harman-everything-not-connected.

Harman, Graham, "Purdue Talk (January 14, 2013)," http://figureground.ca/2013/01/17/video-graham-harman-purdue-jan-14-2013/.

Hart, David Bentley, *Atheist Delusions: The Christian Revolution and Its Fashionable Enemies*, London, Yale University Press, 2009.

Hartmann, Heinz, *Essays in Ego-Psychology: Selected Problems in Psychoanalytic Theory*, New York, International Universities Press, 1964 (original published in 1939).

Hine, Phil, "Some Reflections on Transcendence – II," March 20, 2012, http://enfolding.org/some-reflections-on-transcendence-ii/.

Hughes, Judith M., *Reshaping the Psychoanalytic Domain*, Berkeley, University of California Press, 1989.

Humanum Video on Complementarity with speakers: Peter Kreeft, Maria Fedoryka, Chady Rahme, Fernando Pliego Carrasko, Robert Barron, Thérèse Hargot-Jacob, and Philippe Ariño; URL= http://www.aleteia.org/en/society/article/moving-beyond-gender-stereotypes-video-5771034837909504.

Itao, Alexis Deodato S., "Paul Ricoeur's Hermeneutics of Symbols: A Critical Dialectic of Suspicion and Faith," *Kritike*, vol. four, number two, 2010, p. 1-17.

James, William, *Pragmatism*, 1907, http://www.authorama.com/pragmatism-1.html.

Kalton, Michael C., "Green Spirituality: Horizontal Transcendence," (published as a chapter of *Creativity, Spirituality and Transcendence, Paths to Integrity and Wisdom in the Mature Self,* M. E. Miller & S. Cook-Greuter, Stamford, Connecticut, Ablex Publishing, 2000.

Kaplan, David M., *Ricoeur's Critical Theory*, Albany, New York, State University of New York Press, 2003.

Kaufmann, Walter, *From Shakespeare to Existentialism*, Garden City, New York, Doubleday and Company, 1960.

Kaufmann, Walter, *Existentialism from Dostoevsky to Sartre*, New York, New American Library, 1975.

Kazantzis, Nikolaos, Reinecke, Mark A., & Freeman, Arthur, (Eds.), *Cognitive and Behavioral Theories in Clinical Practice*, New York, The Guilford Press, 2010.

Kernberg, Otto F., *Severe Personality Disorders: Psychotherapeutic Strategies*, Binghamton, New York, Vail-Ballou Press, 1984.

Kushner, Harold, *When Bad Things Happen to Good People,* New York, Anchor Books, 2004; originally published in 1981.

Kushner, Harold, *Who Needs God?*, New York, Summit Books, 1989.

Lopez, Antonio, "Christian Culture and the Form of Human Existence," *Communio*, 40, Summer-Fall 2013, p. 473-509.

Minnick, Chris L., "The Manic Defense," by Chris L. Minnick M.D., 2014; published at *Minnick's Klein Academy: Melanie Klein's Models for Understanding the Baby Core of the Personality* http://minnickskleinacademy.com/module-2-2-kleins-baby-core-coping-defensive-maneuvers/manic-defense/

Moyn, Samuel, "Hanna Arendt on the Secular," *New German Critique*, No. 105, Political Theology, Fall 2008, p. 76-96.

Perlow, Meir, *Understanding Mental Objects*, New York, Routledge, 1995.

Peterson, Christopher, and Seligman, Martin E. P., *Character Strengths and Virtues: A Handbook and Classification*, Oxford, Oxford University Press, 2004.

Philippe Jacques, *Interior Freedom*, translated by Helena Scott, New York, Scepter, 2007.

Philippe, Jacques, *Called to Life*, translated by Neal Carter, New York, Scepter, 2008, fourth printing 2012, p. 5.

Pieper, Josef, *Leisure, The Basis of Culture*, translated by Alexander Dru, New York, New American Library, 1952.

Ricoeur, Paul, *Freud & Philosophy: An Essay on Interpretation*, (translated by D. Savage). New Haven and London, Yale University Press, 1970.

Ricoeur, Paul, "Hermeneutics and Critique of Ideology," in J. B. Thompson (Ed. and Trans.), *Paul Ricoeur: Hermeneutics and the Human Sciences*, Cambridge, Cambridge University Press, 1981, p. 63-100, (original published in 1973).

Safran, Jeremy, "Who's Afraid of Sigmund Freud: The Rise, Fall and Possible Resurrection of Psychoanalysis in the United States," *Public Seminar*, Vol. 1, Issue 1, November 20, 2013.

Sartre, Jean-Paul, "Existentialism is a Humanism"; see: Kaufmann, Walter, *Existentialism from Dostoevsky to Sartre*, New York, New American Library, 1975, p. 345-369 (originally given by Sartre as a lecture in 1946).

Scheler, Max, *La situation de l'homme dans le monde*, translated by M. Dupuy, Paris, Editions Montaigne, 1951.

Schmitz, Kenneth L., "Enriching the Copula," *The Review of Metaphysics: A Commemorative Issue. Thomas Aquinas, 1224-1274*, 27, 1974, p. 492-512.

Schmitz, Kenneth L., "The First Principle of Personal Becoming," *Review of Metaphysics, 47-4*, 1994, p. 757-774.

Schmitz, Kenneth L., "A Not Uncritical Harmony," *Catholic Social Science Review, V*, 2000, p. 17-22.

Schmitz, Kenneth L., *The Recovery of Wonder: The New Freedom and the Asceticism of Power*, Montreal, McGill-Queens University Press, 2005.

Schmitz, Kenneth L., "Transcendentalism or Transcendentals? A Critical Reflection on the Transcendental Turn," *The Review of Metaphysics, 58*, 2005, p. 537-560.

Schmitz, Kenneth L., "The Solidarity of Personalism and the Metaphysics of Existential Act," in P. O'Herron (Ed.), *The Texture of Being, Essays in First Philosophy*, Washington, The Catholic University of America Press, 2007, (pp. 133-145), Vol. 46 in Jude P. Dougherty (General Ed.), *Studies in Philosophy and the History of Philosophy*.

Schmitz, Kenneth L., *Person and Psyche*, Arlington, Virginia, The Institute for the Psychological Sciences Press, 2009.

Scott-Baumann, Alison, *Ricoeur and the Hermeneutics of Suspicion*, London, Continuum International Publishing Group, 2009.

Scruton, Roger, "Confronting Biology," in *Philosophical Psychology*, Craig Steven Titus (Ed.), *The John Henry Cardinal Newman Lectures*, Volume 5, Arlington, Virginia, The Institute for the Psychological Sciences Press, 2009, p. 68-107.

Seligman, Martin E. P. and Csikszentmihalyi, Mihaly, "Positive Psychology – An Introduction," *American Psychologist*, Vol. 55, No. 1, 5-14, January 2000.

Seligman, Martin E. P., *Flourish: A Visionary New Understanding of Happiness and Well-being*, New York, Free Press, 2011.

Sharpe, Matthew, "Jacques Lacan (1901-1981)," in *Internet Encyclopedia of Philosophy*, 2005, http://www.iep.utm.edu/lacweb/.

Sokolowski, Robert, *Phenomenology of the Human Person*, New York, Cambridge University Press, 2008.

Somerville, Margaret, ("Building Ethical Bridges in a Secular Age" *Comment: Public Theology for the Common Good*, published by Cardus, September 1, 2014. http://www.cardus.ca/comment/article/4373/building-ethical-bridges-in-a-secular-age/).

Spadero, Antonio (Interviewer), "A Big Heart Open to God: A Conversation with Pope Francis," *America: The National Catholic Review*, September 30, 2013, http://www.americamagazine.org/pope-interview.

Spaemann, Robert, *Persons: The Difference between 'Someone' and 'Something,'* New York, Oxford University Press, Oliver O'Donovan, Trans., 2006.

Spitz, René A., *The First Year of Life: A Psychoanalytic Study of Normal and Deviant Development of Object Relations*, New York, International Universities Press, 1965.

Tawney, J. Jacob, "Content and Form: From Linguistics to Abstract Art," *Communio*, Winter, 2013, p. 799-832.

Tillier, William D., "Posttraumatic Growth Bibliography," June 2012, Calgary, Alberta, http://www.positivedisintegration.com/ptg.htm.

Titus, Craig Steven (Ed.), *The Psychology of Character and Virtue*, Arlington, Virginia, The Institute for the Psychological Sciences Press, 2009.

Vitz, Paul C. & Felch, Susan M. (Eds.), *The Self: Beyond the Postmodern Crisis*, Wilmington, Delaware, ISI Books, 2006.

von Balthasar, Hans Urs, *Dare We Hope that All Men Be Saved*, San Francisco, Ignatius Press, 1988.

von Balthasar, Hans Urs, "Health between Science and Wisdom," *Communio*, Volume XLI, Number 3, Fall 2014, p. 666; taken from von Balthasar, Hans Urs, *Explorations in Theology*, Volume 5: *Man is Created*, translated by Adrian J. Walker, San Francisco, Ignatius Press, 2014.

Weil, Simone, *The Need for Roots: Prelude to a Declaration of Duties towards Mankind*, preface by T.S. Eliot, translated by Arthur Wils, London, Routledge Classics, 2002; first published in English by Routledge & Kegan Paul, 1952.

Williams, Bernard, *Truth and Truthfulness: An Essay in Genealogy*, Princeton, Princeton University Press, 2002.

Williams, Thomas D. and Bengtsson, Jan Olof, "Personalism," *The Stanford Encyclopedia of Philosophy* (Spring 2014 Edition), Edward N. Zalta (Ed.), http://plato.stanford.edu/archives/spr2014/entries/personalism/.

Winnicott, Donald Woods, *Through Paediatrics to Psycho-analysis: Collected papers*, New York, Brunner-Routledge, 1998, (Originally Published in 1958).

Zaborowski, Holger, *Robert Spaemann's Philosophy of the Human Person*, Oxford, Oxford University Press, 2010.

Zaretsky, Eli, *Secrets of the Soul: A Social and Cultural History of Psychonalysis*, New York, Vintage Books, 2004.

Zucchi, John, "Something Always Eludes Us," *Convivium*, Volume 3, No. 16, October/November, 2014, p. 33-37.

INDEX OF NAMES